A Farm Boy Joins the Navy
An Oral History, Written Down: Cotton Fields, Steel Ships, Airships and Missiles

By Walter Dee Ashe, Jr.
Commander, U.S. Navy, Retired

A Farm Boy Joins the Navy
An Oral History, Written Down:
Cotton Fields, Steel Ships, Airships and Missiles

By Walter Dee Ashe, Jr.
Commander, U.S. Navy, Retired

Copyright © 2018 by Dr. Walter Dee Ashe
Greeneville, Tennessee

ISBN-13: 978-0-692-06783-3

Printed by CreateSpace, An Amazon.com Company
Printed in the United States of America

Author's Dedication

I dedicate this book to my daughter, Susan Lee Ashe Fiedler. She stayed after me until she forced me to write it. Then she tirelessly worked to complete it.

Dedication to this edition,
by the author's son and daughter.

An almost idyllic early childhood was shattered for our father, W.D. Ashe, and his three younger brothers by the death of their father when Dad was barely seven years old.

Their mother's insistence on their education and their duty to each other resulted in all four being the first in their extended family to graduate from high school and beyond. Severe shortage of money and inadequacy of food, lodging and clothing were managed and overcome with hard work, cooperation and help from their relatives.

Dad's unintentional pre-war enlistment in the Navy, combined with his math skills and work ethic took him to Pearl Harbor before the Japanese attack, service aboard an attack cargo ship, then to lighter-than-air anti-submarine duty until the last Navy airship was deflated, and ultimately to missile research and production, with an important support role in the Cuban missile crisis and a related civilian career.

The unanimous opinion of his relatives and descendants was that his story would be of interest and value to a wider audience. For that reason, we prepared this revised edition of his original words.

It was edited by Tom Yancey, a veteran of the Navy and years in journalism, and Walt Ashe, M.D., a former Navy doctor and civilian pediatrician. Production composition was by Richard D. Phillips. We preserved as much of the language of "Dub's" narrative as we could, bearing in mind that not every reader would have heard these stories first-hand, nor would every reader have a naval or airship background. We are indebted to the Naval History and Heritage Command, the Lighter-than-Air Foundation, Airship International Press (especially for the cover photo) and the Naval Airship Association. In revising Commander Ashe's text, we hope we have not introduced new errors.

Contents

1. My Birth 1
2. Early Years 7
3. Dad's Death 13
4. Grandmother Keathley's House, Farris' birth 19
5. Working at the Pie Shop 25
6. The Cat Hole 31
7. Kenton High School 39
8. Working to Survive 47
9. Family Reunions 55
10. Memphis, and a competitive exam 63
11. Memphis State 69
12. School with Evaline 75
13. I Join the Navy 81
14. Northwestern 91
15. Evaline Proposes 97
16. San Diego 103
17. On to Pearl Harbor 107
18. Pearl Harbor Attack 115
19. The Aftermath 125
20. Apply to Flight School 135
21. Flight School 143
22. Lakehurst Flight Instructor 153
23. Flight Instructor 163
24. Ghost Story 171
25. War College 179
26. On the Admiral's Staff 185

27.	Free Ballooning	195
28.	Visits Home	207
29.	Evaline Conceives Walter	215
30.	Post-Graduate School	219
31.	M.I.T.	225
32.	The Gun Factory	231
33.	We Learn to Drink	237
34.	Weeksville	241
35.	We Have Susan	251
36.	Sharing Equipment	259
37.	The NAN Ship Exercise	265
38.	Assigned to the Tulare	271
39.	On the Tulare	275
40.	Japan	287
41.	The Philippines	291
42.	Singapore	303
43.	No More Big T	313
44.	Lakehurst NAS	319
45.	Key West	333
46.	Back at Lakehurst	341
47.	Wind Tunnel Research	349
48.	End of Blimp Program	355
49.	I Leave the Navy	371
50.	Univac	381
51.	Church	387
52.	Farming	397
	Cast of Characters	405
	Glossary	406

Walter Dee Ashe, Jr.

1

My Birth

I was born Oct. 21, 1920, the first child of Walter Dee Ashe and Audelle Keathley Ashe. Right off the bat I was a problem. My dad insisted that I be named after him but my mother didn't like Walter, so they compromised by naming me W.D. Ashe, Jr. I went through high school and college with everyone calling me W.D. or sometimes my nickname, Dub.

Twenty years later I started to join the Navy, but had to have a birth certificate or some proof of birth. I looked up the attending physician, old Dr. Gray at Kenton, Tennessee, and said to him, "Doc, you lazy old goat, why didn't you make out a birth certificate for me?"

He said, "Son, I was too busy."

I said, "Busy, hell. I am trying to join the Navy and I need a birth certificate."

He said, "I can make out an attending doctor certificate."

He went into his office, asking how was school, why was I going into the Navy, etc., and when he got the papers out he said, "Now, what's your name?"

I said, "Don't you know my name? It's W.D." He said, "Aw hell, son, I mean your real name." I said, "That's it—W.D. Ashe, Jr."

He said, "What was your daddy's name?" I said, "Dee."

He said, "I have called him Dee all my life. What was his whole name?"

I said, "Doc, it was Walter Dee."

He said, "That's it, and you are Walter Dee Ashe, Jr." He made out the papers accordingly.

Grandfather John Ashe was a small sawmill operator, sharecropper, small farmer, and during probation days, bootlegger in Macedonia community near Kenton, Tennessee.

He was born just after the Civil War, the son of George Ashe from near Nashville, Tennessee. Great grandfather George Ashe lost everything during the Civil War. He, with a family of four boys and four girls, moved west to the vicinity of Jackson, Tennessee, during the late 1860's, and on to Obion County during the 1870's. One of his sons moved on to Texas, one to Missouri, one to Lake County, Tennessee, and grandfather stayed in Obion County, as did most of the girls.

Grandfather Ashe had met and married Lou Primrose, the daughter of another impoverished Civil War landowner and slave owner. They too moved into Obion County during the 1870s.

Grandmother and Grandfather Ashe had seven children, four boys and three girls. My father, Walter Dee Ashe, was the fourth child.

Grandfather Frank Keathley followed three generations of Keathleys reared and buried in Macedonia Cemetery prior to his birth. Grandmother Ernaline Moore Keathley's father was a Baptist preacher named Allan Moore.

My grandfather Keathley likewise was a small farmer in Macedonia community, and lived about one mile from my grandfather Ashe. My great-grandfather Moore was a Baptist preacher that pastored four churches (one for each Sunday in the month) and lived up near Milan, Tennessee.

It so happened that he was conducting a big meeting the summer that his daughter (my grandmother) turned 16. He took her to Macedonia to play the organ for the church singing. My grandfather Keathley, a widower with two small children, was impressed, and next time her dad came back to Macedonia for the regular monthly sermon, grandfather Keathley asked great-grandfather Moore for her hand in marriage. They set up the time for the wedding to be a month later, and the next Sunday he had church in Macedonia. Grandmother Keathley was informed of this on her dad's arrival back home. She went with her father to Macedonia the next month and her dad married them after the church service was completed.

Grandfather Keathley was a lay preacher, a small farmer and magistrate, but he took time to have a passel of children. Along with his two, he and my grandmother had 13 more. Nine of them lived to have families of their own. He had 32 grandchildren.

What irony! The Ashes—hard drinking, gamblers, dancers and bootleggers, and the Keathleys—teetotalers, no cards, no alcohol, no dancing. How did my mother and father ever get together? It was not easy.

They married November 1919.

My mother and father's courtship was short and sweet. Dad was a gay blade in Macedonia community, a playboy of the day. He had a high-stepping mare and a rubber-tired buggy. He was good-looking and dating a different girl in every community for miles around. He must have impressed several of them, because when I was about 16, several of his old girlfriends would see me, give me a hug and sometimes a kiss, and say how I looked just like my dad. He danced, played cards, shot crap, and drank a lot.

Now my Mom, six years younger, turned 16 and began to blossom, immediately catching my dad's eye. So one day, after church, he strolled up to my mom and asked her for a date. My mom told him she would have to ask her mother first.

Well, come the next Sunday, he asked my mom about the date, and my mom told him that grandmother said no. Actually, in later years, my mom told me that grandmother became quite disturbed and emphatically said no. Mom, as teenagers will do, wanted to know why, and grandmother stated it was not so much what my dad was like as much as what his folks were like. But I am getting ahead of myself.

Dad hit the ceiling. He wasn't accustomed to *no!* As was the custom then, and it lasted for years, Sundays were reunions and family reunion time, down at the Keathley homeplace. My dad, in typical family fashion, proceeded to the homeplace, drove his buggy up the drive and around the house. He got out of the buggy, and grandmother saw him. She pointed her hand down the road and said, "Git!"

Daddy said, "Mrs. Keathley, I want to know why Audelle can't date me."

Grandmother said, "I told you to git—now git!"

Several of my mother's brothers started walking over to where my dad stood.

While my grandmother stood pointing down the road repeating, "Git! Git!," my dad said, "Mrs. Keathley, if you let us date like normal people, I promise we won't get married for at least a year, but if you don't, I won't make any promises."

Grandmother, with her voice getting louder and shriller, shouted "Git!"

Only then did Dad climb into his buggy and drive off. Now you had a pair at odds. My grandmother, the matriarch of a very large family, accustomed to issuing directives and having them instantly obeyed, and my dad who couldn't conceive of anyone saying no to him and getting away with it. As Evaline says, "a chip off the old block," and Jessie (now Walt Jr.'s wife) remarks, that's where Walt, Jr. got that.

Well, anyway, drastic actions began to unfold at the Keathley homeplace. They decided that this little upstart 9th grade, 16-year-old girl would go to Humboldt to live with her brother Henry and go to school in Humboldt. Now realize that in going to Humboldt with bare trails for roads and no telephones, you were indeed isolated.

Dad didn't know about these shenanigans until the next Sunday when Mom wasn't at church, and then the manure hit the fan. He got his sister and her husband, Uncle Wade and Aunt Bonnie, to take him to Humboldt. In due time they found where Uncle Henry lived and drove up the street in Uncle Wade's model T Ford.

It so happened that Mom, who was babysitting with Frank, a year old, was pushing him up the sidewalk in a baby carriage. The car pulled up to the curb and Dad said, "Audelle, get your things and let's go get married."

Now that 16-year-old mom of mine knew how to make a decision.

She said, "Just a minute—I gotta take the baby to the house."

This she did, leaving him with his four-year-old brother, and got into Uncle Wade's car with Daddy, and off to Kentucky they went and got married.

Now Uncle Henry was one pissed off brother, and he never forgave my Mom. Fact is, they continued to feud the rest of their lives.

Now maybe you think the shit didn't hit the fan down on the hill at the homeplace! Grandmother wouldn't admit that her daughter existed. Dad, Mom, and Grandmother continued to go to Macedonia Church, but grandmother wouldn't recognize that they existed. Don't you know that must have devastated my mom, a young girl that had never been away from her mom, now to become totally ostracized.

It spread on to Mom's brothers, too. Only Uncle Maurice, a 14-year-old, and Uncle Elihue, 30 and married to Aunt Ollie, one of Dad's cousins, had anything to do with them.

Dad and Mom moved into the house on the hill, south of the church, and granddaddy Ashe lived next to the church on the north side. Of course, neither he nor grandmother Ashe went to church, but it was close if they wanted to.

One day in the fall about a year after Mom and Dad married, Grandmother Keathley said to Uncle Maurice, "Boy, go hitch up the buggy."

This he did without question. Grandmother came out of the house wearing her long black dress and black bonnet and said, "Let's go to Audelle's."

They drove up to the house and grandmother said, "Audelle, get in the buggy. Let's go home."

Can you imagine the emotions that filled my Mom? She got in and away they went to the homeplace. My dad, now a 22-year-old farmer working in the field, came home at dark and no one was there. He went the couple hundred yards to my grandfather Ashe's house, but no one there had seen my mom. He headed back by the church and saw Mr. Emmett West coming back from town in his buggy, and he told him he saw mom in the buggy with Mrs. Keathley.

Now dad exploded and headed for the homeplace. He came charging in and said, "Audelle, get into the buggy. We are going home."

Grandmother said, "Audelle, you stay right where you are, and Dee, you sit down."

During the ensuing argument, Grandmother told him that the first child of all of her daughters had been born at the homeplace and she was going to stay right there until hers was born. This she did and I can imagine he was mighty glad to have her there with her mom, the mother of 13 children.

I was born 13 days after my mom's 18th birthday, on Oct. 21, 1920. Following at roughly two-year intervals came Malcolm, A.J., and Farris.

My parents, Walter Dee Ashe, Audelle Keathley Ashe, and me.

2

Early Years

Dad had a good life as a small farmer, sharecropper, and very independent truck driver. He was very family oriented. He spoiled his children, especially me, the oldest. He was especially close to his dad. Not only daily contacts, but granddaddy would confer with him on practically every subject of daily life. Granddaddy told his other kids that Dad spoke for him in family matters.

Dad tried so hard to make a living. His desires were bigger than his pocketbook, and Mom had serious illness with arthritis that further complicated things. But by the time I was four years old I would sit all day on the Cullwater tongue driving the mules so he could plough cotton, etc. I was with him all the time except when he went to haul gravel. The minute he left I was ready to go to my granddaddy's house, about a quarter of a mile up the road.

Now as I mentioned, my daddy was lax with his kids. He never spanked me once, and would let me go with him always, except to hunt squirrels. Mom made up for his laxness. She would tell you to do something, and there was hell to pay if you didn't do it. One of those things that you didn't do was to head up the road to Granddaddy's. As far back as I can remember, and certainly by the time I was three, she would tell me to stay at home and not to go up to Granddaddy's. And she would add that if I did, she would wear me out with the razor strap. She never failed to do it, and I never failed to go.

She always tried to teach me some manners—an impossible task. I recall that I had a bad habit when I was about four years old of saying, "I want some meat." Well, you were supposed to say, "Thank you for the meat." So I would be asked to say, "Thank you for the meat," and I wouldn't do it. For a while she tried the old, "You can't have any unless you ask for it correctly."

Of course, I would do without. Then she tried the old razor strap routine. She would whip me until the juice oozed out of my shoulders, and all I would do is hold my lips a little tighter. Dad couldn't stand it. He would turn and twist and finally leave the house. She figured she had to conquer me, so she hit upon putting me into the dark smokehouse. I would scream frantically until my eyes became accustomed to the darkness, then I would watch her worriedly pace back and forth. In other words, I was a pain in the lack of discipline business.

But in other things I excelled, and my dad didn't help things too much by constantly boasting about my mental prowess. I can't remember when I couldn't count to a hundred. I remember trying to count to a hundred when I was about five.

I recall being highly protective of my brothers, a trait that was always a part of my life. This trait spilled over to include my closest cousins.

When one of the neighboring kids would hit Malc (Malcomb), it was "Katy, bar the door!!" It didn't take long to get across my point.

A few occurrences of my early life indicate the course of my heritage.

I recall driving Dad's model T over at Jim Corum's farm through a gate he had opened. Jim was telling him how bad that was, but Dad said, "He can do it—he does it all the time."

Up in the field across the road from us lived a family named Gilbert, and they had about six kids. One day, Mr. Gilbert, sitting on the porch with Dad, saw all his kids coming across the field from their house. On arrival they complained of a problem, where they had let an agate (marble) roll through a hole in the floor. Apparently Mr. Gilbert was to have gotten the marble out, but as he explained to my Dad, the only way he could get to the marble was to cut a hole in the floor, and he knew old Emmett West, the house owner, would not have that. He said to Dad, "How am I going to get that marble?"

Dad said, "I don't know, but I bet W.D. can figure out how to do it."

With Mr. Gilbert and all of his kids along with me leading the pack we headed across the field to their house. With all of the confidence and responsibility of a four star general, I surveyed the situation. I asked for a weed, a string, and Mr. Gilbert's tobacco sack. I opened the sack, tied the string to it, put it down through the crack in the floor, took the weed and rolled the marble into the tobacco sack, pulled it up, and handed it to Mr. Gilbert. Between Dad and Mr. Gilbert, that feat became a community stroke of genius.

I shouldn't forget the mad dog incident. I was, as a four-year-old, proceeding along the road by Tomp Cherry's house when I looked up and saw a big brown dog coming down the road, foaming at the mouth. I screamed, ran to the fence, climbed the corner post, and stood on top of it, yelling, "Mad dog!"

In a bit, Tomp Cherry came out and Dad came running down the hill and took me down from the fence post. In a little bit, as people came along the road and the word spread, a group decided to go after the dog. As the people got their shotguns and were ready to move out into a nearby woods, someone remarked that it might have just been a big dog that scared the boy. By the time Dad finished with him, no one else dared open their mouth.

It was a bad day to be a dog in Macedonia. That group shot first and looked later, and they killed dogs until they had a brown dog that was slobbering. Don't know how long Macedonia Community had a shortage of dogs.

The Ashes, unlike the Keathleys, would drop everything for a special event. For that matter, if a relation from far away came home it was stop all work, the prodigal son is at home. So it was with Dad's cousin Marvin Perriman, that lived in far-away Portsmouth, Virginia. I can recall the joy that permeated around Aunt Molly's house as I went with Dad to visit with his cousin and the families that gathered there when Marvin visited.

Of course prohibition had limited alcoholic consumption to only that obtained from a bootlegger. Grandfather John Ashe was a rather large local bootlegger. His operation ranged from corn planting to half pints. He had a few fellows like Jim Johnson, Nim Dunn, and the like, that took lye to get the husks from the corn. Then they fermented the corn and cooked it off in a still located on a farm that granddaddy leased to grow cotton. After the white lightning was distilled, they put it in half-pint bottles and stored them in a horse trough up at granddaddy's barn. Then, as needed, it was distributed to the mail carriers for them to deliver and sell.

All of this was illegal and the secrecy was carefully guarded. Well, you can imagine the consternation when Dad, leading me, started up the hill one morning to Granddaddy's barn. There were 20 or so men milling around as Uncle T came down the hill shouting at Dad to get that boy away from here. They were verbally at it hot and heavy and about to use their fists, when Grandad came up and said "Hesh." Not another word from his two sons. They "heshed."

Granddaddy took me by the hand and led me up to the biggest horse trough I have ever seen. It was specially made by cutting a large cypress tree down at the river bottom and taking this tree to his sawmill, where a huge plank was cut as a double bottom in this big, long, wide horse trough.

The half-pints were stowed in the trough and covered by this big plank as a double bottom. This particular morning there must have been thousands of these half-pint bottles side by side in this horse trough. Granddaddy said, "Son, they are some men lookin' for these bottles. Don't ever tell anybody that they're up here." And I never did, on through my boyhood days, and through college and through the Navy.

Once I had made lieutenant commander and was 26 or 27 years old, Mr. Corbett, my step-father, once when I was on leave, commenced to pull the razzle-dazzle that he often did to my mom. He rared back and said, "Dub, did you know your grandpa Ashe was a bootlegger?" My mom, in at the sink doing dishes, came up to the door to peep into the living room and said, "You don't know that!" He said, "Yeah, but I heard it." My mom says, "Mr. Ashe was one of the finest men that I've ever known, and I don't believe that he was a bootlegger. I don't care what you may have heard."

Then to my mom I said, "Look, let's cover this once and for all." And I proceeded to relate the story that I just mentioned above. And my mom said, "I don't care if he was, He was still one of the finest men that I've ever known."

I wouldn't want to forget the day my brother A.J. was born. I was with Grandfather and Grandmother Ashe. They were pickin' cotton and I was lyin' on Grandfather's cotton sack as he pulled me along the row as he picked cotton. Someone came across the field from our house to say, "Well, Mr. Ashe, you've got another grandson." That was hardly a month after I was four years old. And to this day, I can't imagine with four boys, why Mom didn't name at least one of them John after my grandpa.

Life moved along and the year that I was five, my mother was unable to pick strawberries for canning. I recall going to the field daily in late spring and picking two gallon-and-a-half buckets of strawberries, comin' home, sittin' down and cappin' them, and giving them to momma to can.

Late in August of my fifth year, lo and behold, somebody decided that I had to go to school. I immediately decided that that wasn't for me. Fact is, it took considerable persuasion on the part of my Dad to get me to go.

He put me on the mule behind him and we rode the half-mile to Macedonia's little two-room school. With reluctance, I got off the mule and walked with him into the classroom with Miss Allie Keathley, the teacher. Boy, did I have a time, and the next morning, didn't have to have anybody take me to school. I walked and was extremely happy to be there. In a couple of days there was a cute little girl named Inez Ladd that attracted my attention. Miss Allie had assigned the kids to the little one-seat desks in the room, but there were four two-seat desks up toward the front. By then, I had learned that when you want to talk to the teacher, you put up your hand.

This I did, wavin' it around a little, until Miss Allie said, "Yes, W.D."

I said, "I want to sit with Inez in one of the two-seat desks." Miss Allie said, "Well what does Inez think about that?" Inez jumped up, grinnin' and noddin' her head yes. Miss Allie said it was all right if we didn't talk. I can assure you that there wasn't any talkin' going on there because I didn't want to lose my seat.

Miss Allie had problems with me, and I look back and think of what an expert in child psychology she must have been. I was bored in some ways because I knew how to do most of that stuff—count, learn ABCs. I did enjoy learnin' those first words. I soon learned all of them. The net result since there were four grades in that room, I spent most of those four years takin' 4th grade arithmetic.

I recall once lookin' out, puttin' my hand up. Said, "Miss Allie, I want to go play." She says, all right. I went outside, walked along the ditch four or five minutes, and learned a great lesson. It's hard to play by yourself. More fun back in the room. Never asked to go play outside of recess after that.

3

Dad's Death

Life was very good until early October. My dad died.

Terrible shock. I wouldn't even look at him in the casket. And I dreamed of him nightly for years. And it seems like an appropriate time to mention the fact that some of my dreams were prophetic.

Of the hundreds of dreams that I had over the years, a few things came out to distinguish the prophetic dreams from those that were just normal, every-day living.

If the dream was to be prophetic, it had to include things that were completely unnatural, and it had to include certain significant items. For instance, if the dream had to do with the death of one of my male relatives, everything would be white—clothes, the dirt. And whomever was in the dream playing a significant part would be the one that the dream would, for me, signify his death. Also, if it was to be one of my female relatives, most everything would be black—the horses, the clothes—and most of the time the individual would be clearly pointed out in the dream.

Now, I had dreams of other than people's deaths that were prophetic in nature. So many times I would dream of little, insignificant things, and know as it was played out in the days that followed just what was going to be said or done. But let me give a few examples of prophetic dreams that I can recall.

For instance, the death of my Uncle Charlie Flowers. I was at Memphis, going to school at Memphis State, when one night I dreamed that I was at the Baptist Hospital at Memphis and that my mother and Buren Flowers were there, and Uncle Charlie was in a room. My mom went out to visit someone. Buren said that he needed to have a smoke, and I stood in the room with Uncle Charlie and watched him as he started to die. I went running out to get B (Buren) to come into his dad's room and momma came running down, and I awakened.

The next day as I rode the streetcar home from school, to Uncle Maurice and Aunt Ruby's, where I lived, my mom was there. And she greeted me with saying that, "Law me, Charlie's up at the hospital. We had to bring him down this morning; he's in very bad shape." She said, "I wanted to come down to see you, but I have to get back up there."

So I went with her on the streetcar and went to the Baptist Hospital.

As we went in, Mom said, "Let me see what room they put him in." I said, "I know what room he's in." She said, "Dub did you dream it?" I said, yes.

We went up to his room. He was unconscious and Buren was with him and events began to unfold identically to my dream the previous night.

Let me mention my dream prior to the death of Aunt Zolie. I was away somewhere in the Navy, and I believe at Navy War College, when one night I dreamed of a large, long column of black horses all being ridden by men dressed in black. And they were comin' down the lane there at the homeplace. No one other than these unknown men was to be seen in the dream until, as they slowly disappeared, Aunt Zolie was standin' beside me as I awakened.

About two days later she was taken to the hospital in Memphis and she passed away.

Uncle Wade Zaricor, the mail carrier, is another. After I retired from the Navy, I dreamed that I was up in the field of the Ashe farm. Uncle T and Aunt Bonnie were hoeing cotton and the earth was white as snow. Uncle Wade came along, got out of his car, climbed the fence over to where they were, talked with them a bit, turned and headed back toward his car, and slowly disappeared into a cloud.

The next morning, I went to work. Called Wade Jr., who lived in Washington, and asked, "How long has it been since you been home, son?" Well, he says, "I went home last week." He said, "Dub, did you have a dream?" I said yes. He asks, "Who was it?" I said, "It's your daddy." He says, "I'll call the office and leave for home in a few minutes." He drove through to Kenton all day and all night, called me the next morning to say "Dub, they've just taken him to the hospital, but I got here in time to see him."

He died shortly thereafter.

And the death of Aunt Bonnie. I dreamed one night that my mother had gone over to Kenton to visit Aunt Bonnie and took her an apple pie and visited with Aunt Bonnie, left and in the dream I was tellin' momma to come back. I turned around in the dream as Aunt Bonnie went back into the house. Then she had a heart attack and died while I'm looking at her and trying to scream, but of course no words are coming out.

Next day, Mom called me to tell me that Aunt Bonnie died last night, "and you know I just went to see her and took her a pie."

The most unusual of my dreams was the death of Anna Hollis. Now as I mentioned before, over the years, those prophetic dreams that I had were more or less limited to things associated with my relatives. I was a midshipman at Northwestern University when one night, about 4 o'clock, I dreamed that I was in a little shack looking down as Uncle Wade and Aunt Bonnie came in to visit Anna Hollis that was ill. They brought her some strawberry ice cream, visited with her, she ate the cream, and then they went out of the little shack to drive away, and my position in the dream continued to be that of being aloft looking down, and I was trying to shout to Uncle Wade and Aunt Bonnie to come back, which of course they didn't. While I was up there looking and helpless, Anna passed away.

About four days later, I got a letter from Mom at home saying that Anna Hollis had passed away, and the unusual thing about it was that Wade and Bonnie had come out and visited with her the night before and brought her some ice cream.

This dream shook me up considerably, because it didn't make sense, because Anna Hollis was in no way related to us. And so, once when I was back on leave, I related the incident as I was visiting Aunt Bonnie at her home one day. I said, "You know Aunt Bonnie, the strange thing about it is, I don't have those dreams except about people that are related to me. She says, "W.D., you don't know, do you?" I says, "What?" She says, "Anna lived with Poppa for several years, and her daughter Robbie Lou is your aunt."

Then, years later, I had a dream that Robbie Lou came to visit my mother, where she lived at the Keathley home place. I remember Robbie Lou only as a little four or five-year-old girl as she came to spend the night as we lived over near Grandfather Ashe while my dad was still alive. But in the dream, I dreamed that she came to visit in the community, and visiting my mother, and me, in my dream, listening on the sidelines as they talked, and then she faded away.

A few days after the dream, Mother wrote me a letter telling me that Robbie Lou had passed away.

The most detailed of any of my dreams came with the one prior to Uncle Elihu's death. I dreamed that Evaline and myself went to visit my mother who lived at the Keathley home place and this was after I had retired from the Navy. The day after arriving at mother's, she wanted to go visit Uncle Elihu, who she said was over at Bobby's. We went to visit Bobby and went in and Uncle Elihu was being nursed by Aunt Ollie and she introduced me to him, asking, "Do you know W.D.?" I don't know whether he recognized me or not. Nevertheless, we visited there for a couple of hours and then went back to Mom's home. The next morning, Mom at breakfast says she feels anxious about Elihu. "Let's go back and see him." We drove back to Bobby's, went in, and from my discussion with Aunt Ollie, I thought Uncle Elihu was worse. But we hung around for a couple or three hours, during which time I noted that his extremities were getting cold and his breathing was getting short. With this, I suggested to Bobby that he might ought to call Harold Lloyd and Geraldine that I thought Uncle Elihu was getting close to death. Well, Bobby went and called them, without any further discussion, and in the dream I also recall that Harold Lloyd came in by plane, and I went along with Roy Manis, and as we came back along Uncle Elihu's bed we watched him draw his last breath.

I dreamed further that the funeral was conducted at the Kenton Funeral Home, but although I had been in the funeral home many times, I just didn't recognize it as the Kenton funeral home. And at the funeral, Geraldine came in wearing a black dress and said to me, "Dub, did you dream all of this?" And I says yes, and now the dream's over, and I awakened.

And of course, to the dot of the I, events unfolded identically as I dreamed it, including the funeral being over as Gerry come in, wearing her black dress, and I said the dream's over.

Likewise, I dreamed a most unusual dream—totally unrealistic of M.A. and Uncle Maurice. I dreamed that they were in a great valley. The valley had snow-covered mountains on each side, and they were racing with each other making giant strides, moving a mile with each stride, racing, with M.A. slowly drawing ahead until it was apparent that he won.

I wakened and that dream bothered me, and it wasn't too long until I learned that M.A. had cancer of the lung and Uncle Maurice had cancer of the prostate. They moved along several years before they passed away, and M.A. passed away several months before Uncle Maurice did.

I could easily write a book about the many dreams. I recall I used to tell my cousins when I was in school about my dreams to the extent that they have about as much confidence in my dreams as I do, except they don't want me to dream about them.

4

Grandmother Keathley's House, Farris' birth

Now enough about dreams. I had a thought. I vividly remember Farris' birth. It was in the spring and we were pickin' strawberries and again momma couldn't pick herself, nor did she have anyone who could pick strawberries for her, and I took upon myself the job of picking strawberries for her. I recall one day after years of her beatin' my butt for goin' over to Granddaddy's, it was suggested—by her—that I go over to Granddaddy's, and while I was over at Granddaddy's, Farris was born. Farris Eugene Ashe, which he was saddled with for a name, came from a little old girl that had married Jim Hayes up from Lake County, and we later learned that half of Lake County was named Farris Eugene Ashe.

In 1926, Dad became ill with something called "locked bowels," which at the time was the name for an infection of the intestine. A cure would have been simple with present-day antibiotics, but at that time, there was nothing to stop the infection, so they resorted to surgery, removing portions of the infected intestine. Dad died on the operating table during the second time in surgery.

After Dad's untimely death, Oct. 3, 1926, Grandpa Ashe moved us in with him and grandmother. We lived with them four months. One cold February, both of them died the same day. They were both sick in separate rooms at the Ashe home place. About 1 p.m. Grandmother Ashe raised up in the bed in her room and shouted, "So long, John! But I'll see ye in a little bit." Everyone knew that Grandmother was seriously ill and the children were all there at the home place gathered around her bed and it was decided to get me over as quickly as possible to represent Dad's family.

As a seven-year old, I was rather bewildered as they lined us up according to age around the foot of Grandmother's bed. We stayed there, watching her, for some time as it got more and more difficult for her to breathe, and finally, in typical pneumonia fashion, she died.

So after about four months, we moved to Grandmother Keathley's where we lived for the next six years.

Down at Grandmother Keathley's there were cousins by the dozens and almost continuously there were visits for special days or special Sundays, or anything else special, like a birthday. Grandmother Keathley was a matriarch, a disciplinarian, who maintained law and order with a peach tree switch. All the kids running around were a varying degree of trouble all the time. And when she saw some hooligan like M.A., she would call the offender over to her chair, and have them stand still while she wore them out with that peach tree limb. Now that happened to me only once. And that was enough for me to learn, no matter what Grandma said, stay away from that chair!

Occasionally she would get furious, and try to catch me. And when my Mom would see this happen, I got it with that razor strap. Because Mom would say, "Don't you ever run from your Grandma."

Life was very good those years with Grandma. And those visits with my cousins cemented the wonderful relations that I have with those cousins even to this day.

There were some difficulties with the Ashe estate settlement and the little dab of insurance that Dad had on his life, with the premium being left to Mom and us boys. The insurance amounted to $250 for her and $750 for the boys. The court appointed Uncle Elihu as the guardian for us boys and Mom spent her $250 buying a steel vault for Dad's casket. The settlement of the Ashe estate added another $555 to this amount and Uncle Elihu, as guardian, was authorized to lend as investment, collect the interest, on this $1155.

My Dad's brothers and sisters were already at odds with Uncle Elihu because the sale of the Ashe homeplace included the house, barn, and 18-acre farm that belonged to Mom and Dad. Uncle Elihu tried to convince Mom to sue the Ashe estate for the house and barn that was sold with the estate and the proceeds retained by the estate. Mom wouldn't let him do this because she was concerned about creating hard feelings in the family.

Already, some of these ill feelings were cropping up because Grandpa had paid for the doctor and hospital bill incurred while Daddy was in the hospital prior to his death. These difficult relations got worse when some of my uncles and aunts wanted to borrow funds from our guardian, Uncle Elihu, and he wouldn't let them have it. Over the years, both my father's folk and my mother's folk did their best to give me their version of several of the things wrong with the other family.

Years later, I spent the night with Wade Zaricor at his home in Knoxville after attending Walt, Jr.'s wedding. Wade looked at me and said, "Dub, why is it that your uncles didn't like my mom and dad?"

I told him, "Wade, it came about because when your Dad bought the Ashe homeplace my uncles were furious that my mom and dad's farm was included in the Ashe estate." I said, "In the beginning, your mom, Uncle Cully and Aunt Lou Ella took the position that the farm should not be included in the estate. But after your dad bought the estate, your mom changed her position and decided to let Dad's farm go with the estate."

Wade, Jr. exploded, came out of the chair at the Senator's Club in Knoxville, saying, "Are you saying my mom agreed for them to steal your dad's farm?" He says, "I'll beat the livin' hell out of you right here!"

I said, "No you won't. We determined that 20 years ago. You couldn't whip my ass if you had a couple of people helpin' you. I was just tellin' you how it happened. And another dang thing. I've told you a lot of things and you never have found me wrong."

He said, "I'll get the papers and I'll ram 'em down your throat!"

Well, I'll say this much for Wade. He went home and dug up the papers, went to Union City and got additional papers. He sent them all to me about two months later in a big manila envelope that I still have. Attached to the papers was a little note.

"You son of a bitch, you're right again."

But before we make the Ashes look too bad, the Keathleys were equally guilty, in that when Grandma passed away they all wanted to keep the homeplace in the family and they agreed to sign over their part for nothin' to Uncle Henry if he would pay off grandmother's indebtedness.

This alone made Uncle Gregory terribly angry and he proclaimed that he and Hetty were giving their part to Audelle and not to Henry.

When I was 15 years old Uncle Elihu took me to circuit court and requested the court to let him, as guardian, start paying some of the principal in addition to the interest on this $1155 fund. The court ruled and directed that he pay us from the principal $15 a month. Uncle Elihu proceeded to pull in the loans to make this possible. Among the loans were people that couldn't possibly pay anything. Some $400 of the funds had been loaned to pay taxes, payments and the like on Grandmother Keathley's farm. When Uncle Elihu asked Uncle Henry for the money, he stated that he wasn't paying any more on that farm. So, Uncle Maurice and Uncle Elihu tried to pay a few dollars, but soon decided that the funds were probably expended for our benefit, so after about eight months, or $120, the payments were completed.

Some fond memories from living at Grandma Keathley's. Winters when her sisters would come to visit. I dearly loved to listen to Grandma, Aunt Tella and Aunt Rosie talk about the days when they were young girls. Momma gave me permission to sit up and listen to them on the basis that I wouldn't say a word. I must've wanted to listen to them something awful!

Poor old Aunt Tella couldn't hear, and some of the most ridiculous misunderstandings would come up as she was listening to the stories. One of my favorites was Aunt Rosie explaining the damage done at a wreck of a truck loaded with watermelon. She used her hands to explain that one watermelon slid across and hit somebody, and put her hands up, showin' the watermelon to be about two and a half feet long. Aunt Tella leaned forward and says, "Brother who?" I can just see it now. Aunt Rosie and Grandma just died laughing, though of course I didn't know enough to laugh.

Stories of their killing hogs, making soap, spinning yarn, and trying to keep their kids from starving all became part of my family tree history.

During those days, every fifth Sunday was a large gathering down at Aunt Em's house (Grandma). Where there's food and a large gathering, you'll always find a bunch of fat preachers. These birds used to collect by the dozens. The kids had to wait until after the preachers had finished eating and moved out into the yard under the shade tree. These preachers, all Baptist, mind you, would have lively discussions out under these mulberry trees at the homeplace.

Frequently, they would quote scriptures to carry the argument for whatever the discussion was, but most of the time, they would quote the scriptures incorrectly. It was with glee, malice and forethought that I would listen to these discussions, interrupt and correct somebody that quoted the scriptures incorrectly. My Mom didn't go for her number one son disputin' the elders, and she'd hear me tell somebody that something wasn't correct, and she'd come out, grab ahold of me, take me inside, and tell me, "Do NOT correct your elders."

She soon learned that I didn't correct them if they weren't wrong, and by the time I was 11or 12 she didn't say too much more about it.

Some of those preachers I knew very well, liked, and respected. And even while I was in high school, some of the time, Brother Duncan, for example, when called upon to teach the men's Bible class, would turn around and look for me, and invite me over to teach the men's Bible class.

I always looked forward to my many cousins comin' down to visit.

But two in particular were especially welcome. Mary Emma, spoiled brat though she was, Grandmother's pet, was a lively and welcome guest. I recall once, during one of her week visits, she ran out, climbed up over the top of the rain barrel, stuck her head down in it, just above the water, and commenced screaming because she couldn't get out. I let her scream a while, and then pulled her out. But I always was very sad when she went home.

Harold Lloyd, when he was down, then at Memphis, back at Kenton, and every other place we lived, was just another brother, and still is.

But as I've said, life was nice livin' with Grandmother Keathley, and it was a terrible tragedy for her to pass away from pneumonia when I was 12 years of age.

5

Working at the Pie Shop

During the time that Grandmother was ill with the flu and pneumonia, Mom also had flu and pneumonia. My mom almost died also, and she had a rather long period of recovery, during which time we visited each of her brothers and sisters for approximately a week.

After she recovered a bit it was decided that we would move to Memphis. We moved into a little shotgun house right next door to Uncle Maurice and Aunt Ruby. I recall the rent was $2.50 a month, and that Mom worked in the pie shop for a dollar a day.

Malc was 10 and I was 12 and turned 13 while at Memphis, and both of us worked in the pie shop both afternoons and mornings. It was especially difficult to get up early in the morning to go sack pies. Life for the year 1932-1933 at Memphis was a terrible economic grind.

It was at Memphis that my capabilities as a military leader came forth. Because at the ripe old age of 13, I organized and led the Philadelphia Gang. We didn't do too many bad things. We'd go over to Orange Mound and take the nigra boys' tires away from them and bring them home. We'd get into fights with the Bruce Street gang, led by an Irishman named Ferguson. I'd call him a "dago," and we'd fight the rest of the day. And he wasn't even a dago!

Then Harold Lloyd came to visit us, and he helped get this gang fightin' on a payin' basis, in that he kicked a Bruce Street gang member off of the car shed, lit out a runnin', and got hit in the head with a large lump of coal that knocked him down in our yard. This prompted him to go into the kitchen and get the ice pick. He come sailin' out, headin' for this Ferguson that I despised, but not enough to ventilate him with an ice pick. So I had to take the ice pick away from Harold. The first time we recalled this together, Harold leaned over, chuckled, and said, "I ought' a stuck him with it!"

Harold continued these visits to be with me in Memphis, even in later years, after I was in college.

Since most of my life has been spent in school, it's only appropriate that I mention a few of the schools, and some good and some bad things.

At almost six years old, it was off to Macedonia School for me.

Macedonia School consisted of two rooms and two teachers. I'm sure that the educators of today would consider those of us destined to be educated in Macedonia as being deprived of many advantages that we could never have. But let me assure you, for myself, for my brothers, for my cousins, and my friends at Macedonia, we were enriched by having Macedonia's two teachers—Miss Allie Keathley for the first four grades, and Mr. Cecil Stewart for the next four.

Miss Allie was truly a patient, talented teacher who helped me cope with always being ahead of my class. Mr. Stewart was the most outstanding teacher I've ever known. Yes, he taught all subjects well. Plus he taught singing, debating, and organized class games. He was a strict disciplinarian. He maintained order by using plenty of corporal punishment, *a la* leather belt. Anyone misbehaving was grabbed up, thrown across a desk top and worn out across the back and the seat of the pants with his belt.

Sure, I was an accomplished student, well-trained by my mother before even going to school. But those two teachers taught more than reading, writing and 'rithmetic. They taught us to live with people. They took us to church. They organized debating teams. They taught us music, choir singing, sessions on special events, far better than anything that I got years later at Memphis schools.

A lot of interesting things happened. I recall that I was a cracker-jack speller in the fourth grade. I went off to Union City, won the county spelling contest. Figured I had it, didn't need to learn any more about spelling, and never did. One of my great literary shortcomings is an inability to spell anything more difficult than maybe "cat."

That reminds me of a little story. We had a very attractive girl in school two grades ahead of me, named Lamyra Little. One day Lamyra came to school with her hair done up in pigtails. She sat across the aisle from me, just in front of Buddy Crabtree. Mr. Stewart was holding forth up at the blackboard, teaching geography to some other class when I reached across, grabbed one of those pigtails, and gave it a tug. I jumped back, and Lamyra thought it was Buddy Crabtree. She stood up and just slapped the heck out of poor old Buddy, and he didn't even know what had happened.

Mr. Stewart looked up, saw the commotion, come running back, grabbed old Buddy, threw him across the desk and out with the belt. He gave him a good whippin' standing 'bout two feet from my shoulder. I assure you that I didn't breathe comfortably for several days.

As I mentioned before, we moved to Memphis in time for the 7th grade. I went to a beautiful new Memphis junior high school called Fairview. Whether it was the lack of organization on the part of the teachers, or whether it was my being thoroughly disgusted with this new school, I learned very little at Fairview.

While at Memphis, we were living in squalid conditions of near starvation, working unusual hours and other disrupting factors. But the chief thing was that, as an outside of Memphis student, I was placed in an unclassified class, which meant that Memphis school system's dumbbells were in this class, called 7-7.

It was during my 7th grade at Fairview that I helped another student cheat. It was in geography class. The teacher always gave true/false tests. She read them to us. I'm sure that was necessary for some of those people couldn't read well enough to take a test. But I always made 100. A boy sitting next to me always flunked. So I told him to watch my thumb. If I let my thumb stay up, write "true," and if I let it lay down, write "false." The teacher "oohed and aahed" and congratulated that old boy for the next several months, and it wasn't hurting my thumb a bit. Later that old boy moved up and became a lieutenant in Memphis' Southside gang, a bunch of hoodlums, thieves, and sometimes killers.

While at Memphis State the gang raided the pie shop one night while I was there alone. I loudly proclaimed that I'd get every one of them. The net result was that I was approached one night about 12 o'clock at the Peabody Theater with about 20 of the gang streaming across the street intent on beating me up and slapping around my date, who was Evaline, to teach me a lesson. This same boy, my former classmate at Fairview, leading the attack, stopped, recognized me, and commenced yelling for the people, "Stop, stop, stop!" and he turned that gang back away and let me go.

It was during the year that we lived at Memphis amid our daily efforts to survive that it was decided that Uncle Maurice would take us all to Macedonia for the church centennial, August 1932. Can you imagine Uncle Maurice, Aunt Ruby, Maurice Jr., Carmen, Roy, Mom, Malc, Jake, Farris and myself all crowding into a 1928 Chevrolet and heading the 106 miles to Macedonia?

We stayed Saturday night and on Sunday afternoon headed back to Memphis. Just outside Brownsville we had a blowout. There in the hot, broiling sun I, a 13-year-old, helped Uncle Maurice repair and pump up the tire. As I was finishing pumping the tire, the other back tire blew out. Oh, I was so glad when two months later it was decided that we were to move back to Macedonia.

We moved into an old house that had three rooms, no running water, no bathroom, and a well for drinking water that was full of old rotted splinters from the well shaft. We had to strain the water through flour-sack cloth in order to drink it. Aside from trying to find ways to get something to eat and something to wear, it was great to be in the 8th grade at Macedonia.

I fell madly in love with Frances Epperson. In the beginning this courtship consisted of note writing, like "Roses are red, violets are blue, you love me and I'll love you," and so on. One day Mr. Stewart called me in and asked me if I had been writing any notes. Of course, I said, "Yes sir, I have."

He then said, "Have you gotten any answers to these notes?" And I said, "Yes sir, I got answers to all of them."

He said Mr. Epperson had complained to him that I had been writing notes to Frances and he would appreciate it if I didn't write any more notes. I promised that I wouldn't and went outside the schoolhouse and told Frances. Lo and behold, Mr. Stewart had had Frances, Ray Dunn and Dorothy Bryant in for the same kind of questioning and they had each told him no, they hadn't written any notes, nor had they received any. Ho, hum. I blamed it all on Mr. Epperson, a tough old World War I veteran. Mr. and Mrs. Epperson were the schoolhouse janitors and daily cleaned both rooms.

I used to sneak behind the curtain that formed a stage in Mr. Stewart's room and hug and kiss Frances each day before going home. I was careful not to be seen by Mr. Epperson, moving around only a few feet away.

Macedonia School was made up mostly of two family groups: the Ashes, including Keathleys, Bryants, Warix; and the Pettys, along with the Littles, Simons, and so on. Most every day there was a feud between the families. Usually it was Farris, age eight, that started the fight by hitting Lloyd Petty, but occasionally Lloyd Petty whacked old Farris one. The fight pattern was repetitious and evolved almost instantly. Farris would whack Lloyd and Haywood Petty would go for

Farris. Jake would be all over Haywood and old Harold Lloyd, who just loved to fight, would plough into the Pettys with both fists flying. At the same time other Petty brothers and Little brothers would enter the act. In less time than it takes to relate, John David Warix would be slamming away at a Petty or a Simon. As these seconds passed, old Malc would be moving into the fray. Malc fought only one way—wide, swinging haymakers. When he hit a boy up beside the head, the head would be forward of the feet as he hit the ground.

The oldest Petty, Grady, was my age, and we didn't fight. The very first day I had told him there wasn't any use in our fighting because I could beat him every time, and if he wanted proof I would give it to him.

Farris usually started the fight to coincide with the bell that ended recess so the teachers sort of looked over what was happening. Even though Mr. Stewart repeatedly told everyone there would be no fighting, as we walked home from school, obeying didn't enter Harold Lloyd's mind. Just as we got out of sight from school, just over the hill from Mr. Hayes, Harold would pick up a clod and whop Laudell Lowe, and by the time we reached Helen Baucom's house, Laudell would have Harold down, just beating the heck out of him. Fists to the face, with bloody nose and so on. Daily I would let it reach this point before making Laudell stop. Laudell was a lot bigger than Harold—Harold never fought with people his size. Mom, one time in later years as we were discussing these long-ago fights, asked Farris, "Why didn't you fight with someone you could whip without help from your brother?"

Farris answered Mom, "There wasn't anyone in school that I could whip."

6

The Cat Hole

Harold would come visit us every time he could swing permission and we always were glad he was there. As I mentioned, his willingness to fight at the drop of a hat didn't include us. I don't remember even a single problem among us as we grew up.

One of the reasons Harold liked to visit us was that he liked to go swimming in Earl Bryant's pond located near the path we used to walk to and from home to school. It was one such day in the spring of my 15th year that Harold left school at the earliest possible moment and shoved off to the pond, walking alone. I messed around school a bit, kissing on Frances and so on, before following the path we used. As I approached the pond I noted that the hogs were in the field. This swimming pond of ours could be used only after driving the hogs out of the water. It was all muddy and smelly, very bad, but it was all we had. When I was about 200 yards away I saw what proved to be Harold coming up and gurgling every once in a while. I ran over, dived into the pond, pulled him out, put his head on the bank below his feet, and pushed on him a while until he could talk. Then we walked on home. I don't know how much I did for humanity, but I did a lot for Harold.

My early life would be far from complete if I didn't mention the cat hole. This historic geographical point was where the Obion River was joined by a swiftly flowing drainage ditch just below Aunt Molly's farm.

The water was deep, flowing swiftly as it sharply turned to the right on down the bottom. It was supposedly full of catfish—so the name.

At every opportunity all the boys would go fishing. I would tell Mom we were going to the bottom to fish and she would always admonish, "Alright, but don't go near that cat hole." Of course, the next stop was the cat hole.

Normal routine at the cat hole was to swim across the swift ditch to a point where you could stand up. We would spend hours diving for mussels that grew in the mud at the bottom of the swift ditch. I recall teaching all the boys to swim—my brothers, Harold, Roland, John David, Charles Edward, Roy Manus, and others—but none of us was expert enough to swim in that swift water with any degree of safety. Several near deaths occurred.

Once Malc saved Roy Manus by running around the bank of the cat hole and pushing a plank out for him to grab hold of. Saved his life!

We caught an occasional channel cat, but we could have done well if we could have had some fish bait. Troy and Millard Bryant locked their boats to a tree and left them at the cat hole, and we came along and either cut the cable or broke the lock. When they got a lock that we couldn't break, we took a single-shot .22 rifle and you would be surprised at how fast a lock gives up the ghost when shot with a rifle. Yes, life was nice back in Macedonia.

The year that I turned 15, we moved into a shack near the Keathley home place. Uncle Maurice had started to build this place for him and Aunt Ruby before they moved to Memphis, but it was never finished. First, there was no well. All water for any use had to be carried from Oran's, who lived in the homeplace. There was no bathroom. We had a little outhouse about 100 feet from the house.

This little shack consisted of four little rooms that were not sealed nor weather-boarded. There was a good roof, but the floor and the sides of the house had been built of green gum planks. They had dried out and left half-inch cracks between each plank. The rafters holding the roof sat on the sill at the top of the walls and a six-inch space allowed snow and rain to blow into the house. A snowstorm covered our bed, but since there was no heat to melt the snow, it wasn't too much of a problem after a storm to take the top quilt outside to shake off the snow. The only heat in the house was generated by burning wood in a little stove in one of the rooms. One of my worst problems was building a fire with green gum wood. But by far my worst problem was trying to keep firewood.

Trying to keep firewood in that house was a continuing, very difficult, job. Without a little fire in the wintertime, it was terribly uncomfortable to sit anywhere in the house. You could make it at night with sufficient covers even though snow collected on top of the beds. We never suffered in the bed. In order to try to keep firewood in the house, we cut wood every day possible during the summertime. Even so, every afternoon, after arriving home from school, it was necessary both to cut wood and to bring wood into the house.

Of course this would not have been possible if it had not been for my cousin Oran Wyricks, who was Mamma's age. Through thick and thin, he worked diligently to see that we had wood to burn. I was able to assist Oran in chopping, sawing and loading wood for both his house and ours. In fact, it was woodcutting with Orin that became a disaster for Malcolm.

Charles Edward was about six years old, and Malc was 13 years old, with all of us down in the Keathley woods, trying to cut wood, when he swung the ax that came over and cut Malcolm's leg. That resulted in his being a permanent cripple.

The accident scared Oran. He picked up Malcolm, put him in the wagon, and I jumped in with him. He raced the team all the way to Kenton to a doctor's office. The doctor did what he could, but it wasn't sufficient. A few weeks later, Malc was taken to the Baptist Hospital in Memphis, where he stayed for months, with the doctors daily debating whether to amputate his leg.

The cutting of wood reminds me of an incident. It was an extremely cold February day. Backwater was out over the bottom. Neither Orin nor I had more than a few sticks of wood. It was impossible to get it from the bottom with the water out, and we were faced with the oncoming night with nothing to burn. Uncle Henry had repeatedly emphasized that we could cut only the gum wood from down in the Keathley woods lot, but I was not about to spend the night without a fire. I went down to Oran's house and told him, "Looks to me like we got two choices. One is to cut that big beech tree up next to our house, or the other is to tear the planks off of the barn and burn them."

Oran says, "Shoot, dadgum, Henry will skin us alive if we cut down that beech tree."

And I said, "It won't be as bad as burnin' the barn!"

Oran got his big crosscut saw, sharpened it, and we went up with him reluctantly sawin' down this big tree that was about four feet in diameter.

After we sawed the tree, we began to cut blocks from the log that we planned to slab for firewood. But, lo and behold, after we cut off the second block, Oran raised his head, looked down the road, and saw Uncle Henry's car comin'. Oran shoved off to the barn, and I proceeded to slab the blocks of beech wood.

Uncle Henry's car came around the homeplace. He got out, and naturally the first thing he missed was that great big beech tree that was already huge when he was born, and he'd watched it all of his life. He walked up to where I was splitting wood, and said, "W.D., what do you mean, cutting down that tree?"

I said, "Uncle Henry, we have no wood, and it was a choice—either burn the planks off the barn or cut the beech tree."

He almost choked. He could hardly speak. He said, "Don't you ever do a thing like that again."

I said, "Uncle Henry, if I'm out of wood, I'll cut another 'un." He said, "You can get your wood in the summertime."

I said, "In the summer, I'm helping Oran plant and gather corn, and while he's growin' the crop, we can't be cuttin' wood. (Note, he never once paid me a dime for helpin' Oran with his crops, even though he paid Oran $30 a month for doin' everything. Of course, he couldn't do it all.)

But Uncle Henry got into his car, drove off. After a bit, Oran came out of the barn and asked me, "What did he say?"

I told him, and told him, "We won't have to worry about it anymore this year, because this tree will last us all winter. But I think he knows that we'll cut down another tree if we have to."

Another rather large problem was trying to, some way, earn enough to buy food and clothes. By the time I reached 15, whenever a job became available, I was johnny on the spot, working as long as the job lasted.

It was necessary to take a job, any kind of job, and stay out of school any time I could get a job. The only reason that I even tried to go to high school was that most of the time, there wasn't any sort of a job available.

Thanks are due to people in the community who would give me a job any time that they had something to do that they could afford to pay for. I recall an instance where the owner of a farm there in the community, a fella named Willard, had crashed and almost killed himself a few years earlier flying airplanes. Mr. and Mrs. Willard came to Macedonia to go through a recuperating period for Mr. Willard.

One day, while sitting under the tree down at Oran's, Mr. Willard met Earl Bryant, stopped him in the road right next to Oran's. He said, "Mr. Bryant, I need a man to help the fellow I have do a little work."

Earl Bryant said, "Mr. Willard, I have a boy in mind that I'll guarantee will do as much work as any man you can hire. Fact is, if you don't think he does, I'll pay for it myself."

Mr. Willard says, "Where can I find this boy?"

Earl Bryant says, "In that house, right next to this one. His name is W.D. Ashe." He says, "You can get to the house by driving across that field down the road."

Mr. Willard thanked him, and I shoved off to the house, keepin' on the dark side of the hill, and by the time that Willard got to the house, I was there, ready and waitin' for him.

He asked me, could I work for him, and I says, "Yes, sir." Didn't ask him what he paid. I knew that. Everybody paid 10 cents an hour, or a $1 a day for a 10-hour day.

Mr. Willard says to me, well, be at his house tomorrow morning at 7 o'clock. You bet your life I was there. Shortly after 7 he arrived with some bird that lived in Kenton that worked for him. Mr. Willard told us to go haul hay. He with his two walking canes sat in a chair under a tree next to his house, watching us. Well, this bird put me to throwin' up the hay with a fork onto the wagon, and put himself up on the wagon, placin' the hay. No trouble at all for me—I just was takin' large forks of the hay and pitchin' up a couple of feet onto the wagon.

After a bit, the hay was getting higher and higher on the wagon and he, apparently knowing nothing about hauling hay, was letting the hayload get narrower and narrower. I got up on the wagon, and by this time, it was getting higher and higher to pitch it up, but I took the fork and spread the hay to have a decent load, practically resting, while the guy was struggling to throw the hay up.

In a bit, a load was on the wagon and we proceeded to the barn, where this bird told me to throw the hay into the loft while he stacked it back. The hay level in the loft was about the same, so it was easy for me to pitch the hay into the loft while the guy was havin' difficulty carryin' it back to the back of the loft, and since he was so slow at it, he soon was gaggin' for air inside the barn.

Well, he soon decided that he'd get down on the wagon, with him throwin' the hay in and me carryin' it back would be a better deal. Again, it was getting higher and higher to pitch it into the loft, and was no difficulty for me. Taking huge forks of hay, I kept the loft door uncovered, had no trouble with keepin' the hay flowing in.

Pretty soon it's lunch time, and for farm laborers, it was normal to work 'til 12:00 and rest and go back to work at 1:00. Momma, poor old soul, had made some cornbread and Irish potatoes for my lunch.

Fortunately, we had some potatoes, since it was summertime. And Mrs. Willard brought us out some cold lemonade. Repeat performance, almost, during the afternoon. And, as the day was over, Mr. Willard asked me, did I know how to drive a team. I told him, "Yes, sir!"

He said for me to be at his place in the mornin' at 7 o'clock, and he took this bird back to Kenton and apparently fired him, because the next morning he said to me, "You did twice as much work as that fella did."

The next morning I hitched up his team and he wanted me to plow his cotton, which I did, until almost exactly 11:00. The mules come up to the fence where Mr. Willard sat, and stopped, and they wouldn't budge.

Mr. Willard says, "They usually balk 'bout 11:00. Unhitch 'em and take 'em on down to the barn and feed 'em."

I said, "Mr. Willard, I can get them over that balkin' bid'ness." He says, "How?"

I said, "I saw, down at the barn, that you have one of those black snake whips. A little of that whip, and they'll go on and work the other hour."

He said, calling the name of that guy who was from Kenton, "He always quit at 11:00 because he couldn't make 'em work any more."

I went after the whip, came back up, looked at him, and said, "Now Mr. Willard, this is not going to look nice."

He nodded, I told the mules to get up, took this whip, cracked it over their heads, making it like a shot. They didn't move. The next time, I came down across the back of one of the mules. He still didn't move. Then I took the whip and brought it around under the stomach, and kept workin' on the same mule. After about 10 or 12 good licks, he commenced to move an inch or two at a time, and he commenced to movin'.

We made another round, and they stopped again. This time I cracked the whip and they turned and proceeded ploughin' until 12 o'clock came and I then unhooked them and took them to the barn.

Needless to say, Mr. Willard wanted to know if I knew how to hoe cotton. I told him I sure did. He asked me did I know anybody to help me. I said, yes, my mom. So for the next two times that the cotton needed to be hoed, Momma, along with all of her boys, would come over and we'd hoe the Willards' cotton. He would pay Mom and myself. Malc, Jake and Farris were there, but they were too little to do any cotton choppin'.

7

Kenton High School

Can you imagine how tough it must have been for Mom to get us all up, have a little bite of something for breakfast, and walk over to the Willard's, to be ready to start hoeing cotton at 7:00 a.m.? We would carry our lunch—cornbread and Irish potatoes—in a dishpan, put it under a shade tree, and have the younger boys try to keep the ants out of it.

Life went on in this manner, as I tried in every way possible to get a job, any kind of job, doing anything, and I stayed out of school for whatever length of time any job was available. Throughout our young days, Mom and all the boys had to rely on what we could make picking strawberries in the spring and picking cotton in the fall, plus any of the occasional odd jobs that I was able to get.

This caused considerable absenteeism from school. In fact, the sum total of days that I attended were less than half. This included the tenth grade, where I was out over 100 days. But when I did get a chance to go back to school, I applied myself diligently, even tried to excel. And, fortunately, my grades were outstanding. But this was with considerable help and cooperation from the schoolteachers.

By now, I was attending high school in Kenton. I recall once returning to school at about the time Mr. Moffatt, a new teacher at Kenton, was ready to give our class a test in math. Mr. DuBow, the principal, came into our class just before the test and told Mr. Moffatt that, since W.D. had to work when he could, we teachers let him decide when he was ready to take the make-up tests. He says in his long drawl, "If you don't have time to do this, let me know, and I'll do it." Can you imagine the young Moffatt's reaction to such a directive!

Early in the 11th grade I got a job working in the grocery store at Kenton. The hours were Saturday noon until Saturday midnight, and the pay was 75 cents for each Saturday. The next year, I was paid $1 a day.

Following my graduation, Malc, Jake and Farris followed me in the job, but by the time Farris graduated, he was making $3.75 a day.

In spite of economic problems, life in Kenton High School was full of fond memories. I went to visit Mary Emma every time I possibly could. In fact, it must have been a pain for Aunt Ella to cook me all of those wonderful meals.

I must jot down one particular incident. It seemed impossible for Mary Emma to get up in time to go to school. Our principal in my 10th grade, a Mr. Caldwell, daily called the roll. Anyone late for roll call was automatically required to stay in an hour after school. So Mary would literally pick 'em up and put 'em down the last minutes trying to be at school in time for the roll call.

One morning as we came in the door, we could hear the principal's voice coming from the study hall. "Mary Emma," he said. From the entrance doorway, Mary shouted, "Present, Mr. Caldwell." Of course, I was already marked late because he called these names alphabetically and the A's had come and gone. But after roll call Mr. Caldwell called off the criminal list of names with Mary Emma on it, and I wasn't on it. Mary Emma stood up and said, "Mr. Caldwell, I was comin' in the door and I answered present."

Mr. Caldwell says, "That made you 'bout a minute late."

Mary sat down and got back up, and asked, "Why doesn't W.D. have to stay in?"

Mr. Caldwell says, "Mary Emma, you caused him to be late, wasn't his fault."

She just dies when that's brought up again, and commences sputterin' and spittin' all over.

Even though I was out much of the time, I still participated in basketball and made my letter in both 11th and 12th grades. And I was a member of the various plays produced by my class each year, and I also was a member of the cast for the special drama classes. And even once, as an actor with a commercial concern that was wintering over in Kenton. In all of these plays, I was the good-lookin' hero that wound up winnin' the heart of the play's heroine.

During the first three years at high school, we did not have a school bus. I didn't enjoy that luxury until the 12th grade. Now, from our home in Macedonia to the Kenton school building, it was 3.1 miles on a clear day, at least 10 miles when it was cold, muddy and raining.

I had a few little misunderstandings while going to Kenton High School. During the 12th grade we continued the girl and boy basketball teams riding together to the school that we were playing each Friday night. As a senior, I took possession of the entire back seat of the bus. And since, riding in the dark, sometimes for 50 miles, offered a splendid opportunity to do some heavy smoochin', I invited Josephine Midget to join me on this back seat.

Shortly after the beginning of basketball season, a big, tall knucklehead called Honkey-Tonk was transferred to our school. He was an outstanding basketball player, at least 10 times as good as I. He was at least four inches taller and soon replaced me as center on the basketball team. The first game I spent mostly on the bench as the substitute. This galling experience was made more difficult when this Honkey-Tonk began to make goo-goo eyes at Josephine, and, what was worse, she was beginning to welcome those goo-goo eyes.

On the Friday evening of the second game of the season, I was late getting back to school for I had to go home to get a little something to eat and walk back before the game. The school bus, with everybody aboard, was parked, waiting for me to arrive. I ran most of the way from home, and went runnin' up to get on the bus, with Joe Fields, the coach, demanding that I hurry. I charged back to the rear of the bus, and guess what! There's Honkey-Tonk, settin' on my seat, with my girlfriend. I said, "What are you doin' in my seat?"

He turned his hands up and said, "I don't see any names on this seat."

I reached out and grabbed him, and pulled him and flung him as hard as I could back over my shoulder in the bus. Just at this time, Homer Ready, the bus driver, was braking the bus at the stop sign in front of the gym. The laws of motion being what they are, this catapulted old Honkey-Tonk down the aisle almost to the front of the bus, creating a considerable commotion. Old Honkey-Tonk came chargin' back to get me.

By this time, Homer Ready was turning left and accelerating down the street toward the highway. Seeing Honkey-Tonk comin' at me, I raised to a crouching position with my fist drawn back and, my ol' buddy John L. Pullen stuck both feet out and tripped Hankey-Tonk. As he fell forward with his hands tryin' to reach something to steady himself, I hit him hard as I could up side the head. Now you know that poor old boy passed out just like a steer'd been pole-axed, wound up in between the seats in the back of the bus. The coach, Joe Fields, got up, turned on the overhead light, looked back, and says, "Honkey-Tonk, get up from there and get in your seat."

Honkey-Tonk was comin' to, but so addled he couldn't find his rear end with both hands, but he did flop into some seat and we proceeded on to Jackson, Tenn., 50 miles away. On arrival we started the ritual of basketball warm-up, but ol' Honkey-Tonk couldn't see the basketball, let alone catch it! And aside from a throbbin' right hand, I was no worse for the wear.

Now old Joe Fields, the coach, wasn't as dumb as he looked. I was always sure that he knew exactly what happened, and even though I was substituted out often, he always kept me as a starter on the team from then on.

One other instance worthy of mention. One Friday night I somehow found myself in the dark back alley behind Uncle Elihu's barber shop. I saw one of the Watkin boys over a fella on the ground literally beating him up, hittin' him in the face with his fists. With my normal willingness to stick my nose in somebody else's business, added to the true compassion I had for the fella that was down, I ran over and pulled the Watkin boy off the top of the boy being pummeled.

The Watkins, along with the Whites, and other ne'er do wells from across the railroad tracks, were all involved in various sorts of crime, and it so happened that one of the White boys had recently returned from reform school. He explained something about my ancestry, including dogs, and that he was going to solve my constipation problem if I didn't get the hell away.

Well I was a long, skinny 15-year-old and small potatoes alongside this hoodlum, but was pointing out that this Watkin boy needed to stop slammin' him in the face. For some unknown and unexplained reason, my buddy Harold Lloyd was out in that same back alley that I was in, and he'd already shoved to the barber shop. He went runnin' in and says, "Daddy, daddy, that White boy is goin' to beat up Dub!"

Uncle Elihu was busy shavin' a customer, but, with the soap still on his razor, he went out the back door, stepped up between me and that White boy. With that razor raised in his hand Uncle Elihu says, "You better leave him alone."

In seconds, the only ones left in that alley were me, Harold Lloyd, Uncle Elihu, and old W.A. Tull, the guy who was getting his nose smashed.

'Bout that time, every town was busy choosing their candidate for the golden glove boxing tournament. Kenton was no exception. The eliminations went forward. Pretty soon, I was distinguishing myself with a few well-placed lucky blows. My manager and coach was none other than Oran Warix. One of Oran's claims to fame was that he was a professional prizefighter that occasionally fought in Jackson.

One Friday afternoon the big contest was between me and the Methodist preacher's son, the Methodist preacher being the coach for his son. They even turned out school for students to watch this fight. Talking about over-confidence, I had a big case of it.

Gong went the bell and out into the ring the two of us pranced.

Before I knew it, that boy had hit me twice right squarely in the nose. I literally couldn't tell which end was up. I did hear the bell go gong, and somehow stumbled to my stool. In the distance I could barely make out Oran saying, "Don't box him, fight him." He was just repeating this because he was looking at me and knew I was about out.

And so, getting a little clearer just about when the bell was about to go off to return to the ring, it finally dawned on me what this, "Don't box him, fight him" meant. I waded in, took the best he had with three or four blows to the face, but with my head down. I caught him a couple of good ones in the stomach, enough to cause him to lean forward. At which time, my old right fist found its mark in that preacher son's mouth and he hit the ground like a sack of coal. That fight didn't resume.

As time moved along, it narrowed to Wade Jr. as the senior, and me as the junior coming up for the championship. One night Uncle Wade said, "I sure hate to see you boys have to fight it out for the championship."

I said, "Uncle Wade, you won't see it because I'm going to withdraw from the fight. Wade Jr.'s arms are longer than mine and he can out-point me."

Wade Jr. was in the front seat and I was in the back of Uncle Wade's car. He turned around and said, "I can whip your ass."

I said, "No, you can out-point me, but you can't whip me."

Wade Jr., Kenton champion, went to Jackson for the regional contest, and he won with a technical knockout, a left to the nose with a broken nose. He went on to Chattanooga.

Again he won. As the state champion he went to Ft. Oglethorp, Ga., where he won the southeast states U.S. championship.

There was another boy there in the 11th grade whose shadow I even despised, and I was always lookin' for some way to have a battle with him. Shortly after the basketball season started in my 12th year, while out flirting and making a nuisance of myself in front of the basketball girls, some kid came running up, and says, "R.J. Dolan is in the vestibule, and says if you come out there, he'll beat hell out of you!"

Now if I hadn't wanted to, my reputation was at stake, and since I really welcomed this opportunity to have a few exchanges with him, out to the vestibule I went. On opening the door I saw not only R.J. Dolan, but two of his cronies from Mason Hall, and all three advancing on me with malicious intent. Knowing full well I was a goner, I planned to get in a few licks, just as the door opened, and in walked Wade Jr. He quickly recognized the situation and said, "Dub, you take one. I'll get the other two."

I don't know whether he could have taken the other two or not, but his golden glove reputation was such that the other two didn't stick around to see.

One other comment on the golden glove business. Later, during my second year at Memphis State I was having an altercation with one of Memphis' football team guards, named Albert Scoggins. My dislike for Albert Scoggins stemmed from his being instrumental in helping the boys hold me down and cut my hair during the freshman hazing days. Try as I would, I could not get into a fight with Albert Scoggins—probably good since he out-weighed me by about 20 pounds.

But one day, in the chemistry lab, I was in a position to call him a liar. Albert Scoggins, wearing his brand-new Memphis State tiger sweater, came around from his side, heading for me. The project for the day had been making methyl orange, so I held up my beaker of methyl orange and said, "Let's make that sweater look like a rainbow." Well, he stopped short because he didn't want that stuff all over his sweater, and he knew that's where it was going.

He backed up, but obviously was waiting for his time, and the very next period was physical ed class. I knew that, during phys ed class, I was fixin' to get smeared. After arriving in phys ed class, one of my buddies, the current Memphis golden glove champion, said to me, "Dub, help me practice preventing getting knocked out. Put these gloves on." He was putting them on for me. He said, "What I want you to do is to hit me, hit me as hard as you can. I'm gonna take it falling back, trying to teach myself how to keep from getting knocked out." Just about the time I got my gloves on, I saw Albert Scoggins with half of the Memphis State football team come through the door. Obviously, he was planning on an exhibition, and I was going to be the recipient of the trouncing.

I put up my glove like I knew what I was doing, and began sparring around, and this old boy, the golden glove champ, was letting me hit him, and falling back each time that I hit him. (I couldn't have hit him if he hadn't been lettin' me do it.) But it looked to Albert Scoggins like I was doing in Memphis' golden gloves number one, and shortly he and the Memphis State football team slowly dissipated.

8

Working to Survive

My dating, because of lack of money, lack of car, and so on, was really limited to riding on the bus with Josephine, or, in our home games, walking her home after the basketball games. This walking her home had become an established ritual. One night after the ball game, I walked up and says, "Are you ready to go home?" And she says, "Yes." And we walked out of the building, down the highway, to about a half-mile-long lane that went up to her house.

A page from the Kenton (Tenn.) High School Annual. Dub is second from the bottom on the right.

Just as we were crossing the bridge going up this lane, up came a car that had some bird I didn't know driving, along with two of my classmates, Pen Martin and Leonard Brown. Pen and Leonard got out of the car and come around toward me. At this time, this fella said he'd teach me to take his date.

Well by this time, she was boo-hooin' up a storm. The guy says he took her to the basketball game and I took her home.

By this time I could smell old Leonard and Pen, and could see they had been hitting the white lightning bottle. I said, "Pen, you come any closer and I'll break your jaw."

I said, "Leonard, if you think you can whip me, boy you've got a surprise coming." They both stopped, and this guy, named Reed, I later learned, he says, "You know, we're going to have a little distant trouble." I didn't know what he meant, but I said, "Yeah, how distant?"

He pulled a .38 pistol out and laid it on the door, pointing at me. And I demonstrated right there that my I.Q. was a whole lot less than I had always believed it to be when I said, "You'd better get closer or you'll miss."

The other boys, by this time, had gotten into the car and they went driving off. Josephine was boo-hooin' at about 90 decibels. I turned and walked back to town and left her there on the bridge in the dark all by herself, thoroughly disgusted with her, too. As I was walking up the highway, on the wrong side of the road, they come a whoopin' down, made me jump into the ditch to keep from getting hit. Then they turned and made me jump into the ditch again.

By the time I got to the restaurant there in town, I was mad enough to eat nails, but I guess, fortunately, they never came in. The next day I learned Leonard and Pen went off to join the Navy. Pen was accepted, Leonard wasn't accepted. He went hitch-hiking to California and was never seen again. I still owe them a kick in the butt.

Once Harold Lloyd convinced me to go to Lake County to pick cotton. Lake County was nice, and it was fun visiting with my folks. Jay Perriman had left several buckets of molasses on Uncle Ike and Aunt Bell's front porch. Naturally, there was no bathroom in their house, so you had to go outside to the privy.

All my life, I've had to get up at night. Such was the case about 2 o'clock in the morning. I got up and left the house, but I awakened Uncle Ike. He got out of bed, got his shotgun, went running in to a window overlooking the porch in time to greet me as I was coming back from the privy.

He said in a loud voice, "Who air ye?" I commenced shouting, "It's me, Uncle Ike, it's me, Uncle Ike." And I could hear Aunt Bell yelling at him, "Ike, it's W.D., Ike, it's W.D.!" She lit a lamp there on the table, and poor old Uncle Ike just sat there and shook.

I can't remember for sure, but I think I had to go back to the privy.

Harold Lloyd and myself got back into bed with the feeling that we'd had 'bout all of Lake County we could handle. The next morning, Harold picked a few bolls of cotton, looked up at me, and says, "Dub, let's go home." I sure wasn't hard to convince.

We went right back to Macedonia and commenced picking cotton for Earl Bryant, twice as good a cotton, easier to pick. It was at least 40 years before I went back to Lake County.

My brothers Malc, Jake and Farris were good workers and pitched in to the best of their ability to help earn a few dollars to buy food, clothes, and groceries. Our ability to earn a few dollars was limited mostly to picking strawberries in the spring and cotton in the fall. I recall hitting the strawberry patch at dawn, picking strawberries as rapidly as possible until they were picked for the day, then walking to Kenton and attending class. Of course, I had to wear the same clothes that I was wearing in the strawberry patch.

This is a good time to say that our baths were somewhat limited and came from water drawn and carried from Oran's to our little shack. Water was rationed and soap was often unavailable. Poor Mom did the best she could to keep our few clothes clean. During those rough days (worst when I was 14, 15, and 16 years of age) we tried most everything to keep alive.

Summers were not so bad thanks to our gardening and fall was very good. In the fall after the weather turned cold our neighbors would kill hogs.

Aside from smoking the hams, salting the side meat and cooking and canning sausages, they had no way to keep the rest of the hog meat from spoiling. Everybody gorged on spare ribs, backbone, liver, kidney, and the like. In these days of plenty, they remembered us and we ate well until about the middle of January each year. We picked green beans, strawberries, blackberries, and Mom canned to the extent of our cans. The cans were always too few due to loss during winter due to freezing. Oh, how I wish I had known what I know now about insulation!! We would have had plenty.

It seemed that everything available to eat became very limited by the end of January. Potatoes were frozen and rotten. Only a few cans of fruit and beans remained, so we existed on cornbread and black-eyed peas. The peas were plentiful. We picked them in Earl Bryant's fields. I asked him once when I was 14 if he would let me pick the peas on the halves. He said yes and showed me where to put his half. In early fall, shortly after the peas turned brown, the four of us boys would take our cotton sacks to his pea patch, fill them and hand carry them to Earl's barn. We would then go back to the field, fill our sacks again, and carry them down the road to our house.

That evening and night we would gather around a wash tub and shell the peas. We then put the peas in flour sacks tied to wires from the rafters in our bedroom. The wires were used to keep mice from eating our peas. A few days of pea picking netted enough for the entire winter.

We didn't eat the peas until we didn't have anything else. I had to have meal to make cornbread. We didn't have a cow; therefore, no milk, so the cornbread was meal mixed with water and fried on the little stove we used to heat the house.

I got the meal by going over to Uncle Henry's barn, filling a sack of corn from the crib, carrying it to town, where Roy Carroll ground the corn into meal for half the corn. I didn't mind a bit using the corn, for I had spent much of the summer and fall helping Oran grow and pick the stuff without pay. Sometimes for days our diet consisted of biscuits and water and flour gravy for breakfast, and cornbread and peas for lunch and dinner. Why old Harold Lloyd would come spend the night with us, I don't know. Rest assured, I visited him often, and partially to get to eat those feasts that Aunt Molly and Aunt Ollie prepared. A real treat was to have a little salt pork to go with the peas.

The only thing we bought on credit was an occasional sack of flour. I would go to Freeman's store and tell Uncle Lunie I had to have a sack of flour. He would get it for me and later on, Uncle Elihu would pay for it. It was about that time that Aunt Ruby would send Mom a letter with a dollar in it.

Clothes were a problem. Cotton picking money stretched thin, and we just didn't have enough for many clothes. Aunt Bonnie would give me a worn out pair of Wade Jr.'s pants when I got to looking too bad. I often sat in the study hall at school during recess because I was too embarrassed to have the seat of my pants waving around for everyone to see. I used to frequently spend the night with Harold, Mary Emma, Wade, Jr., and Roland Bryant. Those feasts fortunately didn't include black-eyed peas.

Having moved from the vicinity of the cat hole, I began to figure out a way to get to the dredge ditch for swimming, fishing, etc. Using the ax that Uncle Elihu bought me, I chopped down long gum trees such that they fell across the Obion River. We then could reach the dredge ditch without wading water.

After a lot of swimming in the dredge ditch, I decided we needed a diving board. Well, there were some fine bridge planks that belonged to the county up in Uncle Henry Moore's yard. I gathered up about a dozen boys and put them to dragging and carrying that plank the three-quarters of a mile to the dredge ditch. The most successful maneuver was to take a stick with a boy on each side of the plank, tie it to the plank with a piece of baling wire with the length adjusted for the height of the boys. With the weight distributed among about 12 boys, the plank rapidly moved to the dredge ditch.

By the time I got that all worked out, I didn't have far to go. Without lumber or nails it was no small feat to install the diving board. This I solved by digging a trench on the ditch bank roughly perpendicular to the ditch.

We then cut gum trees and hauled them into position over our plank. We then moved a ton of black gumbo using buckets to haul the mud and covered the gum trees. After a few days under the hot summer sun our diving board was secure and quite usable.

I then charged any boys using our board 100 buckets of sand from the ditch bottom under the diving board and moved to the area above and around our diving board. After a few sessions of this we had a sandy beach. Such people as uncle Elihue, Oran and Earl Bryant didn't know about this until one fine Sunday, Oran decided to go with us to the river in order to teach John David and Charles Edward how to swim.

John David was about 12 years old and Charles Edward was about 10. I had taught both of them to swim and dive, and with our considerable practice, they were pretty good at it. On the way to the river they asked me, "What are we going to do?"

I said, "When you get down to the diving board, pull off your clothes and go diving in."

Oran was pleased and said, "You boys have been slipping off and going swimming!"

Not all of the things we did were as constructive as building diving boards and swimming. Even though we always worked when we could, sometimes a quick shower would come up and we would all go into the barn loft near the homeplace. Don't know how it all started, but pretty soon we set up a program where we measured the penis of each boy. We set up a plank in the barn loft and nailed it to one of the barn stanchions. Each boy had a line on the plank, all different heights where we wrote his name, marked off the length of the last measurement. These measurements we watched with interest, concern and glee as time and growth added length to each boy's line.

A lot of interesting discussions I vividly recall. Once M.A. from Memphis was so terribly disgusted that two of the boys years younger than he had more to show from it than he. Another, Harold, who was short-changed in that department, was ribbed about it almost all of the time. Years later, prior to a Keathley family reunion, many of the boys that had participated in these activities were sitting under the huge mimosa shade tree at the homeplace when a streak of lightning and thunder ripped out of a little rain shower about to arrive. Old Harold laughingly said, "Dub, about time to go to the barn." All of us exploded in laughter, and as the laughter subsided, A.J. yelled across the group to Harold and asked, "Harold, I want to know, did that little old thing of yours ever grow any?" Without our knowing it, Jenny and Robbie (Harold's and A.J.'s wives) were then coming out the kitchen door. Jenny said, "No, Jake, it never did." The biggest laugh of the entire reunion.

9

Family Reunions

There were many interesting discussions at family reunions. Once, while visiting at the homeplace along with my three brothers, we were discussing various problems while sitting under the mimosa tree. A.J., blowing on his fingernails, said to Farris, "Farris, what was your GCT?" Farris ignored him for a few minutes, and A.J. repeated this question. Farris answered, "It was high enough!" A.J. said, "Well, what was it?" Farris says, "68."

The Navy GCT grades were approximately one-half of the individual's I.Q.

Well, Farris looked up, and asks, "What was yours?" A.J. says, "75." (Which, incidentally, is the highest score you can make.)

This was followed by a short pause, and A.J. says, "Well, Dub, what was yours?" And I said, "I didn't have one." He says, "Wait a minute! Everybody who goes into the Armed Forces gets a GCT."

My brothers and I were serious about life, but we never took ourselves too seriously.

I said, "I went in as an officer candidate. I didn't go to boot camp. And I didn't get a GCT." I said, "One time later, at the graduate school of Annapolis, the Navy was considering a new GCT testing program and they gave a test, made out by Princeton, to determine suitability of the questions on the GCT."

A.J. asked, "Why'd they do that?"

And I says, "I don't know, but I guess that they considered if we didn't know the answers to the questions, they were too difficult to be on the test."

Jake has never said another word to me about GCT.

But back to my story. I think it was in March, but anyhow it was the spring of 11th or 12th grade. In the spring, after I had turned 16, Momma married her old grammar-school sweetheart, Corbett Bryant.

Unfortunately, they had about as much in common as a race horse and a plug mule. Mom was intellectually adept. She had an acute mind, and for years and years wrote for three newspapers. Mr. Corbett was neither scholastically inclined nor was he interested in anything but farming. The poor man could hardly read or write, and he found himself plunged into a family where the most retarded member had an I.Q. of genius or above.

Now you can imagine life became difficult for all hands.

Mr. Corbett believed that families should be run like his old dad had handled things for the Bryant boys. The essence of this management was centered on one purse, with Mr. Corbett planning to dole out as he saw fit. I wasn't about to have any of this, and further stated that neither did it apply to my brothers.

Through Mom's efforts, it was compromised that we would work in his crops for nothing except our food and we would keep the money that we earned picking cotton and strawberries for our neighbors. I'm sure that Mom married Mr. Corbett due to his having been a childhood sweetheart. Mom had dated and seriously considered marrying two other men, one from Union

City named Oscar Owen, and one from Trenton, named Lacey Oliver. In both cases, the four of us boys interfered with any wedding plans.

The situation can best be summed up in Lacey Oliver's own words.

Once, years later, A.J. was a Goodrich vice president, and I was a full commander in the regular Navy. We walked into Kenton barber shop for a haircut. The only barber there was Lacey Oliver. He looked at us quizzically. As A.J. sat down in the barber chair, he says, "Boys, you got me. I thought I knew everybody around here, but I don't know you."

A.J. says, "I'm Audelle Bryant's third son."

Oliver looked startled and said, "I've so often wondered what happened to you boys." He said, "Where are you now?"

A.J. says, "I'm corporate vice president for B.F. Goodrich in Akron, Ohio."

He says, "Were you boys ever able to get through high school?"

A.J. said, "Yes, it was difficult, but we did. All of us went on to college." He said, "My oldest brother went on to college, after two years went into the Navy, became a regular naval officer, and is now a commander. My next brother went to Memphis State for a year and became operations manager for Keathley Pie Company. I got my master's and Ph.D. from Cornell, and have been with Goodrich a number of years. My youngest brother finished college, got his master's degree, and now he's an executive with Frito-Lay."

Lacey Oliver says, "Oh, I'm so glad. Your mother and myself almost got married, and it was my fault that we called it off. I had only sufficient funds to send my four children to college. I couldn't deprive them of going to college, and I couldn't expect to send them and not send her kids."

He then said, "You know, that tall, good-looking oldest brother. How was he able to ever get through high school?"

A.J. says, "Ask him, that's him sitting right there!"

I guess that's enough about that.

Shortly after Mom and Mr. Corbett married, he moved us to a house on Huffman Hill in Macedonia community. Whereas the shack we lived in had never been finished, the shack we moved into had started falling down about 50 years before. We set about making a crop, *a la* Corbett Bryant method. He bought four wild horses, shipped in from the southwest, for $1.00 apiece, and one of my jobs was to break the blasted things to ride. This I did by plowing up a field in February using another team that he had. After a rain in early spring, I would take a horse, lead him out into this plowed field, get up on the horse, hang on to the mane, and let him buck until he didn't have the strength to buck anymore. I used the plowed field for two reasons. One, it didn't hurt so bad to hit the mud when you fell off. And two, it was rather difficult for the horse to buck in the soft mud.

After each of the horses was broken to ride, we then broke them to harness, getting them ready to work. I will say that Mr. Corbett was good at breaking those horses to pull as a team.

Later on in the spring A.J. had harnessed up a team, got on one of the horses, and started to ride down into the fields. The horse got disturbed and began to buck, throwing A.J. up and down amidst the harness. Seeing this from where I was working in the garden, I ran, jumped the garden fence, went down the hill, and caught a line that was dragging from the horse that A.J. was riding. I got the horse stopped and disconnected him from his teammate. I pulled A.J. off. Naturally, A.J., a 12-year-old, was rather frightened. I pulled the harness off the horse, grabbed up a hickory pole about as long as my arm, jumped on the horse, and with one hand holdin' the reins, the other hand I used to beat the horse. Mr. Corbett was yellin' for me to stop, sayin' I was killin' the horse. Between the beating, the riding, and the bucking, about 30 minutes later the horse, all soaked with lather and ready to drop, stopped quivering as I'd lash him again and again. I got off the horse. Mr. Corbett told me,

"You've killed that horse." I says, "Maybe. But if he ever bucks again with Jake on him, I will kill him."

These horses became pretty good riding horses, and boys from miles around would congregate on Huffman Hill, especially on Sundays, where we demonstrated our abilities to duplicate the feats of the Knights of the Round Table. Stupid though it may sound, we would take a two-by-four, get on a horse bare-backed, and gallop toward each other to see who could unseat in Sir Lancelot fashion the on-coming rider. If you ever want a jolt, try bein' on the losing side of two horses gallopin' toward each other, and get hit in the side with a two-by-four.

Our cousins used to come to visit us. The same boys, only bigger.

We would divide up sides to play war. We would use corncobs to throw and hit a man on the opposite side. Over the years, I developed a system of pure honesty on who got hit in our games. We had a cousin named M.A. who lived in Memphis. One weekend, he disrupted our corncob war for a while, and he would disclaim his not having been hit, when everyone knew that he had been. Harold and I solved this by going to the pig lot and getting a bucket of corncobs that were soaked with mud and hog manure. When we hit old M.A. up side the head with one of those cobs, there wasn't any argument as to whether or not he got hit.

One little claim to fame about that Huffman Hill house. Shorty after I left home, I got a postcard from Malc, tellin' me all about his bein' a member of the band and that they were goin' to Trenton to march in a parade. Finally, in a little P.S. over on the side, he says, "Last night our house blew away."

A tornado had hit it. Fortunately, I wasn't at home, and when Mr. Corbett came in yelling for the boys to get into the storm house, they reluctantly proceeded to do so. Had I been home, I'm sure we wouldn't have left to go to the storm house. But, I'm told, as old Malc, grumblin' about his loss of sleep, entered the door of the storm house just as a crash sounded, they remained in the storm house for half an hour. At which time Malc announced he wasn't goin' to stay any longer, and he went out and headed for the house. A few seconds later, he reentered the storm house, went over and stretched out on one of the benches. Mom asked him, "What's wrong? Why'd you come back?" Malc says, "We ain't got no house." It so happened that the tornado had left only the floor and the back wall of the house.

One day the principal, Mr. J.M. DuBow, bless his heart, one of the finest men I ever knew, came out to the basketball court and told me I was the salutatorian. Whatever that was. Not once had I ever heard of valedictorian or salutatorian. It was explained to me that salutatorian was number 2 in the class, and I had missed being valedictorian by 0.2 of a point. Not that it worried me the least bit then, but now, in retrospect, Mr. DuBow had talked me into taking two years of French. Making high grades in French was hardly possible, being out of school like I had been. In fact, out of the kindness of his heart, he had given me 80 each term in French. If you put that through the averages, I suppose it dropped my average by about 2 points.

So now I was salutatorian. The next sentence made me wish I was someplace playing pool. He told me it was customary for the salutatorian to make a welcoming speech. The thoughts of making a speech literally made my toenails curl. No way could I get out of it, and I made the world's worst welcoming speech—certainly, the worst one ever made in Kenton.

But right there I must mention, once when I was playing basketball, Joe Fields substituted me out and back into the basketball game to do something specific, like fouling out one of the other team's high scorers. I didn't do this so well. He took me out of the game, reached over and hit me on the leg, and angrily said, "Dub, you're the sorriest basketball player on the sorriest team Kenton ever had!"

I looked up at him and said, "No wonder, you're the worst coach we ever had." He thought about it a while, leaned over, and says, "Touché! Now get back in there and play ball."

10

Memphis, and a competitive exam

Well, after four long and hard years I graduated from high school. I hitch-hiked to Memphis to live with Uncle Maurice and Aunt Ruby and work in the pie shop. Aunt Ruby was one of the most wonderful people this world has ever seen. She welcomed me into her home, treated me like a son, literally took care of me for the next two years.

Uncle Maurice and Aunt Ruby helped all of us in many ways, often by putting us to work.

The pay scale in the pie shop was 10 cents an hour, and didn't change until the first minimum wage came through sometime that fall, and moved wages to 25 cents an hour. Here I was, footloose and fancy free, except for 10 hours a day, six days a week at the pie shop. I launched into considerable social activity for me, including dating two girls that lived near Aunt Ruby. It didn't take long until I wound up with a date with both of them to go to the same party on the same night. After that escapade, I didn't have but one girl. She was Mr. Noah Ledbetter's daughter. He worked for Uncle Maurice at the pie shop.

A few of them asked me if I wanted to go for a ride. I got into the car, a new '38 Ford, with two other boys and two other girls. They said they were going to Mississippi "nigger baiting." Didn't sound too much like something I wanted to do.

They drove right down into Mississippi. It was after dark. And they would come up to a Negro church, look for a single young girl walking down the road near the church. One boy driving would stop the car. The other boy in the front seat with one of the girls would jump out and grab ahold of the Negro girl, who naturally would start screaming. He would hold on to her while down the road would come Negro men rushing to help the girl, and just before they arrived, he would turn the girl loose, jump into the car, and, with tires squealing, wheel off and down the road to another church.

I was so scared that I couldn't talk. By the time all the churches seemed to be closed, we headed back to Memphis. En route, we ran out of gas. From many miles down in Mississippi we walked toward town, until we came to a filling station. At this point, it was 3:30 in the morning, and this girl, Thelma Scott, called her daddy. He told her for us to stay right where we were and he'd come get us.

This he did, but he was one mad cookie. Although he lived across the street, I had never seen him before, and haven't seen him since. And furthermore, I wasn't looking!

Competitive Exam

It was about this time one afternoon after work that I went over on the porch, reading the *Press Scimitar*. On the front page was an article stating that Monday there was a competitive examination out at Memphis State. Boys from Carroll, Weekly and Gibson counties were taking an exam for a Manning Scholarship award. The article went on to say that Manning had been a professor out at Memphis and left his money for an annual scholastic award for the winner from these counties.

Aunt Rube came out to the porch, apparently looked at me, took the paper, and went on into the house. Uncle Maurice arrived a little bit later, went on into the house, came out, and asked me, "Do you want to go to college?" I said, "Well, of course, I'd like to go, but there's no way I could ever get the money to do so."

He showed me the paper and he says, "Ruby says you read this article and seemed to withdraw into a long dream." He said, "We'll go out and check up on this exam tomorrow morning." I said, "Uncle Maurice, tomorrow's Friday. This exam is Monday. Applicants were to have been received before May1 last year. Even if there's some way to get to take the exam, I couldn't compete with the people that have been cramming all summer."

He said, "We'll go."

Uncle Maurice was busy with running the business, selling pies in the morning, working at night. The poor man didn't have time to take me to Memphis State. Besides, there was nobody to do my job while I was gone. But out to Memphis State we went.

We go into the Administration building, and a receptionist asked what we wanted.

Uncle Maurice said, "I want to talk to somebody 'bout this here exam."

In due course, they ushered us in to see the dean. The dean explained to Uncle Maurice that the applications had been closed, the exams had been printed, and it was too late to try to take the examinations. Uncle Maurice looked him right straight in the eye, and says, "Who's your boss?" Dean Jones, flustered a little bit, said, "Mr. Keathley, the president of the college is Dr. Brewster." Uncle Maurice says, "I want to see him." Dean Jones says, "Well, I'm sorry, sir. He's away for the day." Uncle Maurice thanked him, and as we walked out, we saw a sign that says "Dr. Brewster." So we turned in. Lo, and behold, one of the girls, Helen Parker, that we knew from Temple Baptist Church, was Dr. Brewster's receptionist.

Uncle Maurice says, "Helen, I want to see Dr. Brewster." She says, "Mr. Keathley, he's taken the day off. He's down at his quarters gardening." Uncle Maurice says, "Get him up here. Tell him I want to talk to him."

She said, "Mr. Keathley, I have to tell him what you want to talk about."

He said, "I want him to let Dub take this exam for a scholarship Monday."

In a few minutes, Dr. Brewster came through the door into his office.

Helen says, "Dr. Brewster, this is Mr. Keathley and Mr. Ashe." Uncle Maurice says, "I want to talk with you about this exam." Dr. Brewster says, "Mr. Keathley, just have a seat out here with Helen, and I'll talk with Mr. Ashe."

I went on in. Dr. Brewster closed the door to his inner office, and he says, "When did you hear about this exam?"

I told him, "Yesterday."

He says, "Would your principal recommend you?" I says, "I don't know."

He says, "Who was your principal?" I said, "Mr. J.M. DuBow at Kenton."

"Why," he says, "ol' Jimmy! We went to Peabody College together."

He called to Helen Parker and said, "Helen, get Jim DuBow on the phone for me. He's at Kenton."

We had a few minutes conversation trying to confirm that I lived in Gibson County. I told him that old Huffman Hill house, the county line went through it. He said, "Which side do you sleep on?" I said, "Good, gracious, I don't know!" 'Bout that time, Helen says, "Dr. Brewster, Mr. DuBow on the line."

You can't imagine how smart I was. I got up and graciously walked out of his office and shut the door. After a bit, he invited me back in. He said, "Mr. Ashe, Jimmy speaks well of you. Fact is, he says you were the best student that he's had in all of his teaching career." He says, "After what Jimmy says, I'm going to break a rule and let you make your application now, and you take the exam on Monday."

He took me over to the dean and said, "Dr. Jones, have another exam prepared for Mr. Ashe." Dean Jones had me sit down, and I made out the applications and so forth. He was the most helpful individual you ever saw. He told me that the odds were terribly against me in that I didn't have but just one day to try to prepare for the exam. He says, "Monday, the exams will be chemistry, general science, and physics. Tuesday morning it will be math, and history. Tuesday afternoon it will be English. The math will include trigonometry. Have you had trigonometry?"

I said, "No, sir."

He said, "May I suggest that you go down to the Cossack Library and get a trigonometry textbook and an algebra textbook and a general science textbook. Spend the next two days refreshing general science and algebra and taking a year's course in trigonometry." He said, "Mr. Ashe, trigonometry is the use of four formulas based on sine and cosine, tangent and cotangent. The rest you'll just have to know. I wish you well."

I did as he advised, and Monday morning, off to the races. After Monday I knew I had done well, but Tuesday morning, by the time I finished the math and history, I was rather tired. Tuesday afternoon the test was to write a 500-word theme on why I wanted to be a school teacher.

Well, first, I didn't want to be a school teacher. And second, I didn't know a semicolon from a load of coal. And thirdly, I could not spell anything, even if I was rested. So I went back to the pie shop knowing full well that I blew that English exam.

I couldn't believe it when, two weeks later, I got a letter congratulating me for winning the scholarship. Mr. DuBow later told me that, when Dr. Brewster told him my grades, that I had made in the very high 90s in everything but English, and he told Dr. Brewster that I just didn't have a qualified English teacher, and that I could certainly come out of that.

11

Memphis State

One bright Sunday afternoon, my old buddy, John L. Pullon, came driving up in the field to our house and asked me to go with him with plans to pick up his date, Ethel Linda, and then we'd go by and get her cousin, Josephine, for me. We hurried off to Kenton to pick up the girls. Well, Ethel Linda's mother okayed the girls' going out with us on the basis that we would attend Church of Christ church services that night. It was a far cry from the smoochin' we had in mind. The next thing we found ourselves at big meetin' time at China Grove.

I had had, for several weeks, boils appearing on my neck and other parts of my body, and tried every home remedy you could imagine to improve the situation. Someone told me that if I would take lime mixed in water once a day, it might very well eliminate the problems with the boils. It so happened that a little while before John L. had arrived at my house I'd gone to Uncle Henry's barn to get some lime, mixed it with a quart of water, and drank about half of it.

Not too long after sitting down in the church at China Grove, I began to feel sick at my stomach. About time the preacher had the congregation stand to sing, I could stand it no longer, slid down the seat into the aisle, started down the aisle to the outside, passed out in the aisle, came to with people carrying me down the steps of the church. Some lady experienced in treating drunks decided that she knew just what was wrong with me. She sent someone to a nearby house to bring her a box of soda and a box of salt. She threw together a concentrated mixture of salt, water, and soda, had me sit up to drink as much of this as I could hold, and, shortly thereafter had me do it again.

Naturally, I began to vomit all over the place. Each time, after vomiting, she'd give me another bunch of the stuff. Then I'd vomit again. What neither she nor I knew was that she was saving my life. For a few days later, back at the barn, I noted that, instead of getting lime, I'd gotten cotton poison, and all that vomiting was getting the arsenic out of my stomach. Needless to say, the evangelist inside preaching had changed his sermon to hellfire and damnation for drunks. John L. had left the church to bring his car around to take me to the doctor, but in the excitement, had twisted the key off in the ignition, and he and someone else outside were busy trying to wire his car to start without a key.

Ethel Linda and Josephine were picked up by Ethel Linda's mother. Somewhat later, John L. got his car started and took me to Rutherford, to one of his uncles who was a doctor. In normal fashion, the good doctor gave me a couple of aspirins, told me to go home and go to bed. Well, let me tell you somethin' kiddos, I was sick for eight or ten days, but, thanks to that old woman, I was sick instead of dead.

My mom was, like all of her family, quite a musician. She was an accomplished organist and pianist. It must have broken her heart to have four boys, none of whom could play the radio. She decided she would have an Ashe quartet. Farris would sing soprano, Malc would sing tenor, I'd sing bass, and Jake would sing alto. Often, we found ourselves singing at Macedonia church. This was especially true every time a fifth Sunday came around and they had fifth Sunday dinner, all day preachin' and singin' on the grounds.

We complained bitterly about this singing bid'ness. One day, as I was singing "Down By the Riverside," doing quite well, mind you, throwing in the bass, until my voice had commenced to change, and I bubbled forth with a bodacious croak. I wouldn't sing anymore, and afterwards, I explained to

Mom, never was going to sing again. It isn't necessary to say the other boys wouldn't sing either if I didn't, and the Ashe quartet, like all good things, disappeared.

The Obion River became clogged with debris and created the most massive breeding ground for snakes. Up above the cat hole the river was filled with large colonies of cotton-mouthed moccasins. A cotton-mouth will leave you alone if you do him likewise, but he gets dang-right belligerent and will attack you if you start messin' around in his domain. We used to fish in the open spots of the Obion River, and, naturally, the snakes thought we were trying to molest them. On occasion, they would literally run us away from the river, even though we were doing our best to drive them back with willow poles.

I had this single-shot .22 rifle that I'd bought for $2.50, and it took ten weeks to pay for it at $.25 a week out of my pay with Pat Keathley at the grocery store. I was a crack shot with this little old rifle. I don't know why. No one ever showed me how to fire a rifle. But I could pick up the rifle and, nearly every time, shoot a moving snake and hit him in the head. Well, I could'a cleaned out the snake population, except the box of cartridges cost 25 cents for 50 cartridges. Most of the time, if I was able to get cartridges, I had to buy a nickel's worth, so I never had more than 10 cartridges, and, most of the time, quite a bit fewer. I often remember shootin' those snakes, and wondering if I was a natural-born Davy Crockett.

Now maybe you think going to college with a full scholarship was an easy thing. Far from it! First, I had to work all the time to try to earn enough money to buy books, pay for streetcar fare, and, every once in a while, try to buy a shirt or a pair of pants. I sent an occasional shirt to the laundry, but I never had enough money to get my pants cleaned and pressed. I just wore 'em till they wore out.

Memphis State opened with a bang, and the hazing of freshmen commenced immediately. The year I was a freshman, 1938, it seemed necessary that all freshman boys be given a haircut that included cuttin' it all off and shavin' your head.

With my "don't tread on me" attitude, and willingness to fight at the drop of a hat, I let it be known in clear, unadulterated language, that I wasn't goin' to have a haircut.

After a few days I was grabbed from behind in the basement of the administration building, and, with a football player holdin' each arm and one behind, I was led, pushed and dragged out of the basement toward the dormitory. I saw the basement door approaching and relaxed as if I'd given up, but as they opened the door for me to go out, a boy's head in each of my hands, with all my strength, I cracked those two heads together. Naturally, I was released. I went back and picked up my books and explained to a few other listeners that I was not going to have a haircut.

A few days passed, and lo and behold, they caught me again. This time, they put me face down with a football player holding each arm and each leg. Those suckers used my head to knock open the basement door, carried me across to the dormitory, up to the second floor, put me down into a chair, and held me while somebody with the clippers cut and pulled all my hair out. I was furious, but nonetheless, bald.

One of my first classes was algebra. The professor seated us alphabetically and began an oral test where we voluntarily answered questions that he put on the board. Well, I was used to lookin' somethin' over, runnin' it through my mind again, makin' sure, and then answerin' it. This had worked very well all through high school. But I quickly found the mental prowess of this group was such that I had to answer the question without double-checking it in my mind if I was going to be first.

I kept hearing a girl's voice from back in the back of the room comin' up with the answer just a nanosecond before I did. I craned my neck around to see what the heck's goin' on. There, back of the room, in the "P" section, was some little old girl that looked vaguely familiar, and after a bit, I decided I had met her.

As class was dismissed, I went up and said to her, "I'm Dub Ashe. I b'lieve I've met you before."

She says, "Yes, you were the one kissin' all the girls at Temple Baptist Church's hayride."

I then remembered that she was Estelle Paseur, and at the hayride, I'd sat with her date up in front on the left side, and I couldn't even remember that she held hands with that old boy, George Holt.

Not long afterwards, I happened to sit next to her in chemistry class.

This time, I found out what courses she was taking, that she was a chemistry/biology major. Also found out that she had been an honor student at Central High School in Memphis (only the brains went to Central). A few months passed, and it got to where we sat alongside each other each morning in chemistry. Like brothers and sisters, we discussed practically everything, including her problems with her dates.

At that time, on a regular basis, she was dating seven boys, one for each day. Christmas came and went and she commenced to hint that there was a vacancy, in that her dad ran off one of her boyfriends because he had given her some lingerie for Christmas. I finally explained that I neither had the time nor the money to even have a date, that I worked six days a week, and even on Sunday printed pie wrappers. And, although it was embarrassing to say so, I pointed out that my budget was so tight that I couldn't even buy a Coca-Cola.

The end of the first quarter she showed me her grades and they were all A's. Mine were all A's except English, and it was an ordered-by-the-dean-give-it-to-me C. It was well into the third quarter before she told me of a movie at Peabody Theater that we should see. I said, "Remember, I haven't got the money to even go to a 20-cent movie." She says, "I know, I was meaning for you to be my guest."

That's how it all started. Later years, we got married, had a couple of brats, and now have seven grandchildren, and just finished our 59th anniversary.

12

School with Evaline

But I'd better talk a little bit about that C in English. English at Memphis was a required course. We had an old lady teaching that required a 500-word theme every two weeks. Regardless of subject matter, one grammatical error, including spelling, was an automatic maximum B, two errors was an automatic C, and three errors was an automatic F. I couldn't copy 500 words without misspelling at least three of them! And I just plain didn't know anything about English grammar. So after I rung up my third or fourth 'F,' I knew I was a goner. Flunk English and I certainly would lose my scholarship, and I was sure flunking English.

Evaline at Memphis State, in the days when I had to get in line to see her.

So I decided to do a little filibustering. I wanted the professor to agree to give credit for subject matter, and she wanted me to sit down and hush. I wouldn't let her teach the whole period. I didn't consider that I was endangering my status because I was flunking anyway. It seems, and this I learned later, that the old lady attended a teacher's meeting that evening, conducted by the dean, and she brought up what I was doing in her class and why. Some of the teachers advised that I be expelled. But some others—the chemistry professor, the history professor, and the math professor, talked about what an outstanding student I was. I suspect that Dean Jones, having had his troubles with me when I was trying to take the scholarship exam, decided he didn't want another session with the president, Dr. Brewster, and he advised the English professor to tell me that I was going to get a passing grade so I'd stop my filibuster.

But as it so happened, the next day in class I stood up to start again.

Miss Mays grinned, and she says, "You win, Mr. Ashe. You'll get a passing grade." Can you beat that? They should've just kicked the shit out of me!

Since my scholarship was for only two calendar years, I decided to go to summer school. I chose to take an entire year of physics, plus a couple of courses in psychology, for my summer credits. The first day of the summer quarter I walked into the physics class. About 25 students. The professor, a Dr. Lane from the University of Chicago, was known about the campus as a brain. He looked us up and down and says, "I don't grade on any curve. I'd just as soon to flunk you all as not. And I will, if you don't make passing grades. But no matter what grades are made, there won't be more than one A." Well, I was thinkin' to myself, this is a little stupid, but I just felt a little sorry for the rest of the people. I had no doubt that no matter what it was, I'd make the A. Well, you know what happened? I made three quarters of B+'s, and that little old Paseur girl made all A's. Used to make me so mad I could die to get a lab experiment back and have my grade be B+ and hers be A. By this time, we were physics lab partners, and once, she had a dental appointment, went off to get her teeth filled, while I performed the experiment and the calculations, made mine and her drawings, turned in the two sheets, one that she had signed and I signed the other. And when it came back, and I had a B+ and she had an A, I exploded. Went running up to Dr. Lane and says, "Now why did I get a B+ and she get an A?"

He says, "Hers is neater."

I said, "Derned if that's so. I did them both. She wasn't even here." He says, "You ought to have better sense."

I made 100 on all the exams, as did she, and I made 100 on all the problems we turned in, and I still got three B-plusses.

Next quarter, we went along with our normal courses, except she decided to have American History, and of course, I was a history major. The professor was one Dr. Parks, one of the finest teachers I've even known. At the beginning of the year he announced that he had an unusual grading system. That his quizzes were difficult and extensive, that, if he gave a quiz and the highest grade in the class was less than 95, he would raise everybody's grade such that the top grade became a minimum of 95. He said his quizzes were true/false and multiple choice. He said, "If you guess wrong and miss a true/false, you'll lose twice as many points as you'd lose if you left it blank."

Well, we proceeded into this class. He was a wonderful lecturer. We learned more history than I'd ever been able to grasp before. The first test came out. I had 96 or 98—anyhow, more than 95. And he announced to the class that we had a grade higher than 95 and there would not be any additional points. Test after test after test went on like that for three quarters. Finally, one day, just before the year was out, he handed back our quiz papers. He had me as an 88 and put a +7, making me 95. He announced to the class, "Well, we've gone the whole year, ladies and gentleman, and Mr. Ashe finally failed to make 95, so I've added 7 points to each grade." He had slipped when he had said "Mr. Ashe," and I was *persona non grata*, receiving icicles through eye contact. He said, "Mr. Ashe, what happened?" I said, "Dr. Parks, I hitch-hiked up to Kenton, didn't get back in time to read the material."

All of her life, Evaline has repeated that I got an A in history and she always got a B. But it wasn't enough to salve the wounds of that blasted physics prof.

By this time, she'd been culling her dates back a bit. And also, she was finding ways and means to have lunch with me. But I still just plain didn't have time to do any dating. But one day, I agreed reluctantly to come down and join her for Sunday dinner and to meet her family. I made it up to the porch of her house. I was considering turning and going back, but as I knocked on the door, a little ole girl came to the door and handed me a five-foot snake. This brat was her 13-year-old sister, Gladys. She started out bad and she sure didn't improve with time.

Now, I'm not especially afraid of snakes, but I wasn't happy as that blinking snake crawled up my left arm, come around my head with his tongue forking out on the right side of my cheek. Evaline came running, picked up the snake and handed it back to Gladys. Gladys says, "Poor little thing," and headed it back to the back of the house. The blasted snake belonged to her older brother, Lark. The only thing that I wished was that I could have got that snake into the cross hairs of my rifle.

Well, we had dinner. Lovely dinner. I was scared spitless that my lack of knowledge of appropriate table manners would advertise that I was a country clod. Then, after dinner, we played Rook with her mother and daddy.

Following another dinner, it seemed like I ought to go introduce her to my family. So, one weekend, my cousin, Buren Flowers, and Evaline and myself, set off to visit my folks at Kenton. When anyone arrived down in the Kenton area, it was customary for them immediately to go visit Mom's oldest sister, Aunt Lily Smith. This we did, all of us, including my mother and Buren's mother, crowding into his car. On arrival at Aunt Lily's and Uncle Will's, it was raining. Uncle Will was out milking. He came in, wearing his knee boots, his old hunting coat, chewing tobacco, and carrying two buckets of milk. He looked up at Evaline and says, "Well, Dub, is this here yer woman?"

Well, she didn't chase me so much for a few days, and later said she was considering reconsidering the whole situation.

Life was rather hectic, trying to go to school and work, and, at the same time, worry about my mother and my brothers back at Kenton. But thanks particularly to Aunt Ruby, everything went well. She was a wonderful woman.

Evaline's dad was a postman, and her brother was a substitute mail clerk, so when it was announced that the post office was giving an exam for mail clerks, Evaline and myself proceeded to take the exam. They had a rule at Memphis that not more than two people from one family could work for the post office department, but right away I was notified that I had been appointed as substitute postal clerk.

Came Christmas time, 1939, I was called to work at the post office.

Man, did I welcome this! Because substitute work was at night and the pay was 65 cents an hour. I immediately went on a 20-hour day routine and did my level best to move the Christmas mail. The supervisor used my production figures often to tell the rest of the substitute clerks that they weren't doing such a hot job. As time moved along and the Christmas mail rush was over, the supervisor just kept me on for an extra week. It was sure good for my pocketbook, but I couldn't learn to get along on three hours a day sleep. Even later, in the Navy, when it became necessary, it was a rough chore for me to miss sleep.

By the time the three weeks were over my backlog of pie wrappers had completely been used. I printed pie wrappers on a piece basis so I could work when I had the time. Uncle Maurice had determined that 25 cents a thousand was an appropriate wage. He determined this by testing how long it took for him to do 500, and decided that was a good rate per thousand. I welcomed this because, when I was up to speed, I could do over 2,000 an hour.

I had a few other odd jobs around the pie shop that Uncle Maurice reluctantly let me have. He was afraid that I would commit myself to more than I could do, and sometimes Aunt Ruby wouldn't let him give me the job because she, too, worried about my being overworked.

For instance, I contracted to scrub the floors daily for $5 a week. I also contracted to fill the salesmen's orders and place them in the box each evening for $2 a week. Yes, it was a lot of work for little pay, but a few nickels made a lot of difference. By this time, I had purchased a washing machine for my mom from Sears Roebuck, which I was trying to pay off at $5 a month. Poor Mom surely appreciated that washing machine after all those years of using her hands and a washboard.

Schoolwork was going very well. Fact is, Dr. Parks, the head of the history department, had invited me to join the World Affairs Society at Memphis State. This sounded wonderful until I found out I had to give an hour speech to the society. I felt it necessary to tell Dr. Parks I just didn't have time!

13

I Join the Navy

Realize that this was the spring of 1940. You didn't have to be too heavy with the smarts to figure out that war was approaching. Everything you read, or any time you listened to the radio, removed any doubts that war was imminent.

I had a buddy named J.C. Neal that came by one day and told me that the Navy had a program where you could join for 30 days in a reserve status without pay, but they would send you on an all-expense tour to New York by train, and then on to the Caribbean for a month's cruise. Now I didn't know diddly-swink about the Navy.

The only thing I was interested in was getting that month's Caribbean cruise. So J.C. and myself went downtown, got the papers, but we had to get our parents' signatures in order to officially join up. I hitch-hiked down to Kenton. Mom signed my papers, but J.C.'s mom wouldn't sign for him.

So, August 13, 1940, I left Memphis on a train for New York City with a three-day meal ticket to stay in the Navy for 30 days. Rode that rickety-rack Southern coach all day and all night, and arrived in New York City 'bout 6 o'clock in the morning.

Got off the train, walked out into the big city of New York gawking, asked a few people where was Times Square. They'd look me up and down, wouldn't say anything, and keep walking. I thought these are an unfriendly bunch of Yankees until I looked up and saw a sign that said Times Square. I went into the subway and found out how to get to Columbia University,

106th Street. As I looked out over the beautiful Hudson River, with the Washington Bridge in the background, there swinging at anchor were three of the most beautiful ships that I have ever seen. Three heavy cruisers: the *Quincy*, the *Vincennes*, and the *Witchita*. Well, I saw somebody that looked official, showed him my telegram. He pointed down to the dock and says, "Get one of those boats that's comin' in."

As luck would have it, my boat was heading for the *U.S.S. Quincy*.

On arrival, we were directed to the aviation deck, and there all hell broke loose. First off, they took all of our clothes. Next, they put us in a line to be issued Navy clothing. The storekeeper that issued mine, guessing my size, gave me skivvy shirts and shorts that fit reasonably well. My uniform jumper was so tight that I could hardly breathe, and the pea coat was so loose that I could jump up and turn around and the pea coat would still be pointing in the same direction.

With clothes in hand, the next order of business was to assign you to a division. Right off the bat, I found myself in the 1st division. Nothing spectacular about that, except your bunk was in the bow of the ship, and you got up every morning at reveille to squeegee down the deck.

In a few minutes, as I was straightening up the blanket on my bunk, I noted that some of the regular shipboard sailors put their junk—towels, and so forth—seemingly by force of habit, on my bunk. I told two or three of these knuckleheads to put their stuff on their own bunk and leave mine alone.

Didn't help much until I caught one sailor by the hair of the head and made him remove his towel.

'Bout that time the word was passed for the newcomers to lay up to sick bay. They formed a line, and as it moved forward, the corpsmen gave us shots. We were getting them in both arms and the rump. One among the shots must have been vaccine for typhoid fever because very shortly I began to feel the old feverish ache reaction, enough so that I wasn't interested in going up to have chow. I went and got in my bunk, going to rest a bit.

Along came a boatswain's mate, got me out of the bunk and on deck. The afternoon wore along, and those shots made me very uncomfortable, enough so that I wasn't interested in going to an evening meal. Instead, got back into my bunk. Along came a boatswain's mate, and said, "Mack, you've got the anchor watch, 6 to 8." Since it wasn't long until 6, I got up, inquired where you went for the anchor watch, finally found myself up in the bow of this ship, ready to relieve the guy that had had the 4 to 6 watch. He handed me a 30.06 rifle, and I says, "What am I supposed to do?" He says, "You dumb bastard, don't you know there's a war on?" I said with a huff, "Listen, the war's in Europe. Well, what am I supposed to do?" He said, "You take this rifle, and anybody who comes up that anchor chain, you shoot 'em." And he left me holding that thirty-aught-six rifle. Well, I'd never seen a high-powered rifle before. But, after looking it over, I went on up to the ship's hawse pipe, looked over into the Hudson, and there was this big old chain. I thought, "That's the dumbest thing I ever heard of, to sit and look at that chain. Isn't anybody going to come up that chain."

The more I looked at that chain though, the more I considered that it might be possible, and I got to thinking, "If I let somebody come aboard, I'll be responsible." So I figured out how to load that gun. I rammed a shell into the chamber. And I'll tell you now, it's a good thing that I didn't see anybody messin' around with that chain!

It soon got dark, and since I was feverish, I got cold. And I decided that I could watch that hawse pipe hole from back leanin' against the No. 1 turret out of the wind. As the rifle got heavier and heavier and I got sicker and sicker, I soon put the butt of the rifle on the steel deck, and my foot up against the turret, and leaned back, wondering what time it was.

Well, a snappy-dressed young man come, a-pickin' 'em up and puttin' 'em down, headed toward the bow of the ship. Boy, did he have a pretty uniform. He had a white hat, a dark blue jacket, and light blue pants with red stripes. Well, I didn't know he was a Marine 2nd lieutenant that was the junior officer of the deck up to inspect the watch. When he saw me down there leaning against the turret, he says, "Don't you know how to present arms?"

I said, "Nope." Didn't know anything about saying "sir" to officers, either.

Fact is, I didn't know he was an officer. Even worse, I didn't know what an officer was.

He asked, "Are you one of the V-7s that came aboard today?"

I said, "Yep."

He said, "Somebody should've given you people a little bit of training before sending you to a ship."

He said, "You know how to do the manual of arms?"

I said, "No."

Well, this kid must have been on the Annapolis drill team, because you never saw such handling that rifle with it goin' up in the air, and comin' down, and clankin' the steel deck. Real good show! He pitched me the rifle, said, "Now you do it."

I said, "This gun's loaded, and I don't know how to unload it." That was the most surprised-lookin' Marine I've ever seen.

I got off of that stinking first Navy watch, went down, had a very hectic sleep, got rousted out of bed at reveille to go out and squeegee down the steel deck.

The storekeepers that had done such a poor job of selecting uniforms for me did worse when it come to shoes. In fact, they had no shoes my size.

So the very first morning I lined up in rank, wearing my own shoes, which, incidentally, were brand new and yellow. You should have seen the look on the face of the young ensign division officer when he looked down the line, seeing all of those black shoes, and suddenly, a pair of yellow ones.

He came down and chewed me out for having on those non-uniform shoes. I told him, "They said they didn't have any shoes my size."

He says, "You get down to the ship's store, get some dye, and dye the damn things!"

You know, I ruint my yellow shoes!

During this operation, the coxswain in charge managed to purposely squirt water all over me. I suspect that, by then, he had learned that I was one of the officer candidates on board. Anyway, he had some more learning to do, because I picked up the squeegee handle and told him, "If you squirt any more water on me, I'll break this handle over your head."

Needless to say, I stayed dry the rest of the cruise.

They assigned us what was called "running mates," which meant that I was to go to watches, general quarters, chow, you name it, with my running mate. I was assigned to a big, fat slob from near Atlanta, Georgia.

He was a V-6 reserve, which meant he didn't know much more than I did. We proceeded out of the New York harbor and on to Norfolk. En route, they gave us lectures, gave each one of us a copy of the Watch Officer's Guide. All these things I absorbed, including practically memorizing the Watch Officer's Guide.

Chow was terrible. Good food to start with, I'm sure, but not cooked like Aunt Ruby cooked it. At Norfolk, I was assigned another job as bow hook on the motor launch. This entailed walking out on the boom, climbing down a rope ladder, getting into the boat, making such trips as were assigned, and keeping the boat clean.

On a Sunday morning, our boat made a trip to pick up ward room newspapers and ice cream. Newspapers were late arriving at the pier, and so by the time we headed back to the ship, it was almost 9 o'clock. The boat coxswain says, "Fellas, we missed breakfast, but I got a little pogey bait [candy and crackers] that you can share with me."

Well, I says, "They're supposed to save breakfast for us." The coxswain says, "Well, they never do."

I said, "The Watch Officer's Guide requires the officer of the deck to save a meal anytime a boat's out at meal time."

Well, those boys looked at me like I was Franklin Roosevelt and Einstein at the same time, for they had never heard of the Watch Officer's Guide.

As we went up on the ship, heading down to the chow hall, we went in and told the cook we wanted breakfast. The cook says, "Get the hell out of here."

I said, "Wait a minute. We were in the motor launch at breakfast time. Didn't they tell you to save breakfast for us?"

He says, "Hell, no, and get the hell out of here."

The two experienced sailors in the boat crew were wary enough to keep their distance from the officer of the deck, but they watched and listened as I went up and saluted smartly and says, "Sir, I'm Seaman Ashe. The motor launch was ashore and we missed breakfast. We went down to the chow hall, but the cook says there wasn't anybody who told him to save breakfast."

The officer says, "Boatswain's Mate of the watch!"

The boatswain's mate comes over. The officer says, "Didn't you tell the kitchen to save breakfast for the boat crew?"

The boatswain's mate says, "Yes, sir."

The officer of the deck says, "Messenger! You tell the cook to report to the quarter deck on the double."

In a bit, a very sad looking cook was getting chewed out by the officer of the deck. Now, they may not teach those boys at Annapolis a whole lot, but they got a master's degree in how to chew out somebody.

The Officer of the deck turned to me, and he says, "He'll fix breakfast for you."

My fellow boat crewmen couldn't believe what they were hearing. But we went down to the mess hall, and I said to the cook, "I want sausage and eggs, with the eggs over light."

That cook looked belligerent, but he didn't say anything. Pretty soon, we were eating sausage and eggs. Well, I was really stuffed, but I wanted the cook to get a little more punishment, so I told him I wanted some more sausage and eggs. Well, I had been hungry, and it was tasty, and we hadn't been having food like that, either. Pretty soon, we left the mess hall, went back up, climbed out on the boom, climbed down the ladder into the boat.

The wind had come up, and the sea was getting choppy. Less than 30 minutes later, I was seasick and vomited up every bit of that sausage and eggs.

The next day, I had liberty. And, along with my running mate, got a boat to the pier, got on the bus heading for Norfolk. My running mate couldn't believe that I wasn't going with him to the whorehouse. Now, back in those days, sailors got paid twice a month. This running mate was a seaman 2nd class. As such, he got $30 a month, or $15 every two weeks.

Well he, along with apparently quite a number of the other sailors, would save a dollar from their $15 paycheck for a toothbrush, shaving creme and other incidentals, and take the $14 and go to seven different whorehouses. The frozen price was $2 a throw. When he used up his $14, he'd get on the bus and go back to the ship. That was his liberty.

I looked up Mary Emma, who worked in the 10-cent store, went home with her, stayed all night with Mary and Bronson, and back to the ship the next day before 8 p.m.

The next day's work included painting the side of the ship. It was bad enough to climb out on that boom. But as I looked over the side of the ship and saw those little boards that you had to stand on to paint, I knew that was no place for me. I waited around as long as I could. Finally, this coxswain that was the marksman with the water hose came along and says, "Over the side, Mack."

I said to him, "This is the only uniform I have. I don't have any dungarees. I don't want to get paint on my uniform."

He says, "Over the side, Mack! And that's an order."

"Well," I says, "I'm going to ask the officer of the deck." And so, I headed for the officer of the deck while he squirmed and looked like he was hunting for a place to hide, while I come up to the officer of the deck, smartly saluted, and told him my problem.

"Why," he says, "I agree with you. Who says you have to go over the side?"

I turned, and with a finger-bore sight, pointed out this coxswain, and listened while I got lesson number 2 on how to bawl out a sailor. He called that sailor things that I didn't know how to spell.

By this time, I was getting way too big for my britches. The next morning, before daylight, all hands were rousted out. We went to special sea detail, and, along with the other two cruisers, we headed out of Hampton Roads. We got three miles off shore a little after daylight, and the captain of the ship says, "All hands, hear this! The German pocket battleship *Graf Spee*, location unknown. We're joining the British Navy and searching for the *Graf Spee*. All hands are aware that Congress has declared that the United States is neutral. But the Congress doesn't run the Navy. The president does."

Going through my mind, I was recalling some of the literature that said that the German *Graf Spee* was packing 11-inch guns, and I looked out at these other two new cruisers with us in the line, and I knew we were packing eight-inch guns. And I sure hoped we didn't find that *Graf Spee*!

We headed southeast. A storm came up and I was seasick enough to die. Before long, we moved into the Gulf Stream and entered the beautiful blue waters of the Caribbean. A few days searching with drills of all sorts being constantly run, we were glad to hear the captain give another all hands call and state that the British had found the *Graf Spee*, down off Uruguay in South America.

About this time the officers aboard *Quincy* began individual interviews with each of the V-7s. I had been terribly seasick once, and wasn't so hot at the time when one Ensign Phillips, doing his duty, interviewed me. He asked me what I thought about the Navy. I'm sure I busted his cotton-pickin' heart when I told him the Navy was made up of a bunch of people running around looking for something to do and trying to make themselves look busy as they were doing it. No, indeed, I wasn't interested in the Navy.

A few days later, one of the department heads, a Lieutenant Walker, seemed to enjoy giving me his undivided attention with another interview. I told him I liked the ship, and I was glad we had a Navy, but I sure didn't want to be part of it. I was going to go home, go back to school, be a schoolteacher. By that time, I was thoroughly homesick and was surely glad that we would soon go back to New York, and I could be off to home.

Days passed, and, sure enough, we did arrive in New York City. But before leaving, curiosity dictated that I go down and take a look at the list of the people that were selected and those that were not. First glance at the list, alphabetically, with "Ashe" on top, said "Walter D. Ashe, selected for midshipman training." I went running around all over the ship, telling them it was a mistake, that I didn't want any part of it, and I had told them I didn't want to be selected, and I certainly wasn't going to midshipman training!

I got off the ship and onto the train for the long ride back to Memphis.

Being a natural salesman, I observed the candy and peanut salesman that Southern Railroad had. He was going up and down the train, and wasn't selling a darned thing. I called him over and told him, "That ain't no way to be a salesman." And after a bit, I told him, "Let me show you how."

I stood up, told the people I was going to show this boy how to be a salesman. I sold out his supply of candy and peanuts in less than 10 minutes. Never saw a boy so happy—even considered getting myself a job selling candy and peanuts.

Got back to Memphis, glad to be home, glad to be with Evaline, and was sure that I was never leaving Memphis again, and if so, only on short trips inland!

14

Northwestern

I began to do every job that I could think of for Uncle Maurice, but couldn't earn enough money to pay tuition to enter the winter quarter (my scholarship had expired after two years). Although disappointed that I was missing another quarter at school, I increased my efforts and hours in order to come up with the funds.

About this time Uncle Maurice's contractor for building a new pie shop came up with foreclosures that included taking Uncle Maurice's partially built building. He had to have $25,000 right quick in order to continue on his building. His only source for money was to borrow it from Uncle Gregory who lived over in Arkansas. One Sunday afternoon he says,

"Dub, you want to drive over to see Heddy and Gregory?" Well, I certainly did, and off to Arkansas we went.

It was known that Uncle Gregory was financially well established. As we drove out and on to his beautiful farm, we could see why. But as we got up next to his house, I was terribly surprised. The house was just exactly like two Negro houses

Dub Ashe, Midshipman, at Northwestern University in Chicago.

there close by. It was a little three-room cabin, only his didn't have a floor in the front porch. It had a plank across the porch that he and Aunt Heddy used to go in and out of the house.

First thing Aunt Heddy said was, W.D. I'm sorry for you to see that we haven't got a porch." She says, "I've been trying to get him to put a floor in that porch for six years." Uncle Gregory put his hand on my shoulder and he says, "Now, Heddy, W.D. doesn't care anything about that porch."

We walked around the place, looking at the fine barn, the well-kept equipment, and that two-bale-to-the-acre cotton land. Uncle Gregory said to me, "Why don't you forget messin' around down at that normal school. Come up here and run this farm." He said, "Me and Heddy are getting old and the farm will be yours."

I said, "Uncle Gregory, you have a daughter. When you die, this farm should belong to Floie Mae." He says, "You know that Floie Mae ain't no count, and I want you to have it." After a bit, we got into the car and Uncle Maurice showed me the check for $25,000 that Uncle Gregory had written for him. Uncle Maurice, with tears in his eyes, said, "You know, he meant it when he said you come up and work the farm and he'd give it to you." I said, "Uncle Maurice, I wouldn't come up to live on this farm if he gave it to me right now." And I looked at him and says, "And you wouldn't either."

He put his hand on my shoulder and said, "No, I wouldn't."

The next few days back at Memphis were more or less hectic. I was unable to save much money for the spring quarter of college. It was solved for me when, through the mail, came a letter that directed me to report to Northwestern University, 17 March, 1941, as a midshipman in the United States Naval Reserve. Well, I didn't have any thought about going on to the Navy, but I found out the course at Northwestern was going to give 12 semester hours toward a college degree, and further, I would get room and board and $65 a month. I decided that, you know, I just might do that and save the money so I could go to school summer quarter back at Memphis State.

Course, I learned after I arrived at Northwestern that my letter was not an invitation, and if I hadn't shown up, somebody would've dang well come and got me!

On the 16th of March, I got on the train, heading for Chicago. Good ol' Aunt Rube convinced me to take a little top coat that I had bought for $14.95. The weather was nice and pretty, a nice warm March day, and I didn't much want to be burdened with that coat. But I always did what Aunt Rube suggested. One, force of habit, and the other, she was always right.

By the time we were out of the city limits of Memphis, I had bumped into another knucklehead, James A. Calhoun, that I knew from Memphis State. We were sitting in the coach when lunch time came, but neither of us made a move to go to the dining car. I just plain didn't have any money—$2.20 to be exact. I didn't discuss it with him, figured he wasn't hungry. The afternoon wore long as we were up into Illinois and we noticed the people at the towns we passed through were all bundled up with heavy clothes. On arrival in Chicago, I quickly found out why. Got off of that train, and looked down to see if I'd forgot and left my britches on board! Soon learned from the newspaper boys in Chicago that a deep freeze was expected that night. Old Calhoun and myself ran down the street. The nearest building was a Walgreen's drug store. By this time, we had two problems. We both were about to starve to death, and we didn't have any place to sleep.

A few inquiries established that they had rooms upstairs in that Walgreen drug store building. We went up, rented a room for a dollar. There were two cots, no heat, and no running water. Having established a place to turn in, we went back downstairs and bought a cup of cocoa apiece.

Now I want to tell you, that was a cold night! Wasn't too bad from the top, because we had two blankets, but from the bottom, that canvas cot didn't provide much insulation.

The next morning, we learned it was 1 below zero outside. We likewise learned that Abbott Hall, Northwestern, was about five miles across town to Lake Michigan. We didn't even think of trying to pay for a taxi. We went out into the street, walked awhile, ran awhile, with one hand in the pocket and the other one over an ear. We'd switch hands to warm up the hand and warm up the other ear. Along about 9 o'clock, pooped tired, hungry, and nearly frozen, we arrived at Northwestern University. Man, was I glad I had that little old coat with me!

Of course, we were too dumb to know it, but if we'd arrived at Northwestern the night before, the Navy would've fed us and checked us into a barracks. But as it was, we went in to the main lobby of Abbott Hall, presented our orders, and they took our clothes, put us in a line, and commenced issuing uniforms. Things were different than back at the old *Quincy*. These men were measuring us, making certain that the uniforms fit, and man, what nice uniforms! Blue serge suits, white shirts, turtleneck sweaters, drill trousers, and finally a Navy wool raincoat with a liner. I couldn't imagine that clothes like this existed. Along with another old boy from North Carolina, they sent Calhoun and myself up to the eighth floor of Abbott Hall to our room.

There was a single bed and a double bunk bed in the room. Naturally, I took the single bed, and we got busy helping each other put on our uniform. At exactly 12 o'clock, the bell rang. On inquiry, we found that that meant lunch. We rode down to the first floor in the elevator and walked out into this spacious dining room loaded with food.

Here I was, starved! I went through the line with one of the finest meals that I'd ever had. In the dining room after lunch, with my beautiful uniform, I decided that I'd found a home!

That very day we proceeded with learning the discipline of a midshipman. We were assigned a crash course in seamanship, navigation, ordinance and gunnery, plus a few odds and ends. We were expected to do a condensed version of the Annapolis four-year course in three months.

The place was loaded with lawyers that had finished their law school and had gone into this program to circumvent the draft, which everyone knew was coming.

I was in my glory with these courses, especially ordinance, gunnery, torpedoes, and likewise with navigation, and I became quite a tutor for these law school midshipmen. They worked us hard and meant to, because under the law, they had to flunk out one-third of us. Competition was intense because those not selected knew that they would shortly be a buck private in the army.

The very first few days I observed the instructor solve a torpedo problem for the midshipman class. Didn't take me but a few minutes to see that he hadn't solved it correctly, so I pulled the old routine of standing up at attention, clicking my heals, calling my name, and, when recognized, said, "Sir, you solved the problem incorrectly."

The grading system called for scholastic grades to count 40 percent, and "officer-like qualities" to count 60 percent. Now this instructor was a reserve lieutenant commander called to active duty. His problem was he didn't know how to work the torpedo exercise. So he gave the rest of the lecture hour over to lambasting me for my zero officer qualities for not showing respect to my senior officer.

When the class was over, one of the other midshipmen stood up and says, "Midshipman Folsum. And, sir, the problem is wrong." Ashe and Folsum had our names put on the tree, which indicated that we had flunked ordinance. Our names stayed on the tree in ordinance for a full month, and if I hadn't of had such outstanding grades in the other subjects, I sure would have been flunked.

My room was directly across the hallway from the office of the commandant of midshipmen. The commandant liked to keep his door open, and if you left your door cracked a little, you could often hear some earth-shaking developments, such as the day I heard the commandant offering the midshipman battalion to Secretary of Navy Knox as the only disciplined force ready to be sent to Milwaukee to put down the strike under way in the machine tool plants. The commandant said, "The nation must have those machine tools for us to build the guns, and we've got to stop it." I don't know what Secretary of Navy Knox said, but he must have said we were training to be naval officers and not infantrymen. But the commandant said, "Aye, aye, sir."

Northwestern Law School students occupied a portion of Abbott Hall.

The Navy had about 500 men occupying the other portion. One night, I'm awakened by hearing somebody yelling, "Mary, Mary!" and hammering on doors, and finally to my door yelling, "Mary." And opened the door and came in, and this blonde was in the bed with me, and he told her, "You're in the Navy side of the building." My notoriety rose to new heights as everybody learned that this gal was in the bed with me. Only trouble, I was asleep until her escort awakened me as he was trying to get her out of the Navy side of the building.

In due course, we were getting ready to get our commissions. Some captain from the Bureau of Personnel in Washington came to talk with us. Among other things, he told us that we could apply for active or inactive duty, and those of us that chose to go on active duty could make a request for the Atlantic fleet, the Pacific fleet, or the Asiatic fleet. Some midshipman stood up and says, "Captain, where do you think the war will start?"

The captain said, "I don't know where it will start, but as far as the Navy is concerned, our war will be in the Pacific."

Speech over, martial music playing, I marched down to say I wanted active duty, first choice, Pacific fleet. This, of course, I got. They set our orders as 10 days leave, proceed and report San Diego for further transfer to Pearl Harbor. Report to the U.S.S. Neville. By the time I got to San Diego, the Neville had been sent around to the east coast, and they changed my orders to the Raleigh.

15

Evaline Proposes

Now, while I was back doing all that studying, I first wrote Evaline and told her how checking in went. And later, given a little more information, I told her that an ensign got $125 a month. As I got a little smarter, I learned that an ensign got $125 a month, but he also got $18.75 a month for a food allowance. Then I learned that an ensign that was married got an extra $40 a month for a housing allowance. These letters I was writing for information. But when Evaline received that letter about $40 a month extra for being married, back came a letter saying, "Let's get married so we can get the $40 a month."

Now, boys and girls, that shook me up a little bit. I quickly dashed off a craw-fishing letter that said that I couldn't get married if I wanted to, because I was only 20. Back came a letter that said I could get married, all I had to

Bride and groom and bridal party including best man, Malcolm, and maid of Honor, Gladys Paseur, Evaline's sister.

have was my parents' consent, that she could go up and get the license, take it down to my mom, and my mom would sign it, and we could get married. Well, from my end of this totem pole, I hadn't ever said anything about getting married.

I got my commission on 12 June, 1941. I'd bought a trunk full of uniforms on the credit, and, with my trunk and about $60, I got on Southern Airlines for my first airplane ride. On arrival in Memphis, I walked off the plane. There was Evaline, her mom and daddy, her sister Cubie and her husband Joe, her brother and his new wife, Mary, and her sister Gladys. I walked off the plane and everybody looking at that white uniform—rather impressive. Got in the car and headed to their house. On arrival, her mother told me she was sure I wasn't worth all the trouble that she was going to for us to get married.

I then found out everything was arranged for us to get married tomorrow at their house on Friday, the 13th. Well, I hadn't even thought of buying a ring. And really, if I could've had my druthers, I'd have found some way of getting out of this. I told Evaline, "You know I got orders to go to Hawaii." She didn't care if I had orders to go to the moon.

Next day, I whipped uptown, went over and bought a $75 wedding ring (didn't have the money of course, walked down the street and got my Uncle Allen to come over and sign as a credit reference). Went back out to Aunt Ruby's. My mom had come down. She was eight months pregnant. We all got ready and went down to Evaline's house for the wedding.

I had on my white uniform and I took my sword. Didn't wear it because I didn't know how to unsheath the sword to cut the cake. Shortly, the preacher came in. They normally talk about the scared groom. That preacher was twice as scared as I was. He had never performed a wedding ceremony before.

Mrs. Paseur and the girls had their little home decked out with flowers and arranged beautifully. I set down between Momma and Aunt Ruby.

Shortly, Uncle Maurice come over, set down next to Aunt Ruby. Uncle Maurice, he's a prankster from the word go, and he knew that Mom and Aunt Rube were going to cry, and so he had for himself a red bandanna handkerchief about half as big as a blanket, and as the ceremony started, you never heard such forced crying as he put out into that red handkerchief.

It was a very nice wedding. When the pronouncement of man and wife came, we had to cut the cake. Well, while I'm getting my sword and Joe's getting his camera, Uncle Maurice got the cake in and set it on the table—beautiful cake with several tiers and a bride and groom up on top.

With the camera ready, I took the sword and come down and it went clank as it hit the metal. I thought Uncle Maurice was going to split his britches laughing. He'd gone to all kinds of trouble icing various sized aluminum pans into what was seemingly a perfect cake.

But in a bit he went back to the kitchen and came out with the actual cake. This time, we cut cake with the sword, and gave everybody a piece of it.

After the festivities were over, Lark and Mary drove Evaline and myself to the Peabody Hotel. We went up to our room and, shortly thereafter, she went into the bathroom to put on her gowns and such stuff. I pulled out my bag, dug into it for that pair of blue pajamas I had bought. I'd never had a pair of pajamas in my life. Pulled out those pajamas, and somebody had taken a sewing machine and sewed up both of the legs.

I was exasperated, wondered who did such a thing. Never knew for sure, but I think it was Maxine Flowers. But Evaline, without missing much of a beat, went to her bag and came out with a sewing kit, and she began carefully taking out one stitch at a time. Must have taken a full 30 minutes for me to figure out we didn't need to take the stitches out of that dadgoned pair of pajamas.

Since I didn't have any pajamas, I didn't think that she ought to have a gown, but that's where I made a mistake. She wasn't about to get rid of that gown and that was still true 50 years later.

Well, about 1 or 2 o'clock in the morning, never heard such hammering on the door. Opened the door and the bellhop presented a great big long flower box. I thought that was awful nice of somebody. We opened that box and that brother Malc and her sister Gladys had gone out and picked some of that vile-smellin' dog fennel. We took the flowers and put them in the waste basket in the bathroom, washed our hands and shut the door, but all we could smell was dog fennel.

The next morning, Evaline was about to starve to death, wanting me to get up and let's go have breakfast. I wasn't so interested in breakfast as I might 'a oughta been, but she knew of a good restaurant right near the hotel. Of all things, it was Brettling's Cafeteria. She had about six courses and I wondered how in the world that little ole girl could hold that much to eat.

We soon got packed up, got on a streetcar and rode back out to her house. The only explanation that I can give is, I was stupid.

We had a wonderful few days, waiting to get on the train for San Diego. The lack of a car and money made life a bit more difficult and so did the recognition that I was going to Hawaii without even a guess of when I might see her again.

The Pacific fleet was home based in Long Beach, California. And although it was actually stationed at Pearl Harbor, the government would pay transportation for dependents only to the home port. I didn't know until after I reached the *Raleigh* that the ship was part of the Hawaiian detachment, and as such, home port was Pearl Harbor.

It was late in June 1941 that I got on yet another train and shoved off across the continent to San Diego. Before leaving, Evaline had registered for her final quarter before getting her degree and was back in school. The first day, she asked me to meet her at school after her last class. This I did, wearing the only thing I had, my white uniform. When Evaline got out of class, I was there in the lobby of the administration building, surrounded by a bevy of coeds admiring my uniform and making goo-goo eyes at me.

Evaline quickly decided that after that she would meet me back at her home.

16

San Diego

The trip to San Diego was uneventful but very interesting. On arrival at San Diego, I learned that my duties consisted of calling in each morning at 9 o'clock to see if my transportation had arrived. The very first day, as I strolled around the hotel, I found a bunch of sunbathing mats laid out on the roof, and of course I thought they were there for the guests to use. I stretched out and went to sleep and was awakened surrounded by a bunch of girls.

One of them proceeded to lambast me for having the nerve to use their sunbathing mats. She was a tall, long-legged blonde that was singing with the Fred Waring Band out at Balboa Park. After she determined that I wasn't such a bad guy, she invited me to come listen to her sing. I came up with excuses that you couldn't imagine. I finally stated that I plain didn't have enough money to put her in a taxi to the zoo. She settled that by saying, "We'll go on

Ensign Dub with Evaline in San Diego.

the streetcar." So in a bit, she, wearing a long white evening dress and me wearing a white uniform, got on a streetcar and headed for the zoo.

She was an excellent singer, outstanding musician, and a gorgeous doll. But instead of getting on her chartered bus to return to the hotel, she came over and rode back with me on the streetcar.

I suggested to her the next day that we go to the beach swimming. She said, "Great!" She would prepare a picnic lunch. We got on the bus and went to Mission Beach. We had a wonderful time riding the in-bound waves, using our bodies as surfboards. But by the time we decided to have lunch, she was as red as a beet. It scared me, and I told her she'd better stay out of the sun, that already I thought she was in trouble.

She was. Big, watery blisters came up on her back, arms, and legs, and deep crevices were oozing fluids at any point where she moved her arms or legs.

We went back to the hotel and I told her she ought to go to the doctor.

She asked what could you do for sunburn. I told her that my grandmother and as well, my wife, put butter on the burn. Of course, we know now that was exactly the wrong thing to do. But I went down to the grocery store somewhere and got a quarter pound of butter. I came back up to her room and with her nude put that stinking butter all over her sunburns. You know that girl got up, put on that white evening dress again, and rode on the streetcar out to the zoo, got up and sang, didn't flinch. But her dress was stuck to her back and stomach. It must have been terribly painful.

We got back to the hotel. We went up to her room and I used water that I'd put some salt in that I'd got down at the bar to get that dress unstuck.

Naturally, we didn't go to the beach anymore, but I went another time with her to listen to her sing. She was the lead soloist for the Fred Waring Band in July, 1941.

I mention all this because of what later developed. The next day, I got on a ship, the *U.S.S. Wharton*, and headed for Honolulu. I proceeded on through the attack of Pearl Harbor out to the south Pacific, but in February, 1942, as the *Raleigh* returned to the states, my roommate was a Life photographer that had been on one of our carriers at the Coral Sea. He, Bob Landry, was hurrying back to New York to file his story.

After we arrived in Mare Island, Landry invited all the officers to attend a party as his guests at the Sir Francis Drake Hotel in San Francisco. We went down in 12 taxis, compliments of Life magazine. He got us off to a good bash at the Sir Francis Drake. After a bit, he left, saying he'd be back shortly. I was a teetotaler, quite amused at the antics of some of my buddies, as they became inebriated. After a bit, Bob Landry returned, walked into the ball room with a beautiful girl on his arm. I blinked a couple of times and couldn't believe it, for it was this same Liz Stowkowski, the San Diego singer, that arrived with him. He made quite a to-do of coming along, introducing her to each of the officers. He came to me and says, "Here's my old room mate, Dub Ashe. We slept together for 10 days as I rode with him from Pearl Harbor back to Mare Island."

That girl didn't flinch an eye of recognition or make one single comment until after a bit somebody touched me on the shoulder and I turned. It was Liz, and she says, "Come on, Dub, let's dance." I said, "You know well that I don't dance!" She said, "Yes, but come on anyway."

Of course, anybody could dance with her. She says, "I haven't got but a minute. I know you don't approve, but I will do what's necessary to get my picture on the cover of Life magazine." And she floated off, shaking hands with someone else.

The Raleigh got repaired, and we began escorting convoys to the south Pacific. One night, I went down to see the movies. The movie was Janet Blair in "Anchors Away." First cracker out of the box, here was Liz, now Janet Blair, wearing a sailor's suit, and singing "Anchors Away."

(Editor's note: Efforts to document and/or corroborate this incident proved inconclusive, but in our opinion it's too good a story to leave out.)

17

On to Pearl Harbor

Back to my trip to Pearl Harbor. It was nice. Uneventful, except for my meeting a couple of school mates from Kenton. I got on a taxi from the hotel to the gangway of the *Wharton*. I got out and went aboard the *Wharton* wearing a green civilian suit that I had bought on the credit there at San Diego. This I did after I learned that officers went ashore in civilian clothes.

The USS Raleigh, my first ship, a light cruiser home-ported in Pearl Harbor, Hawaii.

I went up the gangway to the quarterdeck of the *Wharton*, and lo and behold, there was Bill Fowler, from the class behind me at Kenton High School.

He was a first-class gunner's mate, and petty officer of the watch on the quarterdeck. He jovially stuck out his hand and says, "Dub, what in the hell are you doing? Are you going to Pearl Harbor as a yard workman?" I said, "No, Bill, I'm an ensign en route to my ship, the Raleigh." He was astounded, but at that instant, the officer of the deck said, "Fowler, get Mr. Ashe's bags. Put them in his stateroom." Bill left and I never saw him again the rest of his life.

A few days later, at sea, from the passenger deck I saw Warren Ross, a boy that lived less than a half mile from me at Macedonia. He couldn't come to the passenger area, and I wasn't supposed to be in the crew area.

But I went down the ladder to the main deck and visited with old Warren several minutes a couple of times each day. And later, when the *Raleigh* was being repaired from damage received at Pearl Harbor, she and the *Wharton* were at Mare Island at the same time, and old Warren came over and spent the night with Evaline and myself.

I arrived at Pearl Harbor and made my way to a dock, awaiting the *Raleigh* boat. It just so happened that one of my classmates at Northwestern, Jack Scappa, and another ensign from the University of Washington, Hal Johnson, were reporting at the same time.

We arrived on the *Raleigh*, disrupted things terribly because the wardroom was having lunch and we didn't know enough not to go on up. But they put us into our staterooms, fed us lunch, and we were off to a start, no matter how bad it was.

The officers on board received us as friends. Some marveled that our uniforms looked like theirs. And, right off the bat, one of the warrant officers took us on a tour of the island, including driving us up the valley to a pool formed by a waterfall, called Sacred Falls.

The territory of Hawaii had recently enacted legislation that prohibited swimming in the nude. The Portuguese girls that were at the Sacred Falls knew they had to have swimsuits, so they arrived, climbed up on the boulders there next to the falls, stood up, pulled off their street clothes, and put their swimsuits on. Pretty good show, and I was thoroughly amused, and wondered why there were not any Hawaiians. But apparently, native Hawaiians, Chinese and Japanese girls did not frequent the falls.

Back at the ship, everybody pointed out the virtues of going topside at night, getting on a cot, and sleeping under the beautiful moon as we cruised through the waters off Hawaii. I could hardly wait for the *Raleigh* to get under way.

The custom was for the junior officers that didn't have the watch to have the mess boys put them a cot and a couple of blankets up on the main deck to sleep under the bright moon. First crack out of the box, in my cot, looking at the beautiful moon, the wind blowing on me made me uncomfortable. And even though I wrapped up in a blanket, in the middle of the summer in Hawaii, I got cold. Before midnight, I put a stop to that for me. I went back down to my room, and was never interested in sleeping on the deck, no matter how beautiful the moon.

Realize it's only five months before the Pearl Harbor attack. Too little and too late the Navy was urgently training young officers and men to become sailors. Every few days there was an order received by our ship for mandatory quota of officers to go to various gunnery schools.

I was sent to three-inch anti-aircraft school and after a week of firing three-inch guns, and disassembling them to make any necessary repairs, I became quite an experienced anti-aircraft officer. I was assigned the general quarters duties of starboard side sky control. My responsibility was to pick up incoming aircraft, quickly estimate the bearing and sight angle, and call these out to the starboard guns.

Very soon, I was sent to 50-caliber machine gun school. On Sunday night I reported to Fort Weaver, checked into the barracks, was assigned a bunk, and was notified that reveille would be at 5, breakfast at 6, and we would commence firing at 7.

There were about 10 other officers there and we fired from 7 to noon and from 1 to 6 continuously, except stopping to repair our gun when something broke. By mid-week we were also firing at night and were required, in total darkness, to determine the cause of a firing stoppage and repair it. [On the targets they had over there, they had an electric bulb.]

By the end of the week, I was sure glad to get back to the *Raleigh*, but to this day, I'm an expert with a 50-caliber machine gun.

When we were at sea, it was a rough schedule of watches, and as junior officer of the deck, I soon learned that I didn't know nuttin'! An amusing situation. We had an old captain named Simmons who delighted in chasing from port to starboard on the bridge, especially at night. Seeing some unsuspecting junior officer in his path, he would lower his shoulder and lunge into them.

All the junior officers on board were aware of this, and I shouldn't have been surprised when, one night, he hit me in the chest with his shoulder hard enough that it literally knocked the breath from me. To tell the truth, I thought that was ridiculous, and I watched him throughout the watch.

Toward the end, I saw him preparing to hit me again. I dipped my shoulder, and as he lunged, I lunged, and he was the one who had the breath knocked out of him. I never got hit by that captain again.

Soon after arrival on board *Raleigh*, I learned that since she was in the Hawaiian detachment, I could request transportation for my wife to come to Honolulu at government expense. This I did, and on Oct. 3rd, Evaline arrived from the mainland, in company with the wife of one of my buddies, Hal Johnson.

We were lucky to have found a place to live only two days before their arrival. This, our first home, consisted of what had once been a second-story room in a two-story building, and they had put in half a little kitchen, half a little bathroom, and they had hung a curtain down the middle of what was left, with a little bed on one side, and two chairs on the other.

We didn't have any furniture, or for that matter, lamps. It didn't matter. We didn't need any.

The first Sunday morning that she was in Hawaii, Evaline had me up bright and early, insisting that we go to church. We looked in the phone book, and got the address of a Baptist church that was located very near us. We walked to church, went in the door, and I was aghast.

Everybody inside was Japanese.

I turned to Evaline and said, "We're going home."

And I made her turn around and go back out of the church and go home. She was practically in tears because of this unchristian thing that I had done.

Then, and always, I knew that it was an unchristian thing. But I was not knowledgeable enough to differentiate between Japs as the Enemy, and the American-Japanese in Hawaii. Of course, I was very wrong, but it wasn't but a few days until the attack came, and as I went ashore after the attack, walking around Honolulu with my loaded .45, I could've easily and just as soon shot 'em all.

Normally when you're advertising clocks or pictures of clocks, you show them at 9 o'clock. Well, Evaline noted, and remarked that for a few days before the attack came, they were not showing 9 o'clock, but were showing a little before 8. She recalled that again after the attack came, and felt that it was significant and that the Japanese people were being warned that an attack was coming shortly before 8.

[Remember that this is a woman who accidentally found four-leaf clovers as she walked beside a clover patch, not even looking or thinking about clover!]

I don't place any credence in that. I think they just made the ads up that way accidentally.

Very shortly after Evaline arrived, the *Raleigh* went to sea, sailing and drilling off the shores of Hawaii. I think we stayed out about 10 days. By this time, I had become the illumination officer which meant that I directed the movement of the gun firing star shells in such a way as to keep the enemy fleet illuminated.

We came back to port in early November. A high point about that time: Evaline got a job as a control chemist for Kodak Hawaii at $100 a month. We thought we were rich, but we still didn't have enough to even splurge on a Coca-Cola.

Very late in November we went to sea again. This time, we were getting up to fleet exercises. Ours, the blue fleet, were doing drills attacking and defending ourselves from the yellow fleet, American ships simulating that they were Japanese. The drills were getting more realistic and everyone knew that war was imminent.

On December 4th, I was the junior officer of the deck on the evening watch, and was busy writing the log when the communications officer came out of the code room with a message that he showed to the captain. The captain read it and they stuck a match to the message. The communications officer rubbed the ashes in his hands, which caused me to know that it was a highly classified message. I did not know its content.

I went on down to bed glad to get what was called "all night in" because I did not have the mid[night] watch. The next morning I was awakened by a jolt and a roar. I jumped up, put on my clothes, and went topside just as another jolt hit and it was *Raleigh* catapulting our second airplane.

As I looked, the first red streaks of the sun about to rise showed me a mighty fleet that had come together since I got off watch. The *Raleigh* was fleet guide. A thousand yards to port was the battle line—eight battleships in a line. *Raleigh*, the flagship of the starboard destroyer screen, was controlling 16 destroyers, the starboard of the battle fleet, in a position mirroring ours. The light cruiser *Detroit* was controlling 16 destroyers on the port side.

Off to the starboard of the battle line and likewise to the port, were three heavy cruisers. Up further ahead, both starboard and port, were three light cruisers. In the distance, you could see other ships. This fleet in Battle of Jutland formation was heading toward Pearl Harbor.

As the morning wore on, an aircraft carrier met us, moving at high speed, going west, being escorted by cruisers and destroyers. All this time, back and forth, across the battle fleet, about 20 airplanes were flying low with live bombs on board and this old country boy knew right off the bat that this wasn't going to be no Boston Tea Party.

Well, it took a heckuva long time for the battle ships to get into port. Following them came the *Raleigh*, and then the *Detroit*. We tied up at the quays normally allotted to the aircraft carriers. We got this honored treatment because the *Raleigh* was the flagship of a very senior rear admiral. The never-been-right-yet rear admiral Theobold.

In port all hands remained on board on watch. Anti-aircraft guns were all manned, sky control, likewise, was at general quarters. It just so happened that, a few days back, the captain had said, when next we were back to port, he wanted Hal and myself, with our wives, to join him for dinner.

Things were changed a bit in that Hal and myself were on watch, but calls were made. Vivian brought Evaline out. The captain's gig met them and brought them to the ship. It was a very lovely dinner in the captain's cabin. All went well, except the captain got things screwed up and thought that Vivian was Mrs. Ashe and Evaline was Mrs. Johnson.

18

Pearl Harbor Attack

In due time, we put the girls in the gig and they went across the harbor and home, while Hal and myself went back on watch. We were at general quarters an hour before sunrise, and remained so all Saturday morning. It was calm Saturday morning, December 6th.

The big PBYs (flying boats) were having trouble getting airborne. They were fueled to the max and were going north to the limit of their range to be sure no Jap fleet was in that area. To the west and northwest, aircraft carriers were covering their approaches from 1,000 miles out.

At noon time, our PBYs were 500 miles to the north of Hawaii, and they sent the fleet commander a message saying it was all clear. Of course, this message was in code, and the Japs did not know our code, but they knew what it meant, so while our planes are going south, the Japs were going full speed ahead, heading toward Pearl Harbor.

A new ensign and his new bride.

They were up there in the north and they knew from the submarines they have that the planes were in the air searching, so when the code went di-di-dit, they knew what it meant.

Wasn't long until the Pacific fleet went on holiday routine. It so happened that I had liberty and headed home. There was a big party at Pearl Harbor that night. There was a big party every time the fleet was in.

Evaline modeling her gas mask, prior to the Japanese attack.

Evaline and myself didn't even consider going to any party.

We went to bed early, slept some, and the next morning, first thing I heard and felt was a rumble and a jar. I figured that the stupid army was having some sort of a drill on Sunday morning. I rolled over thinking that a little more sleep might be a good idea. Evaline got up, walked out onto the lanai for a few seconds, came chasing back in and says, "People there in the courtyard say the Japs are attacking the island."

I jumped up and went to the window. I rolled the Venetian blinds and looked out toward Pearl Harbor, about five miles away. Just as I did, coming over the house, heading toward Pearl Harbor, came five planes. My first reaction was that the army air force has got some new planes. But instantaneously I saw those planes had meatballs and I remarked to Evaline, as a couple of bursts of anti-aircraft exploded near the planes, "They're shooting real bullets!"

Simultaneously, crashing into our door came Hal and Vivian and the wife of some ensign who was on the *Indianapolis* with the hot news, "The Japs are attacking, the Japs are attacking!"

We didn't have a radio, nor, for that matter, any prospects of getting one. So Hal went running to get his radio. The radio announcer was already droning, "Hawaii is under attack from the imperial Japanese Navy—all military personnel return to your duty station. All civilian personnel remain indoors and stay away from windows." He just continued to repeat this.

The girl whose husband was on the *Indianapolis* was wringing her hands and worrying about her husband, and Hal was telling her that at sea was the best place to be. I noted that Hal had on a pair of his pajama bottoms and Vivian had on the pajama tops. I looked at Evaline and she had on a slip, and that gal from the Indianapolis had on a skimpy pair of panties, and you know, the truth of the matter, to this day I don't know what I had on.

But soon Hal and myself were into our clothes, we hugged and kissed the gals bye, and went running to get into his car. I got down to the car, noted that I didn't have a tie, and went running back up to get a tie. Into his car, down Young Avenue, hard right on Punaho, and left on the highway to Pearl. The traffic was rather sparse, but it was moving fast, so we were surprised to have a Kanaka policeman pulling us off the side of the road.

Another Kanaka policeman was trying to get a Jap florist truck turned around, and the scared Jap had stalled his truck and couldn't get it started. I heard the awfulest sound, and looked to see what was going on. It sounded like nothing I had ever heard before, a grinding roar. Finally, I got my eyes down, instead of looking up for an airplane. Down the road came three army tanks.

The Kanaka policeman grabbed this scared Jap florist, and pulled him out of the truck just before the lead tank hit that truck, and after they passed through the truck was as flat as a tin can. Hal pulled right in behind the tanks and we roared out to the main gate of Pearl Harbor.

The Marine guards had their Thompson machine guns and they were firing at the planes that were coming over the guardhouse. We went whipping down the drive through the golf course. Off to the left came two Jap planes just above the tree tops. They were firing machine guns, and you could see the puffs of the red dirt where the bullets were hitting the ground, and a collision course with us was about to occur. Hal gave that car a hard right rudder. We went off across the golf course and slammed into a tree.

We jumped out and lit out running up for what was called the Officer's Club Landing.

From the landing you could see almost the entire harbor, and what an awful sight it was. Directly ahead of us was the *Oklahoma*, rolled over, and alongside it, the *Maryland* was being bombed. A little to the right was the *West Virginia*, capsized. Alongside her, the *Tennessee* was on fire and being bombed. Just astern was the *Arizona*, still upright but low in the water, and it was being bombed and burning. A little to the left was the *California*, capsized. More off to the left was the floating dry dock and the destroyer *Shaw* that had been blown in two. A little more to the left was the dry dock with the battleship *Pennsylvania* and the destroyers *Kassen* and *Downs*. and they were all on fire and being bombed.

Near us was the dock. The *Honolulu* had been sunk. The *St. Louis* had gotten under way. Ford Island was burning, the hangers were blown up, and across battleship row, I could see the *Raleigh* with a terrible list.

Furthermore, there was a passel of Jap planes like yellow-jackets, bombing and strafing the *Raleigh*. But I could see 1.1 tracers coming up and into those planes, so I knew old Jack Scappa was still in business.

Hal Johnson, who was the other 1.1 battery officer, was standing next to me wishing he was on board ship. Didn't anybody else have any 1.1s except the *Raleigh*. Of course, the training ship *Utah* had a bunch of them, but we learned later that they were upside down in the water. Incidentally, it's still there, upside down in the water at the same place.

There were 30 or 40 officers, all in civilian clothes, milling around in shock. I looked down toward the sub base, and what do you know, I saw a motor launch up against the pier, trying to remain clear of the bombing and strafing.

Well, I knew how to run a motor launch, and I ran the 100 yards or so down and jumped into the motor launch.

I told the coxswain, "I'm taking your boat." I jumped up and grabbed the tiller.

He says, "Sir, I'm waiting for the *Medusa* crew." I yelled to the engineer, "Answer all bells."

And he says, "Aye, aye, sir." I was an ensign, but I was in civilian clothes. I hit the bells for full speed ahead and he gave it to me. I ran alongside the pier at the officer's club landing to pick up Hal. Hal jumped into the boat, so did everybody on the dock, and I yelled, "I'm an anti-aircraft officer. I'm going to the *Raleigh*."

Some fellow looked up at me and says, "I'm the commander of the *Arizona*. You take me to the Arizona."

I said, "I'm an anti-aircraft officer, and I'm going to the *Raleigh*."

He says, "You take me to the *Arizona*, and that's an order."

I'd learned enough to know that ensigns have to do what commanders say. So I gave it the gun and went out through the water past the *Oklahoma* and the *West Virginia* that were capsized, and pulled the bow up against the *Arizona*. Yell as much as we could, nobody answered from the *Arizona*.

About that time, there was an explosion up on the deck of the *Arizona*. I never knew whether it was a bomb or a ready box. But I saw a few sailors going ass over tea-kettle and splashing into the oil on the water.

About that time, up came a PT boat, and he had a man on either side reaching into the water and picking up those sailors covered in oil. I was moving my boat down alongside the *Arizona* when the PT boat turned astern and commenced racing his motor in short bursts. I turned to look, and so help me, that blinking oil was on fire!

With another blast or two of his motors, the screws had pushed the fire out of his way, and he turned and plowed right through it. I gave that motor launch hard left rudder, maximum speed, and I followed right behind that PT boat through the fire with that commander yelling bloody murder.

I pulled around the stern of the *Arizona* to some sort of a pipe coming out of Ford Island. I pulled up against that pipe, and told that commander that the only way he could get on the *Arizona* was to go around and come in from Ford Island.

About this time the *Medusa* gig come up alongside my launch and the captain of the Medusa was in the launch that I had taken, and he had never said a word. He got out and into his gig, and he yelled at me, "Mister, I'll take you to the *Raleigh*."

I turned loose of the tiller, jumped over into the *Medusa* gig, and Hal was following me. We come around the edge of Ford Island and came up to the *Raleigh*, and Hal and myself stepped from the *Medusa* gig to the main deck of the *Raleigh*.

The *Raleigh* had sunk to where its keel had hit the marl. Hal went running to his 1.1 anti-aircraft gun, and I went running to sky control. I climbed a few flights of ladders and out onto the deck of sky control. Ensign Beardahl, whose father was a rear admiral and an aide to President Roosevelt, was standing before me with a steel helmet, a pair of skivvies, no shoes, no shirt, and just as calm as if he had been sitting in my living room said, "Where ya been big Dub? Son, we're sorta needing you around here."

I ran across and looked, and so help me, yonder come a flight of four or five Jap planes. I commenced calling out the bearings and sight angles, and the boy that normally cranked them into the liberscope that we used for fire control stepped up in front of me, and at that instant a bullet hit him. As I was cranking in the sight angles myself to the liberscope, I was thinking that boy was hit with a bullet that was meant for me.

We got off a few shots and the entire Japanese attacking force formed up and flew over us out of anti-aircraft gun range and flew away. We waited for the return. We couldn't imagine why they weren't coming back. By mid-afternoon, all kinds of excitement. A message came through that imperial marines were landing at Barber's Point. Away the landing force!

Now, I commanded a platoon of the landing force. So I put on my leggings, strapped on my .45 and lined my men up, ready to be inspected. I looked out across the mountain range and could see that what was going to happen was that the marines would cross between us and Honolulu, and maaaaaan, I knew what that meant.

I had a gunner's mate named Vinson. I says, "Vinson, go to the armory and get my gun." He said, "Yes, sir."

Well now, my gun was one that I had illegally honed off so that it had a very sensitive trigger firing mechanism. But one thing was sure. When I pulled the trigger of that old 30-ought-6, there was no question of whether or not I hit the target, and I was already mentally tallying up how many Japs were going to get it.

Along came the gun boss. He was a useless lieutenant commander, and he said to me, "Where do you think you're going? Get rid of that gun. You're a platoon officer. You're to command your troops, not to be an infantryman."

I gave my gun and the two bandoliers of ammunition I had around my neck back to Vinson, and about that time, from communications they yelled down, "Cancel launching the landing force. No marines at Barber's Point."

The word got garbled by the time it got back to the aft part of the ship, and old Hal Johnson was back there with his division, and somehow, out of that message he got abandon ship, so he and his whole division went over the side.

They got back on board after a while. We waited and waited and waited, still at general quarters. Night came on, and over the harbor came a flight of airplanes. Suddenly the harbor erupted, firing at those planes. I had the phones on from the bridge, and the captain was saying, "Cease fire."

And I was yelling, "Cease fire!" for all I was worth, but before we commenced yelling cease fire, five Enterprise planes had been shot down, and I was directing our 1.1s. Scappa was off, but Johnson was close, and I recall saying, "Right 50 mils, up 10." And I could see the holes of the 1.1 pouring into our planes. After cease fire, the captain went on the loudspeaker to say, "Men, I'm awful afraid we shot down our own planes."

Let me assure you, it was a horrible, horrible feeling. But about that time, I began to realize that we hadn't had any water all day. Once I thought about it, I concluded we hadn't had any food, either. The prospects for either didn't look too good. But some of those old boys over on Ford Island had been busy getting water out of the swimming pool and making some salami sandwiches. A boat came up. They also had some coffee, but it was slightly chlorinated, too. Nobody bothered. It tasted mighty good.

Across the harbor you could hear, "Halt, halt, halt!" And the rattle of machine guns. It was no night to be out.

I suggested to Ensign Beardahl that we put our people 50 percent on alert and 50 percent of them trying to rest which he thought was a good idea. I pulled off my steel helmet, put my neck over on the life jacket, and in a little bit was asleep. I awakened cold, and it raining. I pulled my head up under a phone box and Beardahl must've put a blanket over me, because I was snug as a bug in the rug, with it raining, until he says, "Rise and shine, you've been asleep an hour."

The damage to the *Raleigh* was very extensive. Although damage control was outstanding, the ship rapidly sank, but the captain was able to keep her from capsizing.

The Jap planes had come over Pearl City and down above the water, heading directly for the *Raleigh* alongside Ford Island. The first torpedo hit the *Raleigh* shortly before 8 a.m. A church party was loading into boats alongside port side. The torpedo ran under their boat and hit the ship and blew a 42-foot hole in her side. They were blown up into the air. The explosion went through the ship, knocked out all engine rooms and boiler rooms.

She received a direct bomb hit back aft that went completely through the ship, exploded into the marl under the ship, and blew a hole 17 and a half feet in diameter, almost directly under the aft 1.1 gun. As a matter of fact, the planes were aiming at the 1.1, trying to knock it out.

In addition to the bombing and torpedo, there was considerable strafing and bomb near-misses. Several of the *Raleigh* crew were injured, but none were killed.

The old battleship *Utah*, converted to an anti-aircraft training ship, was tied up, directly astern *Raleigh*. She was hit seconds after the *Raleigh* with three torpedoes, and capsized almost immediately. Most of her crew was entombed inside the capsized ship and remain there to this day.

The *Raleigh* damage control party on the stern of the *Raleigh* heard clanking noises coming from the bottom of the Utah even during the battle.

They climbed up on the hull of the Utah and cut holes in the bottom of the Utah hull and pulled out an oil-covered man that had been entombed. The Utah man attended Raleigh reunions and was always welcomed and recognized. He passed away last year (1999).

19

The Aftermath

The next day after the attack, December 8th, Pearl Harbor shipyard plunged efficiently into repairing the damaged ships. It surprised me that the first ship they floated was the *Raleigh*. And at the same time, they were clearing the dry docks of the *Pennsylvania*, *Kassens*, and *Downs*. And within a few days, tugs pushed the old Raleigh into the dry dock.

Emergency repairs were commenced immediately. While our gun crews remained on watch, the rest of the crews assisted with repairs. The captain had sent one person ashore to call one of the few wives that remained in Honolulu, and she passed on to the other wives the information that all hands were alive.

USS Raleigh, though half-sunk in the December 7 attack, was the first U.S. Navy ship to be returned to duty afterwards.

About three days after the attack, President Roosevelt made a report to the nation. I was on watch listening to the radio address. He stated that the Secretary of Navy Knox had just returned from Pearl "Haaabah," that our losses consisted of one old battleship, the *Arizona*, and one destroyer, the *U.S.S. Shaw*. He went on to say that the army and Navy were attempting to seek out and destroy the enemy forces.

The crews of my ship and dozens of others were looking at the smoking ruins and capsized hulls of all of our battleships, all of our shore-based airplanes, and many cruisers.

Neither then, nor now, did I consider it necessary to lie to the American people in an attempt to confuse the Japs that we knew had pictures of these sunken ships and other damages to the military installations on Hawaii.

On December 15, eight days after the attack, I was permitted to go ashore for half an afternoon. I was carrying a gas mask, had a loaded .45 around my waist, and I assure you, at the least excuse I would have shot Japanese-Americans as if they were confirmed enemies.

I was home for two hours, and then had to return to the ship. The next opportunity to go ashore was Christmas Eve, and because we had wives in Honolulu, Hal Johnson and myself were granted permission to spend Christmas Eve at home. But, as we were leaving the ship, word came in that all hands would remain on board on the alert for an attack feared for Christmas Eve.

It was over a week later when I saw Evaline again. By this time, she had been informed to have everything packed and ready to leave on four-hour notice and that women and children were being evacuated as fast as possible from the islands back to the mainland, with priority being given to the women that had children.

Now, here I am, not knowing if and when the *Raleigh* would get under way, but I believed that we would be sent to the mainland for more extensive repairs—where to, anybody could guess, and what time, anybody could guess. At the same time, Evaline, at some time in the future, would be sent to the mainland.

I came home some time in February. I left a couple of hours later, thinking I might be back in about eight days. I returned to the *Raleigh* and found we were preparing to get under way the next morning.

Ship movements were highly classified, and we sailed away. I left Evaline and she didn't know the ship was leaving until the next day when Hal had a friend on the *Lurline*, one of the ships that ended up sailing with us, come by to pick up Vivian. He drove by and picked her up and she sailed away in our convoy, and then Evaline knew I was gone.

Right then and there, I learned something that stuck with me the rest of my Navy career. Right or wrong, I didn't wait for bureaucracy to move. I moved.

Along the middle of the afternoon, after we got under way, we listened to Tokyo Rose, making her radio broadcast. She gave her spiel, and ended it with the statement that the battle cruiser *Raleigh* was sunk when leaving Pearl Harbor. She went down with all hands. We joked about it there on sky control, but it showed how rapid communication went from Hawaii to Tokyo.

Late the next afternoon, one destroyer and the *Raleigh*, were the only escorts for five Matson Line Ships and one English ship, loaded with women and children. I had the watch and forward battle control at the tripod, high above the *Raleigh*. My job was to pull the trigger to commence firing when so ordered by the captain.

As we looked out across the blue Pacific, we noted two masts slowly coming out of the water over the horizon. I reported this to the bridge. A flurry of activity. The convoy was turned directly away from the sighting. We came up to max speed, still crippled, heading for these masts. As we moved closer, coming slowly above the horizon came four other smaller masts. As we went further, I could make out the hulls of these six ships, two very large ships and four small ones.

I reported on a continuous basis what I was seeing to the bridge. The ships were not painted the color of American ships, and I had never seen a battleship that looked like these two large ships, but they were far larger than any cruiser I'd ever seen.

In my mind, I was certain that this little plowboy was going to be a greasy spot very shortly. The fact is, I was the most frightened that I had ever been.

It wasn't long until the ships came up over the horizon to a point where they could be seen by the people on the bridge. The secret challenge of the day was immediately sent by search light, and back came the correct answer. A flurry of blink-blink-blinks from our search light and the searchlight on the leading ship, and the captain, over the loudspeaker, said, "Now all hands, hear this. We are first to welcome our two new battleships, the *Washington* and *South Dakota*, that have just come through the Panama Canal out to help us."

We continued an uneventful cruise to the mainland. One of the most thrilling moments of my life was when we entered Frisco Bay and went up the channel under the Golden Gate Bridge. The air was filled with new airplanes, barrage balloons, including the new P-38s. It took most of the afternoon to cruise on up to Mare Island, where we went in to dry dock. The yard commenced working on us before we even got tied up.

I couldn't imagine why such priority for a little ole light cruiser. It wasn't long until I found out. We were fast, and expendable. It was hectic days as all hands turned to, to make repairs, yet condition watches on the guns were continued.

During this time, I almost got killed when a steel beam slipped from the crane and fell endwise down through the ship, through the hole left as our forward turret was removed from the ship. I was down in my room. I walked forward to the bathroom. This steel beam fell and hit the visor of my cap, then between my feet and bounced as it hit the steel deck back up 20 or 30 feet into the air.

My prime business was checking on convoys coming in to San Francisco and trying to determine if Evaline was on any of them. I did this by asking the signalman there in Mare Island to let me know when a convoy came into Frisco. I had bought a little 1930 Model A Ford for $75. I would drive down to Frisco and get the officer of the deck of each of the merchant ships that came in to look at the passenger list, and then turn around and drive back about 35 miles to Mare Island. It wasn't a real problem because gas cost 15 cents a gallon.

This went on and on without success through February and March until, early in April, I followed the same routine, and, most of the time it was the same five Matson Line ships that came over with us.

One day, after looking at the last passenger list without success, the OOD [Officer of the Deck] told me that there was a British ship, the *Aquatania*, that had come over with them. I went over to the British ship, and the OOD wouldn't let me look at the list. I cast some very critical observations about his ancestry. I told him I was going to the captain of the ship. But he settled it by calling one of the supervisory officers that decided to let me look at the list. And there it was, Mrs. Walter Dee Ashe.

I left the ship. I knew that she would have orders and tickets to go to Memphis because she was being evacuated, but I wondered where she went there in Frisco. I walked out to the street. I figured that's what she would have done. I went to a taxi, trying to do exactly what I thought she would have done.

I asked the taxi driver what would be a nice hotel, but one that was not too rowdy. Well, he says, the St. Francis is such a hotel. So I had him take me to the St. Francis. I went in to the desk clerk. I wanted to know if she was in the hotel. That's a no-no. They would not give you that information. Finally, I got the clerk to listen to my story and afterwards, they decided to break the rules and tell me what room number she was in. I went up and went to the room. Evaline was in the bed, asleep.

We decided that I would try to get leave to go with her to Memphis. The next day, I bought a coach ticket at a penny a mile and off to Memphis we went. The government had given her a Pullman ticket, but of course, she rode with me three and a half days by train to Memphis. We stayed there three days and she decided that she was coming back to San Francisco.

I used almost all the money I had buying her a ticket and we, as my leave expired, arrived in Oakland. We checked into a hotel. Didn't eat, because we didn't have any money. The next morning, I hitch-hiked from Oakland to Mare Island, borrowed $25 from Jack Scappa, got my little Model A, drove down to Oakland, paid the hotel room, and we shoved off looking for a place to live.

When I'm looking for a house, everybody knows it. And by mid-afternoon, I had rented a lovely place there on the outskirts of Vallejo. We lived there for a month. The ship repairs were about over and Evaline went down to Frisco, got a job with Kodak Frisco. We rented a little apartment out near the Golden Gate Bridge. I commuted for about a week or 10 days. The *Raleigh* came out of dry dock, and we came down to Frisco.

Shortly thereafter, we were under way escorting a convoy of colored troops to the South Pacific. Again, only two ships—one destroyer and one cruiser—were escorting the convoy of six shiploads of troops. Day and night, all hands had a sharp lookout for submarines. Lack of sleep was the terrible thing to contend with.

We moved into a French-controlled island well south of the equator in the Marqueses group for refueling. We entered the harbor with all guns loaded, ready to fire instantly. We expected resistance from the Vichy French, but with no resistance we pulled around and commenced refueling from one of the transports.

As we were refueling our crew learned from the colored troops on the other ship that drinking water was rationed and other water was nonexistent because they were having trouble with the evaporators. You know that those *Raleigh* sailors were out selling those troops drinking water! The captain had a fit when he learned about it and demanded the money be given back and commenced transferring drinking water to the other ship.

One of the most lonesome times in my life. The moon came up out of the ocean and there was a lonesome palm tree high up on the cliff, and the solitary palm tree looked like I felt.

I decided to do a little fishing. I put a piece of beef on a line and put it over the side. First thing you know, my arms are almost jerked out of socket and my hands were blistered as the line rapidly went out and broke. I'd never fished in the ocean, but I'd learned a bunch right then.

We proceeded westward the next morning, heading for Samoa. On arrival in Pango-Pango, while the ship was refueling, the native chief invited us officers ashore for a little party. He had some native alcoholic concoction that tasted terrible and blew your head off at the same time. I wasn't a drinker, but I had some of that, though.

In a little bit, he brought his 16- or 17-year-old daughter out and introduced her, and she was going to dance for us. The only light was a little fire there on the floor of the tent, and she pulled off her clothes and danced a native Polynesian dance in the nude.

It wasn't long till refueling was finished and we went back on the ship and set sail for Pearl Harbor. At Pearl Harbor, lo, and behold, they sent us back to Frisco to pick up another convoy. It took about two weeks one way.

Two weeks later Evaline was as pleasantly surprised as was I, to get to be back to Frisco. But three days later, we headed out with another convoy, heading for the South Pacific.

We had an airship acting as an escort for our convoy. He stayed with us all day. Just after dark, he sent a message saying he was returning to base. Right then and there I thought how nice it would be to be returning to base. Not only did I dislike the long hours and, each time, considerable doubt that I'd ever get back, but I thoroughly detested being seasick. I was terribly seasick for the first three or four days every time we got under way.

Still thinking of how nice it would be to be returning to base, I went into the wardroom, browsed through the magazines, and happened to see an article on lighter-than-air blimps.

In the meantime, we took our convoy into Suva harbor in the Fiji Islands. While the department heads and duty crews were refueling and replenishing, the off watch junior officers were permitted to go ashore, to be back at 8 o'clock the next morning.

We soon learned that there was a British officer's club high up on the mountain. Ten or twelve of us decided to walk up there. On arrival, we were stopped by two marine sergeants with fixed bayonets that told us that there was not anyone other than commonwealth forces permitted in the club. We later learned the reason for this was that they were having a dance that night and they had pulled in every possible female, nurse, Wren, what-have-you, to be guests at the big party.

Our senior medical officer, a captain, said to the marine sergeant, "Son, we're going in." He says, "Both you and I know that you're not going to stick me with that bayonet, so just move out of my way."

The marine sergeant wasn't about to stick an American officer who was going into the blinking officer's club.

We went in and were treated as *persona non grata*. They wouldn't say anything to us and they wouldn't give us a drink. I looked around and found beer, but the British didn't have the beer cold, and they didn't have any ice, even for the whiskey. I climbed over the bar, found they had two 20-gallon cans of ice cream. I struggled as I poured the ice cream out of one of the cans, rinsed it out a little, put it back in the refrigerator, and commenced pouring bottles of hot beer into it. Long before it got cool, I learned that beer and ice cream go together pretty well.

As time moved along, the British and the Americans got a little lit up on alcohol. We commenced to sing. We were singing British empire songs with gusto about 3 o'clock in the morning, being led by a British sea captain standing on top of a grand piano, when a marine came in, handed him a note, and everybody went quiet. He read the note and said, "All Yanks report to ship immediately!"

We could barely walk, and we had to go down the little road, winding down the mountain in total blackout. Fiji police were all over the mountain, but the only way we made it without falling off the cliffs was to get into a line, locking our arms, and whenever somebody started to fall off on one side, that meant you had to turn the opposite direction.

We made it to the ship, and found it by a light on the quarterdeck that was covered from above. Shortly thereafter we hurriedly got under way and went out through the minefields before daybreak.

At sea we turned to a course of 0-0-0 at top speed. By then I was standing watches in the engine room. Going through the minefields disturbed me somewhat.

Up into the third day, suddenly the ship slowed down and the captain came on the public address system and said, "There's been a great naval battle. We won." The roar of applause from all hands abated and the captain says, "We got here a little late. We're now heading to Pearl Harbor."

Now, man was I ever glad that we got to the Battle of Midway just a tad too late, because that Jap fleet would've removed us from the face of the earth. Fortunately, our aircraft carriers sank the Jap aircraft carriers, and Admiral Yamamoto turned his invasion fleet back to Japan.

20

Apply to Flight School

From the Battle of Midway, we went on to Pearl Harbor and then on to Frisco. Upon arrival in Frisco, lo, and behold, on the 15th of June, an all-nav came out and I was suddenly a lieutenant j.g. (junior grade). A very few days later, a message arrived stating they wanted volunteers from officers that were lieutenant j. g.'s that had a year of sea duty to go to airship flight training.

Dub with his second half-stripe, indicating his promotion to Lieutenant (junior grade). He looks to be one of the youngest.

I didn't need a tutor to tell me what to do. I got the forms, filled out the application, found out I had to have a flight physical. By this time, old Hal Johnson wanted to go to lighter-than-air training, too. I waltzed up to the exec, one commander Cone, and requested permission for us to go to Alameda for a flight physical because we needed to send off our requests for airship training.

He not only said no, but hell no! He was saying that we were getting useful and he wasn't about to let us go off to flight training. Well, that was sort of bad. While we were in port for a few days, I watched, and one day caught the exec away from the ship, and I went down and got permission from the acting exec, Lieutenant Commander McClain, and away we went to Alameda for our flight physical.

We successfully completed our physical and came back to the ship. We sent our request to the captain. Over the exec's objection, the captain signed the request. Well, you wouldn't believe it, that stinking exec told the yeoman not to mail it.

Away we went to the south Pacific. Every day or so, I asked the captain's yeoman for information on our letter. He repeatedly told me that the exec directed him to leave those requests in the outgoing basket until he told him otherwise.

In due time, we completed our round to the south Pacific and returned to Frisco. In a day or two, we were leaving for another trip into the war zone, and I learned from the captain's yeoman that the exec still hadn't permitted him to mail our flight training requests.

Just as we were getting under way from Hunter's Point, I had a bright idea. I went running into the captain's office. Sure enough, there our requests lay in the out-going basket. I picked up the requests, put them into a large manila envelope, grabbed a stapler, and put it in the envelope for weight so I could throw it, quickly wrapped three rubber bands around the envelope, and went running out to my position as a deck officer, third division.

The ship sounded the horn to signal getting under way, and we began to back out. I shouted to a sailor in the line-handling crew on the dock, telling him, "Mail this!" And I threw the package to the dock. An inch shorter, and it would've gone into the water.

I thought a minute and realized what I had done. It scared me out of three year's growth. So I kept my mouth shut.

Away we went down through the south Pacific again, and on back up once again to Pearl Harbor. We had a little dab of liberty and Hal and myself went ashore. We stopped by to look at the house where we once lived. On return to the ship, everybody was greeting us with congratulations for our orders to flight training.

The exec was so mad at his yeoman that he threatened to court-martial him, chewed him out on a daily basis, and I was still the only one who knew how our flight requests had gotten to Washington. And I didn't mention it until many years later at a Raleigh reunion in Las Vegas. I told the former yeoman, now a movie actor, 400 lbs. worth of George Knapp, what had happened. He threatened to kill me right there for all the trouble I caused him.

But the flight training order wasn't altogether over. The exec pleaded with the captain to request cancellation of the orders, since we were about to go to the Aleutians and they badly needed experienced officers.

But the captain told him that orders were orders and we were to be detached a month early because there was no reason for us to go up to the Aleutians and then have to fight to get transportation back to flight training.

I've bumped into a few mean officers in the Navy, but that Commander Cone had the reputation for being the meanest.

[Before I got my orders for flight training.] From the Battle of Midway we proceeded to Pearl Harbor with the hopes of getting a few nights' sleep. But, wham! During the first night the lights came on. A scurry of activity around the docks as the crews were hauled out to commence frantically loading both the *Wharton* and the *Raleigh*. I noted that great quantities of beef were being hauled into the *Wharton* reefers and hundreds of boxes of .30 caliber ammunition were being secured on deck.

A few hours later, a destroyer, the *Wharton* and the *Raleigh* headed for Guadalcanal. Our Marines were out of food and running low on ammunition and I learned later we had unsuccessfully attempted to re-supply the Marines prior to our dispatch. We proceeded at the *Wharton*'s maximum speed, and as we approached Guadalcanal, there were day and night sightings of submarines and airplanes.

As the three ships proceeded toward Guadalcanal, about 2 a.m. the *Raleigh* was diverted northward about 60 miles into Iron Bottom Sound. Our mission proved to be to act as escort for merchant ships that had been diverted to pick up survivors of the Battle of Savo Island, where we lost five heavy cruisers and four destroyers.

The ships were busy picking up survivors. They continued to do so for several hours. About mid-afternoon, a signal light message from one of the ships asked if there was an Ensign W.D. Ashe on board the *Raleigh*. Our signalman sent back a message saying, "We have a Lieutenant (j.g) Walter D. Ashe." A message flashed back, "That's close enough! Dub, tell my momma I'm all right. Wade Zaricor."

That poor old boy was a gunner's mate on the destroyer *Gregor* and he'd spent all the night in that shark-infested water after his ship was sunk and had the unsavory experience of being in the water watching the battle between the Japanese task force and our cruisers and destroyers in Iron Bottom Sound.

After nightfall the *Raleigh*, along with the four merchantmen, headed for Pearl Harbor.

The next day after arrival, I learned that Wade and his fellow survivors were in a barbed wire, heavily guarded compound over on the main base. The complex was a double-fenced, sailor-guarded outside, Marine-guarded inside, making certain that these survivors didn't make contact with anybody. The Navy did not want news of our disaster to leak out.

With difficulty, I got through the first gate and told the duty officer that I wanted to see one of the survivors, Wade Zaricor, gunner's mate first class. I was informed that no visits were allowed. I couldn't see him. I asked permission to see the command duty officer, and in a bit, a Lieutenant Commander arrived from inside the compound. I repeated my request and was again informed, "Absolutely no visitors."

I said, "Sir, the *Raleigh* arrived on the scene and participated in the search for survivors of the night battle. I know what happened. The survivors can't tell me anything, and of course, I can't tell them anything. But I want to see my first cousin, Wade Zaricor."

He said, "Come with me." He took me inside the second fence, and I saw Wade over there. I said to the command duty officer, "There he is, over there." I went over to talk with Wade a bit, and the poor boy was still wearing the skivvies and dungarees he had on the night the *Gregory* was shot out from under him. He said that he'd been washing them every night, sleeping naked while they dried, and wearing them the next day. He said there was no small stores [clothing] on the ship that rescued him and they had just gotten in that morning and were told that small stores were being brought over to them shortly. I asked him if he needed any money. He says, "No. I haven't been paid for three months, and if I had a tub full of money, there isn't anywhere to spend it."

I left and shoved off to San Francisco and didn't see him for about two years.

From San Francisco, Evaline and I got into our little '38 Chevy and headed to Memphis on ten days' leave.

At that time, getting gasoline sometimes was a problem. And getting a place to stay was likewise difficult. Tires were extremely difficult to obtain, so you would carefully reduce the pressure in the tires for daytime driving, and, then in the evening, add some air.

We were in a hurry to reach Memphis, so we drove until we were about to drop before trying to get some sleep. Somewhere in Arizona, just at dusk, we pulled into a filling station, filled up with gasoline, and then I drove over to an air pump, intending to adjust the pressure. Just as I went around to the right front tire, up drove a touring car going the opposite direction. In that open car was a swarthy white man driving and three colored men as passengers.

The passengers got out, came around their car, and, though I was scared to death, I yelled to Evaline, who was inside our car, "Evaline, lock the doors!"

I said to one of these birds, "You can have the air pump in a minute." I bent down and put I don't know how much air in that tire, got up, and walked back to the filling station.

The filling station operator, like myself, was scared, and when I asked him how much I owed him for the gas, he says, "Forget it." I walked back to my car, and came up to the door. It was about three feet from the touring car, and said, "Evaline, let me in."

She opened the door, I got in and started the car, feeling badly that I was leaving the filling station operator to an unknown fate. But at that instant, going the same direction that we had come, an open-top blunderbuss of a car came driving up with six or seven cowboys in it.

I saw through the rear-view mirror the filling-station operator come out and commence shaking their hands while the touring car, with wheels spinning, headed down the road.

Now Evaline and myself had been very sleepy, but that was over. We drove all the way to Albuquerque, New Mexico, arriving at 3 o'clock in the morning, before we even commenced to discuss finding a place to sleep.

Another little thing I recall about that trip. As we came into Little Rock, Arkansas, almost dead from loss of sleep, and it raining, I considered stopping for the night. But Evaline wanted to go see her momma, so we continued on. Hour after hour, and I saw nothing that indicated we were approaching Memphis. Then, suddenly, out of the night, there flashed a sign that said Texarkana, 9 miles. We, in our stupor, had driven all the way across Arkansas, the wrong way.

We turned and retraced our steps, and on to Memphis, arriving just a little before sun-up. And after listening to Mrs. Paseur give me ten minutes worth about being such a cheapskate that I wouldn't even stop and get her daughter a place to sleep, we had a wonderful leave at home visiting the folks, enjoying that blue October weather. The only thing, we had a problem with the tires on our little Chevy. Those were the days of the O.P.A. (Office of Price Administration) At my Uncle Elihue's barber shop, I was recounting to many of his customers about my problems with the tires. He says, "Why, go down here to Jess Finch's store. He can authorize you to get some tires."

I hurried down to see Mr. Finch, who happened to be the father of one of my high school classmates, and told him my story. You know that son of a gun looked at me and said that he had to keep his allotment of tires for the folks there at home.

Just back from the war zone, I could easily have cut his throat. I went back to the barber shop and my Uncle Elihue asked, "How many tires did he give you?"

I told him what had transpired. He looked around and says, "I have half a notion to go down and give him a good whuppin'."

After a bit, he looked up, addressed the several people in his barber shop, and said, "If any of you ever set foot in Jess Finch's grocery store, don't ever come into this barber shop again!"

I really don't know what caused it, but the next time I was home, Finch Groceries had closed.

But I still had the problem. I went on to Memphis and decided to trade my car for one that had some good tires. I bought a '41 Ford. The tires looked good. And in a few days, Evaline and myself headed for Moffatt Field, California, to begin flight training.

The second morning, about 50 miles east of Sauncey, Texas, the right front tire blew out. As Evaline and myself were sadly surveying the damage, down the road toward us came a pickup truck. The driver got out, looked at my tire, and looked at my spare. He says, "We're going to have to fix that tire."

You know, that gentleman took the wheel off, put it in his truck, and put us in the truck, and drove back down the road about 30 miles to his filling station. He got out his equipment. He didn't have any tires, but he repaired the one that had blown out, and I left Evaline at the filling station, while he took me back out to my car. He put the wheel back on the car and led the way, again back down the road as I followed him, to his filling station. And on arrival, his wife had just finished cooking a Texas-sized breakfast of ham and eggs for Evaline and myself.

And you know, when I pulled out my wallet to try to pay him, he wouldn't take a cent. I've had a soft spot in my heart for anybody from Texas ever since.

The gentleman told me that that tire was liable to blow out anytime and my spare wouldn't drive very far. So as I headed on west, every place with any size, I attempted to get local O.P.A. approval to buy two tires, always with the same, "I'm sorry, but we have to keep them for the local people."

On arrival in San Jose, California, my first order of business was to go to the local O.P.A. administrator and tell him I needed two tires. He asked me what I was doing. I told him I was a lieutenant reporting for flight training at Moffatt Field. Without another word, he authorized me to purchase two tires.

The next order of business was to look for a place to live. We saw a little sign on a house that said For Rent. We asked about the rental and moved into a fully furnished, two-bedroom house that had orange trees, walnut, plum, and grapefruit trees in the back yard, with the rent $50 a month.

And do you know, a few days later, the owner came back, gave me $15. He said the O.P.A. had frozen the rent at $35 a month because one time he let a girl stay there and charged her only $35.

I says, "No, I won't take it. It's worth three times that."

"Oh," he says, "Lieutenant, I'm not doing anything for the war, and 1sure wouldn't want somebody to think that I charged more than the O.P.A. rental."

The next day his wife brought over a pack of venison steaks and showed Evaline how to cook them.

The next day I reported to Moffatt Field. All these big airships all over the place. Man, was I ever tickled to be there!

21

Flight School

In a day or two, they gave us our first flight. Hal and myself and another fella named Ray Gardner got in this airship with a pilot named Amarind and away across the beautiful Santa Clara valley we went.

In a little bit the engine started to sputter, then quit, and the airship started to fall. The ground was coming up at us. I wasn't the slightest bit frightened because I thought that pilot was trying to scare us. Just before it hit the ground, he got the engines going again and we climbed back up.

Only then did we realize that those engines did quit!

Flight training and ground school was a wonderful experience. We were Class 1, Moffatt Field. We had five officers back from sea duty along with 25 cadets, and it was decided that we would get our wings on February 22 and the cadets would get their wings and commissions on the first of March.

This K ship photo gives a good idea of its structure.

Three of the officers were to go to each of the three squadrons on the west coast: Santa Anna, Moffatt, and Tillamook, and the other three were to go back to the east coast.

Lieutenant Commander Epps decided to do this by drawing straws. The shortest straw had the first choice and on down. But I drew the longest straw and got Tillamook, Oregon, which was already known as the worst possible place airships had ever been.

These K ships were like the ones I flew toward the end of the war and after.

On the first of March, I was promoted to full lieutenant, and I had just, a few days previously, learned that we were getting flight pay, and I learned that I was going to get sea pay for being in the squadron. So, here we were, suddenly jumped from $183 a month to $432 a month.

I was tickled about that, but terribly unhappy about the housing situation in Tillamook. I flew up there and worked myself to death, and with difficulty I finally found a Swedish woman named Farmstrom who let us share her house.

I flew in the squadron airship to Eureka, California. A few days later, I got on an airship with the squadron commanding officer, Lieutenant Commander Sullivan, to fly to Tillamook.

Tillamook was a little spot tucked in a valley with mountains to the west rising to 1,400 feet, sheer cliffs, and to the northwest, rising more slowly to 3,000 feet, and to the east, to 5,000 feet.

Captain Sullivan was flying us in one of the new K ships. We came in over the air station. They were working on a hanger, and they didn't have any runways. They were building fences around the air station, and they had a great big graveyard close to the administration building.

The captain started his approach three different times and couldn't make the landing. Finally, he came around over the administration building with the long lines out. As the lines were tumbling along, they somehow took a half-hitch around the wheels of the commanding officer's sedan, lifted it up into the air and dragged it along across the field. We finally were pulled down on the mat and put on the mast.

I must say I was depressed. I thought to myself, "Man, if this experienced pilot has that much trouble up here, how am I ever going to learn to handle these airships."

Well, I didn't have long to wait. Two days later, I'd been put into Lieutenant Keim's flight crew. The weather was pouring down rain. You could hardly see the ground-handling crew in front of you. And, except for that ride up the coast with Sullivan, I'd never been in a K ship, and I had never touched the controls.

Keim came aboard and said, "Dub, you take her off."

Now, mind you, that ship was too heavy to fly, and it was pouring down rain, and there were mountains all around. I had read the handbook, and I remember it saying that the engines were so powerful that you must push the nose down with controls in order to compensate for the engine thrust that would throw the nose into the ground.

I really thought Keim must be kidding, and I didn't feel any better about it when I found out he wasn't. We were all set and ready and I gave the signal to come off the mast. We were sitting on the circle that was connected to another circle by a little gravel mat. I pushed the throttle slowly forward, pushed the nose down, and began to roll. The gravel was coming up and hitting the car as we rolled down this little road. There was a let-up in the rain, and up ahead that graveyard had one of those Washington Monument-type tombstones directly in my path.

I was continuing to push the throttles wide open, and as the airship gathered speed, I began to let the nose rise. We were barely climbing, if any. I yelled to raise the wheel. We went directly over that tombstone with one engine on each side of the tombstone and disappeared into the overcast.

I slowly turned to the west, climbing as fast as I could, expecting to hit those 1,400-foot cliffs any second. Old Keim came forward, chewing on an unlit cigar and says, "Damn, Dub, what'cha tryin' to do, kill us?"

The plane captain turned around and looked at old Bill, and said, "Mr. Keim, I'm sure glad Mr. Ashe was on the controls." He said, "If you'd a been flyin' it, you'd a killed us all."

Keim slapped me on the back and says, "Good job." To Lambert he says, "You're probably right."

We flew in this fog westward a couple of hundred miles, then north, then headed back to the little entrance at Tillamook Bay. I had been navigating the whole time after take-off. Everyone was nervous as we approached the shore, because if I'm wrong, we'll fly into the mountains.

So every little bit, Keim would say, "E.T.A. [estimated time of arrival] coastline?'" And I'd get down and give him my calculations. He was flying a few feet above the water, trying to maintain visual contact. And so be it, I crossed the land spit exactly to the second of my ETA.

We flew every third day, and I established a reputation of precision navigation. Enough so, that when an especially important flight came up, the captain's special crew would fly—he as pilot, the operations officer as co-pilot, and me as their navigator.

After one such day of socked-in conditions, we were returning to Tillamook and the captain frequently was asking me, "How many minutes to the coast?"

Evaline dressed up in front of our house in Tillamook, Oregon.

A few minutes before my estimated time of arrival, the captain, with a little pomp and ceremony, says to all hands, "Let the navigator into the look-out seat, because if he's wrong, he'll the be the first one of us to die."

We crossed the coast exactly on schedule.

There was no work available for Evaline. I came home every third night, and meantime she and Mrs. Farmstrom tried to get into whatever trouble was available. There was a movie on Saturday and Sunday nights, but Mrs. Framstrom thought movies were a terrible sin.

We moved there in March, and it was the latter part of April before we ever saw the mountains behind the house. It rained all the time.

There were three little rivers coming through the valley to form Tillamook Bay. We lived about 100 yards from one, the Wilson River. It was literally teeming with trout and salmon. Every third day, when I came home, I'd step over to the river, catch a mess of trout for breakfast.

Immediately after reporting to ZP-33, I flew on one of our airships to Eureka, California. The weather at Eureka is, at best, bad, but more often, worse. The airships would come in from sea, and fly back and forth just above the sand dunes, until they could spot the landing crew, be landed, and be put on the mast. A lot of mishaps.

Our little air base was out on a peninsula covered with sand. Being an old farmer, I thought it would be nice to plant some vegetation around the barracks. Somebody had left a bulldozer near one of our landing circles. I decided to take that bulldozer and level off an area to set out some little ice plants.

Nobody knew how to operate that bulldozer. On a try-and-try-again basis, I was able to start it, raise and lower the blade, make it go forward and backwards, and, I might say, did a pretty good job landscaping the barracks area. Until one day, I was putting on the finishing touches, somehow lowered the blade, and at the same time I let the clutch move forward, and I moved the barracks off the foundation. I didn't want anybody to know and I didn't have any authority to be out there, so I went back and moved the barracks back on the foundation. End of the landscaping business.

On arrival at Tillamook, Squadron ZP-33, Captain Sullivan brought the four ensigns along with me into his office. He was a little, short man and he walked up and down in front of us, rocking back on his heels, pushing out his lips, and through pressed lips, said, "Welcome to Tillamook." He says, "If you are here a year, you'll either be dead pilots or damn good pilots."

He dismissed the new ensigns, looked at me and he says, "I don't know what I'm going to do with you. When I was your age, I was a plebe at the Naval Academy."

That remark pissed me off. So I says, "Captain, yes I'm only 22 years old. But I've seen more action in the last year than you've seen all your life."

Needless to say, we were off to a running start. And the next thing that little turd did was made me a member of a courts martial board, which itself was routine. But the squadron had a sailor on board that was 35 years old from Virginia, a farmer, whose wife had died of cancer, and he'd enlisted into the Navy and been sent to our squadron without any training whatsoever. Z.P. 33 was a hot outfit, and Captain Sullivan wanted this misfit sailor out of his command.

Well, this sailor went to Portland one weekend, rode a bus over, got ready to come back on the only bus leaving Portland at midnight, and it had mechanical troubles, resulting in this old sailor getting back to base the next morning at 8:20, when he was supposed to be there at 7:00.

Well, the captain convened the courts martial board. And he told his administrative officer, Hughes, a lawyer in civilian life, that he wanted the board to kick this sailor out of the Navy. When Mr. Hughes apprised the other member, a lawyer in civilian life named Atley Arnold, of his desires, I bolted, loudly proclaiming that wasn't anybody going to tell me what punishment I would vote for.

Within the board there was a battle royal all day and into the night, Mr. Hughes voting for discharge, me voting for a few days' restriction, while Arnold just couldn't make up his mind. The next morning, Arnold came in sad and bedraggled, but he told Hughes that he'd just have to tell the captain that his conscience wouldn't let him do it.

So we gave the sailor a week's restriction of liberty. The captain was furious, and of course, his anger was pointed at me because I wouldn't carry out his wishes.

All these days, we had the duty one 24-hour period during which I ground-handled the airships; we had standby during the day and liberty at night on the second day; and the third day, we flew.

I went two months before it stopped raining long enough for me to learn there was a mountain right behind our house.

One day, while on standby, down came a message from the sea frontier that stated a merchant ship, going down the Columbia River into the sea, was sunk by a submarine. We were urgently requested to send an airship for an anti-submarine search.

Out of the ready room and out to the field, a quick take-off, and we were wide open heading up the coast to the Columbia River, 60 miles away. Already there were three small surface craft on the scene—two sub chasers and one P.C. (patrol craft or sub chaser) boat. We joined them, crisscrossing back and forth, trying to get a submarine contact.

I was flying at 60 knots at 50 feet above the water. Pretty soon, from one of the boats, voice radio, "Submarine periscope!" a couple of thousand yards away.

I pushed it wide open, headed straight for the bearing and range of the periscope. First sighting, sure enough, there it was. Those surface craft were firing 20 millimeters at that periscope and the tracers were coming under the airship. They seemed like they were coming in the window at me as I looked toward the ships.

I started to climb immediately. Lieutenant Keim, the command pilot, back on the M.A.D. [magnetic anomaly detector], yelled, "Keep it below 50 feet!" As I pushed her back down, getting ready to drop depth charges, so help me, that reputed periscope became nothing more than a swab-handle [mop] floating above the water, held upright by the wet swab.

Back to the crisscrossing. Before long the P.C. boat had sonar contact on a submerged target. I went a-whoopin' over forward of the P.C. boat, and about that time, we got M.A.D. contact. Smoke floats were ejected, we roared into a hard circle to the right, and began tracking the submarine. Shortly, a second M.A.D. contact. As tactics prescribed, I circled the last contact and got another one.

I peeled around, came directly down the line of the three contacts, and Mr. Keim yelled to the ordinance man, "Man the depth charges!"

He told the ordinance man, a boy named Lambert, to drop two on contact. "Stand by! Contact!"

Well, at 50 feet, going 60 knots, two depth charges make you think you've been blown out of the air. The helium valves pop, your ears pop, and your throat feels like you're trying to swallow a mouth full of cotton.

We come around, and sure enough, there was debris. And the P.C. boat kept right on getting sonar readings on a submerged submarine. We worked all day trying to get another contact. We just were not successful.

The sea frontier ruled that we did not have a submarine. At the same time, the Coast Guard, who owned the P.C. boat, was still getting submarine contact every once in a while. The Navy called it a non-kill. The Coast Guard called it a probable. However, for nearly a week, they kept coming over, and every once in a while got contact and dropped ash cans on it.

Fifty years later, at Pensacola at a Lighter-Than-Air Reunion, there were some of the new airship members trying to bring up again that we had sunk a submerged submarine.

And they had a copy of this top-secret Coast Guard report that they were using to substantiate the claim.

I read the Coast Guard report, declassified the report because of the time, and wrote the time and date on each sheet, stating that I declassified. [In other words, who am I to have the authority to do it? I just took the authority.]

By then, we were aware, thanks to old Gordon Vaith's research, that the Japs said that they didn't have a sub in the area at that time. But, you know how the little bastards lie!

Another little thing—that report that we received of our ship being sunk wasn't so. I don't know what I think. You can fool sonar, but it's pretty hard to fool M.A.D. At the time, I thought we sunk a sub. Now, I don't know.

22

Lakehurst Flight Instructor

By this time, I'm getting to be sorta useful around the place. I'm a pretty good pilot, and even better ground handler, and a cracker-jack navigator. In came a message from the admiral back at Lakehurst, N.J., directing each squadron to send three pilots back to the training command at Lakehurst to be flight instructors.

The captain carefully considered the request for 30 seconds and put me and two ensigns on the list. I definitely was happy to be going to Lakehurst, but as I was out landing airships that afternoon, the executive officer drove out, called me over, and told me that the department heads had told the captain that he was making a mistake to send me. And the captain had agreed that if I requested to stay, he would remove my name from the list to go back to Lakehurst.

I says, "You tell the captain I didn't request that he put my name on the damn list and I'm sure not going to request that it be taken off."

So, shortly thereafter, I had orders to report to training command at Lakehurst as a flight instructor.

I put Evaline on the train for the long ride to Memphis. And because of a desire to have a visit at home for as long as possible, I went by air. I got on the plane, American Airlines, at Seattle. It was to be the maiden flight of the airplane, going from Seattle to Washington, D.C. This was not non-stop. It was just the same plane, and it required three stops.

We landed at Boise, Idaho, about midnight. And a Lieutenant (j.g.) that had been up in the Aleutians 18 months and I walked off the plane to stretch our legs. The governor of Idaho, along with his chief administrator met us at the foot of the ladder, and proceeded to read the state of Idaho commendation to American Airlines. We couldn't stop him until it was over. I told him we were Navy pilots, and in a little bit the airline pilots came down and he did it over again.

One of the stewardesses on the plane had really been trying to get me to stop over and spend the night with her at the next stop, Des Moines, Iowa. She couldn't believe that I wasn't interested in staying over with her. But when she found out that the J.G. had been up in Alaska for 18 months, she dropped all of her efforts to woo me and spent her time in his lap trying to get him to stop over in Des Moines with her. The old boy told her, "I can't do it! I haven't seen my wife for two years, and she will be at the airport in Chicago waiting for me."

Uneventful flight on to Memphis. And a very fine leave in August of 1943.

My first free balloon ride was an eye-opener for me. A 3,500-cubic-foot racing balloon inflated with flammable hydrogen. Inert helium was in short supply because the demands of a rapidly expanding L.T.A. [lighter than air] organization exceeded the Navy's processing capabilities.

My trip over Sunnyvale, Palo Alto, and the beautiful Santa Clara Valley entrapped me for life. There is nothing that compares with the soundless ride with a bird's eye of the scenery. What better place to practice flight than over the peach and orange orchards of the Santa Clara Valley, now called the Silicon Valley. I managed to get many extra flights and soon became quite an expert balloonist. Now our operating procedure dictated that we fly up and down the valley and in no wise go to the mountains.

One day while instructing a group of five cadets, the wind took us up the mountains above a place called Mountain View. There was a qualified pilot, a warrant officer named Stillman, on board to make it legal (I wasn't yet a designated pilot). He said nothing as I went up and over the mountains and down into an enclosed valley where we slowly drifted around at 500-foot altitude at a speed about three times a normal walk.

The balloon drifted over a little farm house with a woman in the back yard doing her wash with a tub and wash board. A little soap and swish, swish up and down the wash board, then do it again. It so happened that one of the cadets had a deep bass voice. So he cupped his mouth and shouted down to her, "Prepare yourself! The Lord speaketh. Prepare yourself! The Lord speaketh."

That woman stopped the washing and went to the corner of the house, took a look, then looked to the other corner. Another look, and the cadet, once again, said, "Prepare yourself! The Lord speakest."

That woman pulled off her apron, went over and sat down in a swing where she stayed as we drifted out of sight.

Well, down the valley a bit, we drifted into the top of a giant redwood tree and came to rest. I threw out sand ballast, jumped up and down in the basket, but to no avail. I couldn't dislodge the basket for the longest time.

I finally climbed out of the basket, and while hanging on the outside, I kicked around enough to get dislodged. We drifted out of the tree on down to the end of the valley.

And this time, the balloon began to slowly rise, bumping against the side of the cliffs. When we reached the top of the mountain, the wind coming in from the sea threw us like a giant slingshot out toward a reservoir. I threw out all the ballast I had, including my leather coat [which someone later picked up for me], but we still came crashing through the tall fir trees, smashing off limbs until we hit the ground.

I still have a bad back from it.

Not all of our free balloon rides ended so violently. Once, on a perfect morning, I was free-ballooning over the peach orchards just outside Sunnyvale. We were at about 500 feet, practically standing still, enjoying the beauty of the Santa Clara Valley with the peach trees in bloom. Just below us was a beautiful estate with a swimming pool.

While we were admiring the estate and the swimming pool, a gal about 18 years of age came walking out of the house, walked up alongside the pool, pulled off all of her clothes, and stretched out on some mats to do a bit of sun bathing. She stretched out face down, and therefore was totally unaware that we were hovering just above her. We quietly waited, and intently watched for a rather long period before she decided to turn over on her back to sunbathe on the other side. After a bit of turning and twisting, she happened to look straight up and there we were, two officers and five cadets.

Like a shot, she charged up and into the house. I valved the balloon down into the peach orchard (although I was not yet designated a naval aviator, I was flying the balloon with a L.T.A. qualified warrant officer on board as pilot).

Well, the people in the house, as well as quite a few surrounding, invited us into the pool area and began serving drinks, and the butler and the maid were serving us fine sandwiches. After a bit, the recently nude girl sheepishly came out to the pool area, dressed in shorts.

One of the cadets got a date with her to go to the movies before we left. Well, guess what! A few months later, he was commissioned an ensign, got his wings, married that girl, and they moved to Santa Ana, California.

I went the other way, to Eureka, California, and Tillamook, Oregon, but in time was transferred back to Lakehurst, New Jersey. Along the way, he likewise was transferred to Lakehurst. One night at a big party, with more booze than food, one of the friends of this girl was admiring her new dress. She turned and said to me, "Walt, doesn't she look attractive in that dress?" And I says, "Yes, but she looks even better without anything on."

The friend's eyebrows went up, and, in a huff, she walked off. I said to this lady, "Gee, I'm sorry! Why didn't you tell her what I was referring to?"

She says, "It would've made no difference. She wouldn't have believed anything I said!"

Well, most of our flights at Moffatt Field were in the little L ships. But one morning, I went flying with Ensign Williams as pilot of the old army airship, TC-13. Pretty soon, it was completely zero-zero [no visibility], and Williams was trying to fly up and down that valley at 2,000 feet, totally on instruments, and scaring me to death.

Mt. Tantalus had a near peak of 2,500 feet, and I tried to get Williams to increase the altitude. But he was at pressure height, and couldn't do so without valving helium. Helium was scarce and expensive, and a pilot needed a very good reason to valve helium.

The only time I ever put on a parachute in an airship was while we were flying in this fog, and I surely was relieved when a few hours later the sun began to peep out.

About mid-February, each of us had our solo in the L ship.

The few times that it was not foggy, the view in the Tillamook area was breathtakingly beautiful. One such day, while on patrol, moving north 125 miles west of the coast, I was flying at 300 feet, literally breathing in the beauty of the snow-capped glaciers on the Olympic mountain range. Suddenly, both engines quit.

While falling, I desperately tried to re-start the port engine. It so happened that the mechanic, who, bless his heart, had been asleep, awakened instantaneously, hit the wobble pump, transferring fuel to the service tank, and, just as I was about to hit the water, the engine exploded into life.

And to this day, I go around with my heart just a little bit higher than is normal. I did not chew out the mechanic. In fact, I blamed only myself for not noting that the service tank had run dry.

After a bit, the mechanic, a chief petty officer, came forward and said, "Mr. Ashe, I'm not fit to fly. I went to sleep and almost killed everybody."

I says, "Chief, it was me. Admiring the scenery was our chief problem." But I want to tell you something. I've watched the fuel tank ever since.

Just before leaving Tillamook for Lakehurst, I learned that Mom and my brothers were back in Kenton after an aborted trip to visit us in Tillamook. Would you believe that Mom purchased tickets for them to go by train to Chicago and from Chicago across the plains and mountains to Portland and bus to Tillamook. She wanted to surprise Evaline and myself.

I learned about it when I called Mom to tell her that we were about to leave Tillamook for Lakehurst and were coming by Kenton on leave.

Mr. Corbett happened to answer the phone, and gave me a thumbnail sketch of the situation. I immediately called Uncle Elihue, told him the story, and asked him to try to find Mom en route and turn her back home. Good old Uncle Elihue found them in the train station at Chicago about to get on the train going west.

Mom and the boys made the trek back to Kenton and never made a trip anywhere again on this "surprise 'em" business.

Evaline and myself had a wonderful visit at Memphis and Kenton. I left Evaline at Memphis to go to Lakehurst and find a place to live. It was August. The temperature was terrible, and I was wearing the heavy Navy green uniform. I almost burned up. Finally, I reached Lakehurst by tramp train through Red Bank, New Jersey.

I went over and reported in to the training command. Now, what a mess! Flight training was headed by a former Goodyear pilot, Commander Verne Smith. He had a group of former Goodyear pilots and earlier lighter-than-air classes.

The recent group consisted of those of us that, for whatever reason, were made available from their squadrons.

The commander greeted this new group with the words that he didn't care what our rank was or how many ribbons we had. The only thing that counted there was, "Could we fly an airship?"

There were maybe a dozen or more lieutenants that were senior to me.

We were all put into four duty sections. Rank didn't count, and some lieutenants were working for ensigns. Most of the new lieutenants managed to get themselves transferred to the ground school. The others, like myself, were placed in a duty section.

My duty section consisted of one lieutenant (j.g.) command duty officer, one ensign as operations duty officer, another ensign as assistant operations duty officer, and me as ground-handling officer. Talk about Hooligan's Navy or Cox's Army! We were it.

Although I recognized that this was a mess, and was terribly unhappy about it, there was nothing I could do. I was bitter at this ridiculous set-up of lieutenants working for ensigns.

The daily routine: first flight's take-off at 5 a.m., five cadets on each flight plus a pilot and co-pilot and a crew of three men. There was a crew shift for new instructors and new cadets at 1 0 o'clock, at 1500 (3 o'clock), and commence landing at 2100 (9 o'clock). By the time they got the ships landed and into the hangar, it would be approaching midnight.

We flew one day, had the duty one day, and were on standby one day, with no days off. Officers could go home after the last flight had landed. They had to be back out for their flight on the flight day, except they could not go home on their duty day.

This mess didn't improve when, shortly after arrival, we were going to have our first day of free ballooning. The wind was gusting at 25 knots. I was placed in a balloon with Lieutenant Ray Gardner. They launched us. We went dragging out across the mat, unable to get airborne. The basket smashed into the trunk of a large dead tree near the balloon hangar.

Ray, the designated pilot, valved down the balloon and it drooped over into the swamp. We went back to the duty officer, and I volunteered to take the next balloon. Meanwhile, Commander Smith had reported us to Captain Cockle, the flag training officer, stating that we had deliberately scuttled the flight. Captain Cockle came down to the hangar 4 and ordered us to take the next balloon.

I stood my ground, and stated I'd already volunteered to take the next balloon, although I knew it was too windy. But I was ready and able to do it. This time we took off with my being the designated pilot, and we flew 37 miles in 47 minutes. I had the audacity to come back and go up and report to Captain Cockle that this wasn't an estimate of wind, but this was actual miles flown.

I had to check out as the first pilot and flight instructor. My check pilot was the same ensign that I was working for in the duty section as ground handling officer.

Time moved along while I fumed at the worst situation that I ever experienced in the Navy.

One foggy morning, with visibility zero-zero, I was ground handling the training airships. I had the operations jeep. I tuned on the radio monitoring the squadron take-offs. As the squadron airship came out on mat 3, about a half-mile from I where I was, I stopped any further take-offs of training ships.

This ensign, Dorner, came shouting at me, "Continue taking off our ships!" I told him this I would do after the squadron airship was airborne and had cleared the area. Out came his boss, one Ensign Bodeck, gesturing and shouting, "Get that airship in the air!" I told him, "There's a squadron airship on mat 3 getting ready to take off. After it's cleared the area, I'll commence taking off again."

He says, "Get that ship in the air!" And I didn't move. In a bit the command duty officer, Lieutenant (j.g.) Punderson, came driving up and said, "You must take that ship off."

I says, "Pundy, I'm not going to do it until the squadron ship is cleared."

He disappeared into the fog, heading back to Dock 1. Shortly he came back, saying, "Commander Smith says you get that ship in the air immediately!"

And I says, "Tell Commander Smith if he wants it in the air, he can take it off, but I'm not going to."

Again Punderson disappeared, and when he came back, he says, "I'm sorry, but Commander Smith has ordered me to get the airship airborne. And you report to him in his office."

This I did. I defended myself by stating that the squadron airships have priority and it was not safe for two airships to be in that close proximity in zero-zero weather.

Well, what I feared could happen, did happen. Our airship, the K-5, collided with the squadron airship, split the bag of the squadron airship, and it went into the ocean off Barnegat Light, all hands lost.

Admiral Rosendahl, on learning of the terrible accident, had the responsible people report to his office in the flag building. Of course, I was too far down the totem pole to attend this meeting. After hearing the story, Admiral Rosendahl hit his desk, and said, "Didn't anybody over there have sense enough to stop the take-offs?"

After a long wait, finally Punderson said, "Lieutenant Ashe refused to take the airship off, admiral."

It was then that the admiral learned that lieutenants were working for j.g.'s and ensigns. After biting the rear end out of a few people, he ordered that the command duty officers would be lieutenants, and that I would be command duty officer of section 1, and I would have Punderson as my operations duty officer and Bodeck and Dorner, in turn, reporting to him.

Commander Smith was livid with anger at these developments and he told Punderson that what I said didn't have any weight unless he ordered it, and that Punderson was to keep him informed.

Punderson told me, he says, "I'm sorry, but I gotta do it."

I said, "You can call Commander Smith as often as you like, but I'm not calling him at all, and I'm directing the operations of this duty section."

They transferred the rest of the lieutenants to ground school and shortly thereafter they transferred Commander Smith.

23

Flight Instructor

Being a flight instructor had its problems, of course. But the thrill of watching students learn to fly was a wonderful experience. And I have many friends in the airship organization that I taught to fly.

Many interesting, hazardous, and amusing incidents occurred during the time I was a flight instructor. For instance, I recall landing a balloon in the front yard of the multi-millionaire parachute maker Stanley Switlik's estate. What a beautiful place. Lakes stocked with fish, peacocks as guard dogs.

Shortly after we landed, Switlik and his daughter invited me and the cadets up for drinks. With his butler catching the fish, one of his cooks cleaning them and another cook broiling them on the grill, we had a wonderful time.

Along about midnight, I decided that we must return to base. Switlik had three big Cadillacs parked in his garage. He took one of them, along with the five cadets, had his daughter take another one with me as the only passenger, and away we went.

I had heard that Switlik was trying to find a husband for his daughter and first-hand saw them in action. That poor girl, aged about 25 and uncommonly ugly, was terribly disappointed when, just outside Lakehurst, I told her I was married. Bad, bad. Shoulda waited awhile!

One night, after an all-day flight with myself as the only pilot and five cadets, we landed a little after midnight. We got caught out in a wind that was hovering slightly above 60 knots. We slowly drifted backwards until we were 60 or 70 miles at sea. Very low on fuel, and the airship extremely light, I struggled to land her and get on the mast.

A few minutes later, across the field came a jeep, and as we were getting out of the airship, someone yelled to the duty officer, "There's a wolf pack attacking a convoy in the slot! They have no air coverage, and there's no available squadron airships."

Commander Smith happened to be there, his purpose being to bore my butt anew for letting myself drift so far from land. He told the officer in the jeep that training did not have any airships, that this one that had just landed was overdue for 120 hour check that was to commence as soon as we got in the hangar. I spoke up, "Commander, refuel it and give me a crew, and I'll take it."

He says, "You know it's overdue for a check."

And I said, "Yes, but we can't leave a convoy without air coverage."

My crew turned around and filed back on the airship. We grabbed one of the duty officers to be co-pilot. They pumped it full of fuel and put four torpex depth charges on board. I had the airship unmasted and gave it the gun for take-off.

Approaching the Cathedral of the Air, I started pulling her up and the port engine conked out. I was afraid to drop the depth charges, so I gave the starboard engine wide open while the mechanic got the port engine started, during which time, I took off the top of a few pine trees with the airship's tail.

I pulled up to 1,000 feet in altitude and headed out the northeast leg of the beam. The slot was about 65 miles due east of Asbury Park. A little past Asbury Park, we could see two burning ships. The convoy was about 35 miles away. In a few minutes, I arrived, went down to 50 feet, and began I circling the convoy. The subs went deep, we didn't get any contacts, but again, our purpose was served because the subs couldn't fire their torpedoes at the convoy.

It hurt those of us airship pilots that surely would have liked to sink a submarine not to be able to do so, but our mission was to protect the ships of the convoy. This we did because, just our presence caused the subs to break off their attack and go deep and the convoy could sail away. This happened as airships escorted over 89,000 ships during the war and never lost a one.

One day someone came out to the mat to tell me that the exec of the air station wanted to see me. The exec, one Commander Winetraub, greeted me in his office, and says, "Mr. Ashe, I have an additional duty for you. As you know, we've recently organized a colored division. We're having too many troubles with the men in this division. They are unmilitary. They come back over leave (late). And already I've had four different division officers and they have not been successful in leading the division. I want you to take that division and whip it into shape."

I said, "Commander, I'm a flight instructor. I fly every day. I'm the ordinance and gunnery officer, and every day I instruct the students in small arms. And sir, I don't really have time!"

He said, "Do the best you can."

Now, I want to tell you, I didn't like that job. But the next morning, I arrived at quarters for muster. As I walked up, the chief called the division to attention, and you really couldn't tell any difference in the looks of the division before or after they were supposed to be at attention.

I walked out in front of the division, introduced myself as Lieutenant Ashe, their new division officer. I said, "It's reported that you men are the sorriest division on the air station. I understand that after a weekend, there is a large percentage of you who come back late. I understand that you can't keep your hair cut, and I can see that you are as sloppy-looking a bunch of men as I ever saw."

I said, "That's all for the past. You will shape up and stay in shape or you'll never set foot off this base. At first, I will have marine sergeants to come and drill you. And, oh, you'll learn to march all right. The sooner you do it right, the sooner you'll knock off marching. In the beginning, the three sections will march until lunch and at 1:00 you'll commence marching again. You'll march till the evening meal, and then you'll come back, and you'll march from 7 until 11 at night."

I said, "That will be done every day until I determine that each of the sections can qualify for a day's rest." I said, "The best section will be granted weekend liberty, and the other two sections will spend the weekend marching."

I said, "Each morning at quarters for muster, any man whose hair is determined as being too long will be escorted to the barber shop and have it all cut off. Any man that hadn't got his shoes shined will spend lunch hour shining them. Any man that arrives back from liberty A.W.O.L. [absent without leave] will be placed in a special section to drill until midnight the next week."

"Now, 'ten-shun!" And you can bet your life some went to attention that didn't even know how to spell it.

Without dwelling on the subject, a month later, Commander Winetraub called me in to tell me he didn't want to know how I did it, but I had the best division on the air station.

We were taking off and landing at 9 o'clock and 1500 and 2100 every day, but in between time, the airships, one after the other, were having their cadets practice-land on the airfield. Sometimes that became very hazardous.

One day, as I stood in the open door of hangar number one, I looked up to see an airship heading directly for the hangar with his engines roaring as he attempted to climb above the hangar doors. The airship nose plowed into the hangar just above my head, and with a crunch, it fell backwards, tail first, to the mat.

The fuel tanks broke open and raw aviation gasoline poured down on the hot engines. Fuel drenched me and actually ran several inches deep down the tracks into the hangar. Why no explosion, I'll never know. All hands except for a passenger riding in the bunk perished on the crash.

The body of the pilot, Lieutenant (j.g.) Kilpatrick, a classmate of Roland Bryant, was twisted around the rudder pedestal. And the crews that tried to extricate his body spent most of an hour cutting cables and the like.

After his body was removed, I went on into my office and changed clothes.

Other mishaps that come to mind include a day in which I was taking off with a load of parachute rigger graduates, letting them make their graduation jump, quickly returning, and picking up another load. On the third load, as I come around and came over the field at 1,000 feet, I watched them as they jumped from the rear of the car.

One parachute didn't open at all, and one parachute partially opened. And the two parachutists hit the ground feet first and literally went into the ground several feet. We knocked off the graduation exercises for that day. The graduation exercise, incidentally, was for the parachute rigger to pack his own parachute and jump.

Shortly after arrival as a flight instructor, I was designated ordinance and gunnery officer. I immediately added to the curriculum that every flight group of cadets would experience dropping a depth charge. I was scheduled for most of these flights because the other instructors didn't like to do it.

Likewise, one day as I strolled by the pistol range, I stopped and observed the station warrant gunner teaching a group of officers to fire the .38 pistol. Somehow, he must've noticed that I was drooling, because, on completion of one of their rounds, he asked me, "Lieutenant, would you like to fire?"

I said yes, and he asked me if I had ever fired before. And I said, "Only a .22 rifle back at home."

He showed me how to hold the gun, where to hold the sights, and said, "Fire in half a dozen rounds."

This I did. I put them all in the bull's eye. And he says, "Lieutenant, you were joshing me about not firing before."

I said, "No, that's the first time I ever fired."

We re-loaded, and he told me that rapid fire was in 25 seconds, and you also had no time and slow fire. So I proceeded to put six more in the bull's eye rapid fire. He got interested, and had me fire the whole expert course. And I made 220 points the first time practicing. A score of 211 was expert.

He fired off from the station a request to the Secretary of Navy for me to be given the official expert pistol course designation, which the Navy did, and I became an expert the first time.

The station newspaper headlined "Two-Gun Ashe Escapades with the Pistol," and I automatically became the small arms instructor.

To get the cadets' attention, I would hold two guns and tell them how to hold the gun and aim, come up with my right hand, put six of them into the bull's eye in 10 seconds, and with my left hand, put six of them into the bull's eye in 15 seconds, and you know, those old boys would pay attention to me!

A little more on firing. The F.B.I. from Newark would come down to use our range to qualify their agents with rifles and pistols. Since I was the range officer, I had to observe these firings. The very first day, the director asked me, would I like to go with the next group. Of course, I excitedly stated yes. The firings consisted of four men walking parallel up the range and, electronically, each of their targets would fly up for a second and fall back down. In this second that your target was up, hit 'em in the head or in the body, 10 points. Hit 'em in the leg or in the arm, 5 points. Miss, no points.

As I marched the length of the range, I had six targets fly up, and I put a .38 bullet hole between the eyes of each target. The F.B.I. director asked me, "Lieutenant, how do you do that?"

I says, "I don't know. When the pistol comes up, it just seems that the bullet comes out when it's lined up with the middle of his head."

I became equally proficient with the Browning automatic rifle and the .50 caliber machine gun. Of course, with the .50 caliber, I was already an expert from my pre-Pearl Harbor training.

A few years later I was teaching Susan and Walter how to fire pistols and rifles. I got Walter a new .22 rifle for his birthday. We arrived back at my mother's and the kids looked around for targets to fire at. I told them to take a match and stick it up on a post and fire at the match head. Walter groaned and says, "Daaaddy! You can't do that!"

"Why," I says, "You surely can!"

He handed me the rifle. I fired, knocked the end off the match. While he was surprisedly looking at the results of my firing, I said, "Now, if you want to be extremely accurate, you can fire, hit the white part of the match, and it'll blaze up."

I proceeded to demonstrate, and for the next three shots caused a match to flame up. In later years, Susan was in Canada, firing at a turkey shoot. A few of the people fired. Susan's turn came, and she put one exactly in the corner of the triangle. The manager of the shoot proclaimed, "We have a winner! This gal has got a perfect hit!" When they found out she was from Tennessee, they had her sign the target and put it up in the clubhouse.

24

Ghost Story

Back to the story. One day, I got a call to report to the flag building, that Admiral Rosendahl wanted to see me. Let me tell you something, boys and girls, admirals don't waste time seeing lieutenants.

With considerable trepidation, I headed to the flag building. Now, I'd seen Admiral Rosendahl before, but always from a distance. When I was ushered into his office, I had difficulty breathing, and don't know what would've happened if I had had to talk.

He got up, shook hands, and said, "Would you like to go to the War College?"

People said our house at Middleton, R.I., near the Naval War College, was haunted. They may have been right.

I said, "Yes, sir!" And I didn't have the slightest idea what it was!

He told his yeoman to get Ernie on the phone. Ernie, of course, was Admiral King. In a bit, I heard a little bit of discussion about how Mrs. King was and that Jean was fine, and he says, "I have a Lieutenant Ashe I'd like to send to the War College." I couldn't hear the other end, of course, but Rosendahl says, "I know he's a lieutenant. I want him to go anyway."

They exchanged pleasantries, hung up the phone, and he says to me, "You'll get orders this afternoon for the War College." He says, "But the classes start two days from now."

Well, I thanked him, went looking up Lieutenant Commander Koff, who was a Naval Academy graduate, and asked him, "What's the War College?"

He gave me a dissertation about it being the school at Newport, R.I., where officers were sent for training, normally before going to the staffs of admirals throughout the Navy. Then he asked, "Why do you ask?"

I said, "Admiral Rosendahl is sending me to War College." He says, "The hell you say!"

Farris was up visiting us, but the next morning, Evaline, Farris and myself got in my little ol' Chevy and headed for Newport, R.I.

The war made housing at Newport terrible. We couldn't find a hotel, but were luckily steered to a fourth floor rooming house. We moved in, and began frantically looking for a place to live.

I went out to the War College, and they gave me a list of people that rented to War College students. Why the people would rent like this, I don't know, because they had somebody moving in and out of their houses or apartments every six months.

We got the address of a place overlooking the reservoir at Middleton, R.I. We were met by the daughter of the owners, who told me that it was part of a house that included a living room, dining room, kitchen, two baths, and four bedrooms. But she was quick to point out that it had been once used as a nursing home and several people had died while living in the bedrooms.

Now, at this point in time, with no place to live, I'd have taken the place if there had been a couple of corpses still hanging around.

We moved in.

The ghost story I'm about to set forth makes my hair stand up even now.

Nothing happened until Farris had gotten on the bus and headed back to Kenton. We had been given free use of the Third Beach facilities there at Newport. These facilities were exclusively for the Newport high society crowds, but they graciously invited the War College students.

Evaline and myself went swimming each afternoon. And when we came back, we would hang our swimming suits up on a sun porch that was off one of the bedrooms upstairs. After hanging out the suits one evening, the next morning I went upstairs looking for part of one of my uniforms. And I looked and saw the door from the bedroom to the sun porch swinging, and I knew damned well I'd closed that the night before. So I shouted down to Evaline, "Leave the door closed!"

She came up and assured me that she hadn't touched the door. Well, with just the right amount of pomp and ceremony, I closed the screen door and hooked it top and bottom. I closed the door and turned the lock and left the key in it. Then for good measure, I put a straight chair under the doorknob to keep it shut. I told her, "Now leave it that way and don't open it anymore!"

You know, that afternoon when I come home, I went up to get the swimsuits, and there that blinking door was, swinging open. We both looked at the door, and couldn't imagine what happened.

We stayed there five and a half months, and that door never stayed shut.

Two or three days after Farris left, our collie King, who always slept next to Evaline's bed, was sound asleep while both of us, who were in twin beds, sat up at the same time. We were apparently awakened by King's growl. For there he was, silhouetted in the moonlight with his fangs bared and his tail a-twitchin', emitting low growls. We heard the front door open.

We distinctly heard and felt the steps of a person cross the living room and go up the stairs, by which time, I had my .45 with a round in the chamber. I was over at the door and had turned on the light, looking up the stairs.

I said, "King, go get em!" He scurried upstairs. You could hear him go to each of those four bedrooms. He came out and looked down the stairs at me and wagged his tail. Holdin' my .45 with a round in the chamber and the hammer back, I cautiously went upstairs and into the first bedroom. And there was that door to the sun porch swinging slowly on its hinges.

I came back downstairs, went over to shut the living room door, and it wasn't even open.

Well, Evaline and myself had a little difficulty sleeping that night.

But the next night, we had somewhat the same experience, except that instead of teeth bared and tail a-twitchin', King, that never showed fear of anything, was over in the corner, crouched down like something was going to get him!

I decided we needed two more guns. I got Evaline a .32 automatic and I got a repeating .22 rifle. We'd go through an evening ritual making certain everything was closed.

One night, after Evaline had spent the day cleaning the pans and aluminum, she put them in a dishpan on a chair in the kitchen. We distinctly heard something. Instead of turning on the light to investigate, I moved slowly into the kitchen in the dark. Well, naturally, I bumped into the dishpan, and all of those pans hitting the floor sounded like a volcano hitting the place.

I heard something that sounded like steps running down the two flights of stairs that were outside of the house, leading up to the sun porch. I quickly unlocked the door, opened it and says to King, "Get 'em!"

He went running down across the lawn toward the reservoir with such snarling and growling as if he was tearing something to pieces. He came back up with a smile on his face and his tail wagging, holding a little piece of cloth in his mouth.

I decided that maybe the landlord and landlady knew a little bit about what was going on up there, so I went down alongside their house overlooking the lake, took a plank, and set 12 Coke bottles on the plank.

And with both the man and the woman watching intently, I pulled out my two automatics and burst those 12 Coke bottles. And then, rather belligerently, walked over and told them, "That's exactly what's going to happen if I find somebody in my house."

I told them a bit of what had been going on, and the lady went in and called the police. A police lieutenant and a sergeant came out. As they interviewed Evaline and myself, we told them of the practically every night occurrences of hearing doors open, with it not necessarily being open, of having doors open without hearing it, but that I never had actually seen anything, although I'd sat on the stair steps and had disgustedly talked to something as if I could see it, saying, "If you let me see you, I'll pop you one!"

I said to the lieutenant, "Something's going on in that house." I said, "I'm not scared of ghosts. Fact is, I don't know of anything I am scared of. But I can't find anything to shoot at!"

The sergeant says, "Come on, lieutenant. Let's get out of here!" The lieutenant says, "Didja ever consider movin'?"

And I says, "Yes, but there's no place to move to. Besides that, I take a dim view of ghosts makin' me do anything."

He asked would I want police protection? And I says, "If you want to put police out surveying the place, it's all right with me." I said, "You can tell them that I have guns and they're loaded, but I won't shoot them as long as they stay outside the house. But I sure won't look the second time if I see somebody in the house."

I had begun to report this every morning at the War College. It became a laughing matter among many of the students. But over home it was not a laughing matter.

Once, I went to South Weymouth, stayed overnight to get some flight time, and Evaline remained at home alone. She took the position that there wasn't any ghost goin' to run her out of her house!

But on my return, she reported that she didn't hear a darn thing the night before.

Weeeeelll, pretty soon Evaline's mom came to visit us. And we concluded that the best move would be to keep this all top secret from her.

Well, the first night there, King, who didn't care any more about Mrs. Paseur than she did about him, went up and parked himself across the doorway of the bedroom that Evaline put her mom in. This was the first time that he'd ever slept anywhere except next to Evaline's bed.

Do you know that cotton-pickin' dog spent every night lying outside Mrs. Paseur's bedroom door the whole time she visited? It's worth noting that, after we'd moved from the place, Mrs. Paseur began to babble about, "There's something wrong with that house." She said she could see things that looked like devils in the room with her. She said once she went to the door and opened it, and there was King, and she could have hugged him.

Since she hadn't said anything, I commenced to think maybe if I wasn't around nobody'd hear and see that stuff. But about that time, A.J., who was an aviation cadet, got some leave and came up to visit us.

Well, Evaline put him in the same room that she had let her mother use. Of course, King didn't bother to go offer any protection to A.J., and A.J., while there didn't say a word about seeing anything remiss. But, like Mrs. Paseur, after we moved away, he commenced tellin' us what he thought was wrong with that place. He said in that room he'd cover himself up with the sheet, the quilt, scared to death, take his eyes out to look, and there'd be a bunch of eyes out in the room looking at him.

Years later, when I was stationed at Lakehurst, one night while flying to New England, we came near to Newport in one of the huge, million and a half cubic foot airships we had at that time. I told members of the crew about this house, went over Newport and into Middleton, found the house, put the searchlight on the house, and began to slowly circle it from about 1,000 feet with the searchlight beam pinned on the house.

As I told crew members of incidents that occurred down there—doors opening that you couldn't see, hearing things that made no sense—one of my chiefs looked up at me and says, "Commander, let's get the hell out of here before whatever's down there comes up that beam at us!"

I don't know what the problem was in that house, but the very last night we lived there, we were expecting Commander and Mrs. Peterson to be over to play bridge. After hearing what we believed to be them in their apartment, which adjoined ours, Evaline sent me over to check if maybe we were supposed to be over there for bridge. As I went out the door, Pete and Madelaine came driving up. I asked if they'd been home. He says no, and I says, "There's somebody in your house!"

He jumped out of his car and ran in to his front door, while I ran through my house, picked up my .45 and ran out the back door. I could hear Pete inside his house with the doors slamming. As I came running up to his back door, and while standing there, his back door flew open, and I could almost feel something come running by me, and the screen door flew back shut. And Pete arrived and says, "Where'd he go, where'd he go?"

I said, "Pete, the only thing I saw was the back door fly open and something go running by me."

Whatever it was, maybe it's still there.

25

War College

I arrived at the War College July '44. On reporting I learned that they divided the class into two groups and for five and a half months, with the students in command of various sections of two fleets simulated doing battle. I also learned that they let the two senior officers that were students choose, one at a time, the students that were to be on their team.

I already had an inferiority complex, hobnobbing with the Navy's social elite. Most of our class were from families that frequented Newport. On the class roster, where we listed the school from which we graduated, I saw the Harvards, the Yales, the Princetons, with an occasional University of Pennsylvania. My little three years at Memphis State made me feel rather insignificant.

But, crack out of the box, the third night after arrival, they had a big party for the students to meet the president of the Naval War College. Vice-Admiral and Mrs. Fife were in a receiving line, with the admiral's aide attempting to introduce the students and their wives as they came through the line. The aide, in an effort to assist with the introductions, asked the senior student there, Captain Fuqua of the Atlanta Fuqua department store clan, to pass on the names of the students.

It seemed that Captain Fuqua was having difficulties, and since I was the junior officer, he told me to get the names of the students and tell him who they were as they arrived in the line. We'd been there two days.

I'd had a couple of bourbon and ginger ales, and I proceeded to call them all by name, and he shortly put me to just directly introducing the students to the admiral.

The next morning, back at the War College, the two senior officers that were to head the respective fleets were selected, and everybody stood by as they commenced their choice for their team. I got back out of the way, alongside Robert Taft, Jr., who was the only other lieutenant there. Bob, obviously feeling somewhat as I did, remarked, "Well, they'll have to select us sometime!"

They flipped a coin. Captain Fuqua won first choice, and he looked around the room, pointed his finger at me, and says, "I want Lieutenant Ashe." I almost "swallered" my tongue.

It became apparent shortly thereafter why he selected me, when he put me on his personal staff to be his aerial observer. The rules of the game were such that the aerial observer could simulate aircraft searching by stepping out over-looking the maneuvering room, looking at the fleet for 10 seconds, and coming back into the board room to advise the fleet commander on suggested maneuvers.

Captain Fuqua, watching me with the names of the students, figured I had a photographic memory and could, in a few seconds, determine the fleet movements. Well, I could. And I did. And we just beat the livin' heck out of the other fleet.

The Naval War College instructors were some of the world's best international specialists. The course was most interesting, highly informative, and since we were cleared into what was called the holy of holies of classified material, we studied the actual battles. We even participated in making our personal input into planning some of the battles that were about to occur.

My claim to fame came when I presented the plans and schedule for the attack on the Palau Island chain and it proved to be almost identical to that prepared by Admiral Nimitz's staff.

Outside reading was unlimited, but I must admit that I was more interested in afternoon swims and being home than I was in studying. But you know, one night I did drive back to the War College to get some research material. As I walked in, at about 2300 (11 p.m.), the loudspeaker blared "Long distance for Lieutenant Ashe. Admiral Rosendahl is calling."

I picked up the phone, said, "Good evening, Admiral."

He said, "I was just checkin' to see how you were getting along." Naturally, the old man thought I was really burning the midnight oil.

A few days before the end of the course, we were handed a paper telling each of us where the next tour of duty was to be. Old Bob Taft and Walt Ashe had orders to go as control officers for the seventh fleet.

Everybody knew that the life expectancy of a control officer during an invasion was something between 10 and 30 seconds. So we weren't too enthusiastic as we discussed our future.

In a few minutes, the loudspeaker blared, "Long distance for Lieutenant Ashe. Admiral Rosendahl is calling."

I went over and picked up the phone. Admiral Rosendahl told me, "Some bastard down in Washington thinks he's going to send you out to the south Pacific. Those orders are going to be canceled, and you'll be coming back to my staff."

Well, I went walking over, looking like the cat that swallowed the canary. Bob Taft went over to the War College director, requested permission to go to Washington. They wouldn't let him go. He said to me he needed to see his father, then-U.S. Senator Robert Taft. I told him, "Get in your car and drive down Friday night. Do what you can and be back Monday morning, and nobody'll know the difference."

I never did meet ol' Bob after he, too, became a senator.

Each of the War College students was required to write a bit of a thesis and to give two speeches of 20 to 30 minutes each. One of my speeches was, "Do not listen to either Churchill or Stalin. Do not invade Europe. Continue to build as rapidly as possible the forces in England. Watch and wait, and whichever one, Germany or Russia, defeats the other, attack the winner with all our might."

Later, back at Lakehurst, a multi-millionaire owner of a radio chain, and later TV chain in Pennsylvania, one Captain Sam Townsend, chewed on me every day for months, pointing out the need for me to realize that Russia was our ally. Eighteen years later, I got a phone call from the Marines at Lakehurst's main gate, saying that there was a Sam Townsend who wanted to see me.

He and his wife, Wanda, had located me in the Navy, and had driven over so he could personally tell me how wrong he was.

But before I leave Newport, I want to mention that, during A.J.'s visit, a full-fledged Atlantic hurricane hit us dead center. The hurricane moved up the coast at a surprisingly rapid rate. The forecasters in early morning thought the hurricane would arrive off Norfolk by night. But by 1 o'clock that afternoon, Newport was battened down, War College students were released, and the forecasters expected it to reach Rhode Island by midnight.

On arrival home I told Evaline and A.J., "Let's go over along the high cliffs of Newport," to watch the grandeur of the waves that would be pounding into the rocks. They didn't want to go on any such excursion. In fact, the radio was warning all hands to stay indoors. But they went with me, and A.J. chewed on me the whole time to get back home.

The waves and spray as they pounded the rocks and sometimes practically obscured the Newport mansions were thrilling for me to watch. Well before dark, we got back to the house, made sure everything was secure, got out the candles and began to play checkers.

A.J., never having been in a hurricane, was rather apprehensive, so I chronologically listed what happens as a hurricane approaches you. I told him not to worry until the wind started whistling. That meant it was barely reaching hurricane force. But that somewhere around 76 or 77 mph, suddenly the leaves would leave the trees. I said, "We'll watch out the window because there'll be lightning, and if the leaves leave the trees, the hurricane will begin to be dangerous. If it goes up much from there, suddenly the huge oak trees will be blown over as the roots give way, and all power will go out and we'll need those candles. Soon A.J. decided, no more checkers, and from there on, step by step, I told him what was happening, and a pretty good estimate of what the wind velocity was.

After two big oak trees near our house came up by the roots, suddenly everything was quiet. I said to Jake and Evaline, "Come on, come on! Let's see this!" They reluctantly stepped out. There it was, calm, stars above us, clear skies. A.J. says, "You mean it's over?" I says, "No, it's not over. We're in the eye of the hurricane. In a bit, you'll hear the awfulest roaring you ever saw, and it'll hit again."

As advertised, the roar occurred, and back in the house we went. The next day, we learned that the wind hit 105 miles an hour as it passed over us.

While A.J. was visiting we had a few occasions where some of the Newport drivers were plain disgusting. So, I stopped my car each time and got out and explained the errors of the ways of the driver that was creating my problem. One day, as I drove up to a stoplight, less than a second after it turned some bird honked on his horn. I stopped the engine, got out of the car, walked over to the driver and asked him what was his problem? He says I was blocking traffic.

I said, "Keep your shirt on, fella. Don't give me a horn blast!"

I got back in the car, and A.J. gave me one of his "father to son" lectures concerning holding my temper and just not being worried about what was going on. In other words, take it easy.

The very next day, he was in the car with me as we arrived at an intersection and almost collided with some bird. Before the car stopped, A.J. was out of the car and over to the driver of the other vehicle. He reached out and grabbed him by the coat while he lambasted the driver concerning the errors of his ways. I was laughing so hard that I could hardly control myself. In a bit, as A.J. got back into the car, mumbling and grumbling, I told him, "Yeah, what about that lecture you gave me?"

Within a few days, graduation time at the War College. Why, I do not know, but I went to my graduation wearing aviator greens. We had 96 students plus the staff, all in blues. Little ol' Lieutenant Ashe goofed up and was wearing greens. Our speaker was none other than Admiral Earnest King, then Chief of Naval Operations, Commander in Chief of the Atlantic fleet, and Commander in Chief of all allied naval forces. After his speech, he presented each of us with our diploma. Presenting diplomas moved rather rapidly until I walked out on the stage.

The admiral stopped, put his arm around my shoulder, walked out to the front of the stage, and said, "You destroyer men and you submariners are doing an outstanding job. But it's these boys wearing the greens that are beatin' the hell out of the Japs."

Dub is wearing the green Navy uniform reserved for aviators during World War II, as Evaline looks on with pride.

26

On the Admiral's Staff

The next day I was detached and shoved off to Lakehurst to report to Admiral Rosendahl's staff. Rear Admiral Rosendahl was the same for lighter-than-air as fleet Admiral King was for the entire Navy. At Lakehurst I was royally welcomed and immediately assigned the task of looking into the crash of the Hindenburg in 1937 and reporting to the admiral what I believed happened.

After reviewing the findings of the U.S. Navy Board and the German Board, I concluded that the rigger whose station was just aft of midship, high up in the girders had planted an incendiary bomb timed to go off after the Hindenburg had been put into the hangar at Lakehurst. The admiral told me that he completely agreed with me. Then he told me that he wanted me to write training pamphlets for use by the airship pilots for searching, tracking, and attacking submarines, and to expedite this because the airship Navy had never had such instructions in writing.

I hired a stenographer who could take dictation as fast as I could talk and a typist that never made an error. I had a Navy yeoman who had her master's degree in English from Cornell University, and my secretary, who was good at being my girl Friday.

I talked, the stenographer took the dictation, typed out what she thought I said. The Cornell yeoman corrected my English, the secretary-typist double spaced it, I reviewed it, often put it back into my English, and my secretary typed the final and went about printing up the booklets.

It was indeed a giant step forward for airship efforts in anti-submarine warfare. It became a lesson in how to win friends and influence people.

When some poor command pilot, in the middle of the night, with the winds blowing and the rains pounding the airship picked up a contact and proceeded to attack the sub, if he missed, he needed to report and be debriefed. And he always missed. Such contacts occurred rather frequently. The command pilot would return to his squadron, be debriefed, then he and his commanding officer would report to the wing commander. Then shortly thereafter the wing commander, the commanding officer, and the command pilot would report to Commodore Mills. They would get their story together and go to report to Admiral Rosendahl.

He would have me stand beside his chair while we listened to the command pilot's report. Then he'd look up at me and say, "What'd he do wrong?" It's a wonder to me that I ever made lieutenant commander.

The admiral called me in and stated that, "We get a wealth of information from the tenth fleet. All of it's secret and top secret. I want you to review those reports and inform me of anything you think I should know."

Now, maaaann, if that wasn't a wonderful position to be in! A young lieutenant reading all the reports from the tenth fleet! The tenth fleet was stationed out of Norfolk, but included Washington, and its intelligence reports were considered outstanding. They included actions and capabilities plus indicated plans of all the Axis powers.

I recall as Christmas approached Evaline continued to ask me what I was worried about. One of these reports had stated that the Germans were expected to make a drive against the channel ports in order to capture launching sites for a new weapon that they had for bombing London. The weapon would go above the atmosphere, move several times the speed of sound, and rain devastation down on London. It would hit before the recipients had even a sign of an incoming weapon. The report further stated that the Germans were working on a weapon that was expected to travel from Europe to New York City in 33 minutes.

When I briefed the admiral, he says, "Don't bother me with that crap. They ain't nothin' goin' across the Atlantic in 33 minutes."

I went home for Christmas lunch. Evaline still thought I looked sad.

In a few minutes the radio blared forth the details of the Battle of the Bulge. I told Evaline, that's what I've been worried about.

As we know, the V-2s did their work on London. And a few years later, the German scientist von Braun helped us create a missile that crossed the Atlantic in less than 33 minutes.

There were a lot of other things a-poppin' around that staff. First thing you know, we had a couple a dozen Brazilian pilots up for flight training. I was rung in as a flight instructor, and teaching Brazilians to fly was a hazardous occupation.

The Brazilians, from the senior colonel on down, seemed to admire and respect me, and I imagine the reasons were twofold. One, I was attached to the admiral's staff; and, two, I had a few ribbons depicting Pacific fleet naval battles.

But it didn't stop with the Brazilians. The next thing you know, we had a passel of Coast Guard men. They were a fine bunch of boys. Good pilots.

Now, on the admiral's staff, there was a lieutenant commander O'Brien. And that turd was an avowed Communist, a lover of Russians, and an all-around antithesis of me. First thing you know, President Roosevelt authorized delivery of 25 PBYs to the Russians. Well, that mighta been all right except he included delivering our top-secret MAD [Magnetic Anomaly Detector] with the planes.

I had been constantly involved with the scientists at Humm Lab as we worked and developed the MAD for anti-submarine warfare. It broke my heart for the stinkin' Russians to be getting the MAD.

But the Russians arrived at Lakehurst for training. O'Brien decided to welcome them with open arms. And they threw a big party out at Rova Farms (a Communist farm in Lakewood, N.J.). O'Brien especially wanted full representation of people like me involved in anti-submarine warfare, knowledgeable and experienced on the MAD.

He made a point of personally telling me that he wanted me at that party. I told him he could sure look for me but I wouldn't be there. And he said, "You damn well better be!"

Comes Monday morning, with blood in his eyes, he came to chew me out. A verbal battle commenced that lasted all week, during which time I said a lot of things that you shouldn't say during wartime when you got a bunch of Russian stinkin' Communists as allies. Among them, during the heat of our arguments, I told him that, if faced with a choice, I'd rather right then be living in Nazi Germany than in Communist Russia. I also told him that I wasn't the slightest bit impressed with American Communists from the Hollywood theater guild, of which he was one. I told him that no way would I ever show a Russian how to work MAD. And, a thousand other things were thrown back and forth.

The only thing that we really could agree on was that each of us had a canine ancestry, and that we didn't care any more about each other than I did about the Russians.

I helped him along a little by saying that in a speech at the War College I had pointed out that we should hold our forces in abeyance and let the Germans and Russians fight it out, and then destroy the one that won.

But, by the end of the week, he had the audacity to order me to be at the Friday and Saturday night Rova Farm beer bust and barbecue.

I didn't go. Monday morning, there was a repeat of the previous week and I walked out on him, telling him that I'd go anywhere the admiral told me to go, but his two and a half stripes was a disgrace to the Navy and human intelligence.

Well things skidded along for a few weeks, and one day Captain Cockle, the admiral's chief of staff, asked me to come up to the admiral's office.

This I did, with pad and pencil. The admiral looked up at me, and I could tell he was terribly agitated. He says, "I got a letter here to the Secretary of Navy, reporting you to be a Nazi sympathizer." First looking at the letter, then asking me if I ever said, for instance, "I'd rather live in Nazi Germany than Communist Russia," on down through many of the other things I had said. I told him in each instance that I had.

After a couple of pages, he looked up to Captain Cockle, and says, "Art, if you got any more Nazi sympathizers like Walt, get 'em ordered to my staff." And he says, "I want that O'Brien ordered out of here today." He paused a minute and says, "No, I'll do it." He called Washington to some admiral he knew, and says he has a Lieutenant Commander O'Brien on his staff and he wanted him ordered over to help MacArthur. And he added, "I want the bastard away from here today!"

He got up and slapped me on the shoulder and said, "Keep up the good work."

Now Evaline was a cute little girl being welcomed by the wives of the senior officers. And right off the bat, she was invited to join them for bridge. Now Evaline didn't know anything about playing bridge. She was scared to death, playing with Mrs. Cockle, Mrs. Rosendahl, Mrs. Thornton, the wife of the commanding officer of the air station, so she could hardly sleep before going over the day of the bridge game. She didn't know there was such a thing as counting points and Culbertson I'm sure she'd never heard of.

Anyway, she sat down with the big wheels for an afternoon of bridge. Just beat the tar out of them! Getting grand slams, and she didn't even know how to bid. Well, you guessed it. This prompted our being invited to the Wednesday night club bridge night.

Now I didn't know any more about bridge than a load of coal. They had a routine that the woman high score got a bottle of bourbon, the man high score got a bottle of scotch, and the second place got a bottle of wine. Long before Evaline and myself learned how to play bridge we had our little bar completely stocked with scotch, bourbon and wine.

We were so lucky that different ones would try to get to have each of us as partners as we floated through those Wednesday night bridge games.

One evening I had the staff duty and was surprised to get a phone call from Jean Rosendahl asking me to come by her house, pick her up, and take her to some party. I got into the staff car, drove up to flag quarters, went in, asked if she was ready to go to the party. I hardly knew her, and was further surprised when she said, "Let's go up to Helen Smith's. She's having a party." It so happened that Commander Smith, the admiral, the flight surgeon, and a few other dignitaries had flown off to Europe to inspect the lighter-than-air facilities in North Africa.

We went in to Mrs. Smith's quarters, found two other wives along with escorts, and they announced, "Come on, sit down Jean. We're about to play strip poker." Imagine my confusion when I learned that the poker game required each player to ante any garment from their body or from their winnings for each hand. I didn't know how to play poker well, but my chief problem was that I knew we didn't have any business at that party, and I didn't know what to do about it.

As the game progressed, neither Jean nor I were losing, but others were. And finally, Mrs. Smith had lost all of her clothes except a slip. At that point, she announced that she wasn't going to play the next hand. Her escort, an assistant public works officer, said yes she was, reached over and pulled her slip over her head. Suddenly standing completely nude, she went running upstairs, with him running after her.

I turned to Mrs. Rosendahl and said, "It's time for us to leave." She got up and we went out to the car. On the way to her quarters, she just chewed me out unmercifully, telling me that I should have had us go home when they announced they were having that strip poker game.

I told her, "Well, I knew it at the time, but I was at a total loss what to do about it." I said, "Young lieutenants can't go tellin' admirals' wives when they got to leave a party."

Needless to say, I was terribly worried about the incident and confided my worries to my buddy, Bob Kilcourse. He had a good laugh and said, "You don't have to worry about it, because she sure in hell is not going to tell the admiral!"

Bob and myself used to schedule an airship flight two or three times a month. We rotated signing for the ship with the other being copilot. And my, oh my, did we bump into some stories. One, for instance. Old lady Hitchcock, the senior wave on board the station and a former school teacher, was a strict disciplinarian and quite concerned about what the waves on board actually did. One day, we decided to take two of the wave yeomen from the staff on a joyride in a K ship across New Jersey. In time, I flew the airship back and forth across a nudist colony. Well, this wasn't s'posed to be done. But I put the two girls in the lookout seat, armed them with 750x binoculars, and at 200-300 feet, we viewed the sights.

On return to base, those girls spread the word about the flight. And the next morning, Bob told me, "You're in trouble."

I said, "How's that?"

He says, "You flew the waves over the nudist colony and old lady Hitchcock is madder 'n hell, and she plans to go see the admiral this morning."

"Why," I says, "you were with me!"

He says, "I was the copilot. You signed for the ship."

I was very concerned at this development, and more so when, out the window, old lady Hitchcock could be seen approaching with her measured 30-inch step. She went around to the front entrance of the flag building and up to the admiral's office.

A little bit later, she came out, reversed her course, heading back to the Lakehurst administration building. About that time, I practically wet my pants when on the squawk box Captain Cockle said, "Walt, can you come up a minute?"

I went into his office and he says, "Did you take some waves flying yesterday?"

I said, "Yessir."

He said, "Did you take 'em over the nudist colony?" With a sinking feeling, I said, "Yessir."

He said, "The next time you take another flight like that, let me know. I'd like to go with you."

Other goodies. Once flying at 2,000 feet, heading toward Barnegat Light I noticed in the sand dune area south of Seaside Park a boy and a girl on a blanket makin' love. With the help of my 750x binoculars, a better look proved that the situation should be investigated, and with all hands on board armed with binoculars, we proceeded south with the engines in idle, and losing altitude.

I turned and come over the sand dune at 50 feet with the engines just enough to equal the wind speed, and hovered right over the blanket. They were busy, and didn't notice us for a bit. But when the girl became aware of the airship just above her, she jumped out from under the fellow and got under the blanket.

The boy, with his fist wavin', stood up, obviously cussin' us out, but we held our ground for some time, and finally, he picked up the girl's clothes and put them under the blanket. She came out shortly with her clothes on, obviously made him put his on, and they walked out to the road among the dunes, got into their car, and headed north toward Asbury Park.

Another little funsie was flat-hattin' at Atlantic City. I thought it was great to take a K ship, put it about 10 feet above the water, fly directly toward the two ferris wheels that were in the amusement park on the steel pier. As I would head directly between the two ferris wheels, pandemonium would set in among the ferris wheel riders. Just before crashing each time, I would pull slightly to the starboard, fly close alongside the ferris wheels, laugh, and wave at the people riding the ferris wheel as they obviously were scared to death.

Boy, oh boy, big fun! Until one day, after landing I went to my office, and the admiral called. Somebody had called and reported me. The admiral said, "You been flat-hattin' down at Atlantic City?"

I said, "Yes, admiral, I have."

He says, "I used to do that when I was a kid." That's all he said.

Didn't need to say any more. My swings at the ferris wheels stopped right then.

27

Free Ballooning

One of my duties on the staff was reviewing the specs and investigating any new weapon. The admiral was constantly after the Bureau of Ordinance to get replacements for those depth charges. Finally, they came up with a weapon called a scatter bomb. They sent a truckload of these scatter bombs to Lakehurst. The weapon consisted of eight 30-pound bombs in a cluster. When dropped from the airship, an explosive charge blew the bombs into an ellipse, thus greatly enhancing possibilities of sinking the sub.

The only problem is these bombs became depth charges that were detonated on contact with the submerged submarine by a small arm projecting from the bomb. I looked at the weapon, looked at the specs, and it seemed to me that there was a very good chance that one or more of these bombs could go off under the airship when the explosive charge kicked them into the ellipse.

I pondered this a day or two. I went up and told the admiral, "Admiral, these scatter bombs are not safe."

But he didn't like that. He was very glad that the bureau had developed this weapon for us, so he looked me in the eye and said, "The Bureau engineers have tested this weapon and declared it safe. I don't want to hear any more about it."

Well, my poor old mom did a good job of teaching me on most things, but she never taught me to keep my mouth shut. So after a bit, I wrote him a letter, really an internal memo from me to him that said the dang thing wasn't safe and why.

Man alive! He didn't even bother to call me up. When that memo hit his desk, he come chasin' down from his office on the second floor to mine on the first, came a-stompin' into the office I shared with Bob Kilcourse, threw that letter on my desk and said, "I told you I didn't want to hear any more about it!"

Even Kilcourse lectured me on my stupidity.

Time moved along and one day an Italian sub had been captured. So I did a lot of scheduling and arranged for the admiral's ship, the K-91, to take a flight, search, track, and attack that submerged Italian sub being towed, and then drop a scatter bomb on it.

The big day arrived. I as pilot, Punderson as copilot, with a crew along with the admiral and Captain Townsend as passengers. I was excited. I went chasing up the stairway to the admiral's office in flight suit and told the admiral we were ready for take-off. On the way down the stairway, I blurted out, "I'll tell you one more time, admiral. This bomb's not safe!"

He changed from laughing to angry and told me, "That bomb is safe, but you're not going on the flight. Punderson will be the pilot."

Well, I knew I had blown it for sure, and I knew what happened to people for less, and that soon as he got back he would transfer me to the south Pacific. I went into our little wardroom and began to plan how best to handle our situation, concluding that it would be necessary for me to convince Evaline she had to stay at Memphis with her folks and not go to San Francisco.

Needless to say, I couldn't believe I had been stupid enough to tell him one more time that that scatter bomb wasn't safe.

I sat in the wardroom and moped. After several hours, the crash alarm for the air station sounded. As a course of habit, I called operations to see what the problem was. They told me that the King-91 was approaching the air station losing lift so fast it was about to crash. I didn't need any more information.

I hurried up to Mat 1, watched ole Punderson bring the K-91 in for landing. As always, he did a good job. The O and R helium trucks along with their repair ladders went running out to the K-91, where, while they were pumping helium into the airship, they were putting pressure patches in the ship to stop the biggest holes. Some of them big as a desk, many of them big as a basketball.

They got the ship on the mast and stabilized. The admiral got out of the airship. His aide drove over with the sedan and he climbed in. He drove right by me as I was standing there looking like the cat that swallowed the canary and disappeared over the hill to the flag building.

But in a bit, the sedan rolled up alongside me, the admiral rolled down the window and says, "Get those god-damn scatter bombs off of this air station!"

That's all he ever said about the matter, and rest yourself assured I never said anything else.

Not too long after V.E. Day, New York City decided to have a huge Eisenhower ticker tape parade. In those days—no TV—the prime coverage for a special event was newsreel coverage presented at movie houses throughout the land. Some enterprising newsreel companies—Pathé, 20th Century Fox, MovieTone—got permission from the Pentagon to fly on one of the Navy's airships to take pictures of this very large and worthwhile event.

As was customary, I flew as pilot for these special flights. The time was set to take off from Lakehurst at about 8 o'clock in the morning. So I found myself briefing the news cameramen and telling them that I intended to fly up the Hudson and come up and over the city just short of the Empire State Building and down into Central Park. Then and later, they all seemed to be concerned that I wouldn't get close enough for them to get good pictures of the parade.

As advertised, I flew between the Empire State Building and the Chrysler Building and down into the park. I was flying a K ship about 600,000 cubic feet in volume and slightly shorter than a football field in length. I flew down among the trees and shrubs of Central Park, back and forth between 5th and 8th Avenue, and up to Harlem on the north side, and down to the south end of Central Park. The city fathers had set up a large reviewing stand at the southeast corner of the park.

I made a few practice runs up 8th Avenue toward Harlem, making sure that I kept my tail out of the second floor apartments. There was a rather brisk wind from the northwest which required a little "crabbing" as I moved up the street. In order to be sure the airship tail didn't hit the apartments, I had to move along just above the sidewalk on the west side of 8th Avenue.

On reaching Harlem, it was necessary to climb because the buildings were mostly eight stories high. Flying was a little more difficult as I moved south because I had a tail wind and it was the nose of the airship that I had to keep out of the buildings.

As I moved backwards and forth, I managed to get closer and closer to the buildings. Frequently diverting and flying out over the park, waving at the millions of people, I was having a gay old time. On schedule, the parade started. At first, I went up the parade route and flew directly over the convertible in which Gen. Eisenhower was riding. I even got a wave from him. Then, as I descended from my swing over Harlem, I attempted to maintain an altitude of 50 feet and keep my nose as close as possible to the buildings.

This worked rather satisfactorily and the three newsreel cameramen were getting a wealth of pictures. But as I approached the reviewing stand, I got into some rather bad turbulence and found myself being thrown to the left, almost into the buildings while I was frantically giving full port engine with the starboard engine pulled back to idle and my copilot holding hard right rudder.

Just as I thought I'd surely hit the buildings, the airship turned slowly and commenced to rise slowly, and I roared over the reviewing stand only inches above the heads of the dignitaries. I understood that the president wasn't there, but every East Coast general and admiral surely was.

I continued my climb from the reviewing stand up to the right of the Chrysler Building. These news cameramen were in unison from all angles telling me that they had sufficient pictures.

After an uneventful flight I landed at Lakehurst. But the next morning, Admiral Rosendahl called me to his office. He was holding the New York Times when I entered. He said, "The headlines say A Million People Saw Ike! But," he said, "two million people saw you damn near kill me in the reviewing stand!"

I said, "I surely thought I was a goner. With full up, hard right and wide open on the port engine, I wasn't too sure that I hadn't hit that building."

"Look Ma, no hands!" Dub in the cockpit of a K-ship with an unidentified sailor.

He says, "Neither was I. And I saw where you had the controls."

Not all my cotton-pickin' free balloon rides were nice enough to write home to Mom about. One day in early October of 1944, I took a group of five student officers on a flight, intending to show them some of the fun things you could do with the balloon. Oh, what fun it was as we moved slowly above the New Jersey treetops! Until I began to get low on ballast, and I let out the long line in order to show them how you could use this line to maintain rather accurate altitude without valving helium or dropping ballast.

This worked fine until the long line took a half-hitch around a mesh wire fence, and as we slowly drifted along the fence was going poing! poing! poing! as it was being yanked off the posts. After drifting along and collecting another fence, I managed to cut the long line and drifted on away. But as the morning moved into afternoon, the beautiful day turned cloudy and the wind commenced to pick up, and I began to search for a place to try to land.

I came down into a peach orchard up in west central Jersey, but found the wind moving us so fast that the basket was knocking the tops out of the peach trees. I threw out a little ballast and climbed a bit to look for a better place.

Lo and behold, about this time we started to have a little snow squall.

I figured I had to land as early as possible. Up ahead was a fine looking estate that had a lovely front yard. I gave the valve a couple of pretty good tugs and began to drift in for what looked like a pretty fair but fast landing. Just before the basket set down, the balloon was hit by a tremendous shear that threw the balloon into a path almost 90 degrees from the original course. The basket hit one of the beautiful tulip poplars growing alongside the driveway. The poplar was about 18 inches in diameter. It snapped off just like a match stick and moved along with us.

Suddenly, I was hit with another wind shear that threw me more than 90 degrees to the right again, directly toward the barn. The balloon caught on a maple tree, and the basket went in an arc up and through the top of the barn. The limb of the tree tore a hole about ten feet in diameter along the equator of the balloon. The basket was being bounced along the ground through a field of late green corn, and as I was desperately trying to reach the ripcord (each time we bounced, being knocked back down into the basket), we plowed into a thicket and the balloon draped over one of Jersey Central's Power and Light high tension lines.

The basket was on its side in a briar patch, and as I cautiously tried to get out, the electric wires would contact each other and fireworks went all over the place.

What made this a little more tedious was the fact that our balloon was filled with hydrogen.

After a bit, we were all out, alongside the road, in reasonable shape except for bruises and scratches. An old boy, a Lieutenant Gillespie from Mississippi, was quivering all over. One of the visiting spectators said, "Daddy, I bet it's cold up there. Look at that man. He's still shaking!" It had scared the living shit out of everybody.

About this time, some irate turkey farmer came up and announced that I'd killed all his turkeys. Do you know that those turkeys must've thought that balloon was some kind of a huge hawk, because they had all piled headfirst into one of the buildings and smothered to death!

I don't know how much the Navy had to pay for the turkeys. But it was not near as much as it was taking care of the lawsuit from Jersey Central Power and Light.

The K-91 was kept equipped with the very latest in electronic developments—new radars, new engines—just whatever looked the best, we had it. We were also sitting right on top of the latest intelligence from the 10th fleet. One day the hot poop was that there was an enemy submarine operating in the Long Island Sound.

We quickly loaded the airship with the then hush-hush, top secret homing torpedo. A crack crew from Lakehurst Experimental with Lieutenant Commander Don Winton as command pilot set forth to Long Island Sound with me on board as vice-president in charge of the torpedo. The fact that we had these new torpedoes was a very recent and closely guarded secret. And even the command pilot didn't know anything about what I had on board.

We searched through the late afternoon and night, moving further and further out into the Atlantic. Through the next day, about the time we were 100 miles off Cape Cod, it became necessary for us to refuel.

The weather was bad. It was beginning to snow. And I suggested to Mr. Winton that he send a message to South Weymouth that we wanted to land there and remain for the night. He sent the message, but some dumb ass at South Weymouth answered by saying that they were sorry, they were unable to take us. We'd have to return to Lakehurst.

Winton showed me the message and I says, "You tell them they damn well will take us!"

And he sent back the message that was often quoted up and down the coast: "Lieutenant Ashe is on board and he says you damn well will take us."

As we came in for a landing at South Weymouth, I was on the controls, moved just above the revetment on the east side of the field, and came down into the snow, which was five or six inches by now. The landing party, accustomed to handling airships with regular engines, scattered, thinking I would run over them. But surprise! surprise! Those who had never seen reversible-pitch props in action, were probably stunned as I just lifted an engine into reverse, stopped on the mat, and waited until they collected their wits. They came out, put me on the mast, and moved the ship into the hangar.

Once in the hangar, I had a problem in that I had that secret torpedo on board. I told the command duty officer, a Lieutenant Morelander, that I wanted two Marine sergeants who were cleared "secret."

He says, "We don't have any Marines."

I said, "Notify the commanding officer of the air station that I want two Marine sergeants cleared for secret."

It wasn't but a bit before the commanding officer, tall, thin and red-headed, arrived in his sedan in the hangar in person. He came on board and told me, "Your Marines will be here shortly."

The Marines came on board and I told the two sergeants that I had a secret weapon in the bomb bay. The bomb bay doors were not to be opened, the airship pressure watch would be on board ship, and they were to be the only ones allowed on board. I told them that one of them was to be on watch and the other one could sleep, and they could rotate as they saw fit until I came on board and relieved them.

The next day, we took off again to continue our search, but unfortunately, we were unable to locate the enemy submarine.

About five years later, I reported in to ZP-1 at Weeksville, N.C., as exec of the squadron. A day or two later, Lieutenant Morelander, now at Weeksville, told me that the night that he was command duty officer with the K-91 in the hangar at South Weymouth, he decided to go on board to see what was so hush-hush on that ship. As he was climbing up the stem ladder, after a step or two, the Marine sergeant says, "Halt!"

He says he told the sergeant that he was the command duty officer and he continued his climb up the ladder. The sergeant ordered him to halt again. He repeated that he was the command duty officer. Just as his head got on the level with the deck of the airship, the sergeant slammed a shell into the chamber of his .45 and says, "Halt!"

He says he turned loose and slid down the ladder. By then, the homing torpedo was still a confidential weapon, but didn't require the extreme security that we previously had to employ, so he knew what it was that he had missed.

Another special flight that I thoroughly enjoyed and was fortunate enough to get to take in both '44 and '45 was the Army-Navy football game at Philadelphia. Believe it or not, taking a K ship in and over the giant stadium filled with most of the high brass of the armed forces was a tremendous thrill. I took a K ship, flew from Lakehurst to Philadelphia, a distance of approximately 50 miles, and took a position at approximately 500 feet altitude, almost directly over the 50 yard line, or as near to it as I could keep it positioned.

Remember everything was radio and there was no worry about having an airship directly over the playing field. It was most interesting to watch in the third dimension a football play develop and be executed. The radio announcer would excitedly describe each play to his radio listeners and would be blasting away with his description well after the play had been completed. In fact, sometimes he had to stop in order to start describing the next play.

I certainly enjoyed piloting the airship on these flights and can't to this day figure why the other pilots ran like the devil from these special assignments.

For memory's sake, those weather buffs may recall a terrible hurricane in October 1945. It hit the air station at Richmond, Florida, dead center. It blew down all the hangars, destroyed 25 airships, over 100 airplanes, and 300 automobiles. Of course the commanding officer of Richmond was blamed, however, the court of inquiry declared that he was not guilty because the Bureau of Yards and Docks, the builder of the hangars, had certified the hangars safe to 125 knots wind velocity. The only trouble is that as the wind blew over the cigar-shaped hangars, the ventura (Bernoulli's effect) of the moving wind created a lift that lifted the hangar tops up and away. The hangars, full of airplanes and automobiles, quickly ignited, and there was one howling inferno.

The only casualty was the fire chief, who happened to step outside at the wrong time, and a flying two by ten moving end ways knocked his head off.

A couple of days after this catastrophe, one of Jack Nahagian's airships was on night patrol in the Florida straits. Nells Grills, the pilot, looked toward the moon and saw the silhouette of a surface submarine. Although it was contrary to orders, like any good blimp pilot, he went wide open to attack the submarine.

As he went in, flying at 50 feet with his one machine gun sweeping the decks of the surfaced submarine, the sub was pouring the bullets from 12 machine guns and a 4.1 right into the oncoming airship. Neils flew directly across the sub, released his four depth charges, and saw two of them fall on one side of the submarine and two of them on the other side, but there was no explosion.

The next morning the admiral came charging into my office and said, "Get down to Richmond. Find out what the hell's goin' on. Take my plane and my pilot and shove off immediately."

Away I went. And as I came over Richmond, as we circled for our landing, there before me was the utter devastation left by the hurricane. On debarking from the plane, Captain Nahagian said, "Dub, I want something done about those bombs. And don't tell me it was the crew's fault."

Jack and I had been students together and knew each other well. I says, "Jack, it'll be easy to decide. If the arming wires are still on the bomb rack, they armed the bombs before dropping them. And if they're not there, they failed to arm them."

He says, "We'll know soon because they've located the ship, which incidentally slowly fell to the water about an hour after the submarine had filled it full of bullet holes. All hands went into the water and only one was lost to shark attack.

Well, you guessed it. There wasn't any arming wire on the bomb rack. And I was very unpopular for stating the obvious. The crew was at fault.

A day or two later, I got on an Eastern airline at Miami, ready to proceed to New York. I had a wartime "priority three" that had permitted me to kick off other passengers, but a bit before take-off, somebody with a priority two kicked me off.

I went over to Miami Beach to spend the night, ready to fly on a plane taking off the next morning at 9 a.m. During the night, the plane that I was bumped from crashed near Cape Hatteras, N.C., leaving no survivors. With that bit of news, I put my airline ticket in my pocket, went over and got on a train and spent the next two days and nights going to New York.

On arrival at Lakehurst, I told the admiral, a survivor of the Shenandoah crash, what I had done. He just nodded his head, listened to and accepted my report of why we missed killing the sub in the Florida straits.

28

Visits Home

Along about this time I made lieutenant commander. At the ripe old age of almost 25, I pinned on my additional half stripe. Man, was I proud of that uniform with two and a half stripes! The Navy decided to send out requests for those reserve officers among us who would like to apply for commission in the regular Navy. Thanks to a pr etty good record, and the admiral's recommendation, in due time I received notification that I had been accepted.

Shortly thereafter I went back to Kenton on leave. When I told Uncle Maurice that I had joined the regular Navy, he seemed to be terribly unhappy. He told me that he had always planned for me to come back and run his businesses.

I told him, "Uncle Maurice, Malc has been here and knows the business. rAnd in addition, you have two sons that are grown and will soon be taking over the running of the company."

The four Ashe brothers: from left, Farris, A.J., Malcolm and Dub, on a visit home looking sharp.

He told me that he didn't know of anybody that could do as good a job as he knew that I could, and he wished that I would reconsider making a career of the armed forces.

I told him that if I had come back, he and I would've been into it half the time. Because if I had the job of running the business, that I would do it, and I wouldn't let him interfere with how I did it.

And he says, "I know that. And really, that's what I need."

After all that he had done for me, I surely felt badly not to come work for him. But I knew I was right, that Carmen and Junior should be in line for running the business.

It's appropriate to mention some of the good times I had while on leave visiting Kenton and Memphis. For instance, this time it so happened that Harold Lloyd was back home. And A.J. hadn't gone back into the Navy.

We all decided to spend the weekend picnicking and fishing near the cat hole on Obion River. We seined the bait, rounded up the hooks, collected enough food to last a month, and shoved off to camp and fish on a Friday afternoon.

A.J. had his Navy hammock tied up real short. I took a hammock, and stretched it out real long. Carmen took a blanket, Malcolm took a blanket, and Harold Lloyd had a blanket. We practically melted in the hot afternoon sun trudging from our cars to the river, during which time Carmen spilt a can of bait fish. A.J. still laughs as he remembers Carmen trying to pick 'em up in the grass.

Harold Lloyd and Malc took a boat and set out the trot lines. I took two rods and reels, threw the hooks over in the li'l ole creek 'bout 6 inches deep. Wham! Caught two large mouth bass in quick succession. As it got dark, we built a big fire alongside the blown ditch [they had dynamited it to let the water run fast], and began to cook such goodies as pork and beans.

Harold Lloyd was dippin' the beans from a pot into pans that each one of us held. Only, the pan that Malc had was one of Aunt Ollie's holey ones. As the hot juice poured down on Malc the expression changed from "What's happening?" to "Oh, NO!"

We ate, told stories, frolicked, had a most wonderful time. By then it was so dark you couldn't see your hand before you, and we were trying to make our way to our previously planned sleeping quarters. Harold and Malc had no trouble. They each had a blanket, and judiciously decided to put one blanket on the ground and had the other one to spread over them in case they needed it.

Little did we know, as the night grew longer, it turned cold.

A.J. had his hammock all set. I thought I had mine stretched out between two trees, rigged so it wouldn't make my back bend. The only trouble, I got into the hammock, lyin' there lookin' at the stars, and that hammock turned me upside down and I hit the ground.

While I was tryin' to figure out how to stay in that thing, two hoot owls began to carry on a conversation. I heard Carmen in the dark say, "Dub, you mind if I come over there where you are?"

I told him, "Naw, come on."

He had a blanket. We felt around in the dark and I took down that hammock, and put it on the ground. We both got on it, and used his blanket to put over us. We probably slept like babies—for five or ten minutes all night.

The next morning at first light we were a sad bunch. But Malc and Harold got in the boat to pull in the fish that we'd caught. I went over and pulled in a couple o' bass. We looked the situation over as to where we were sitting last night, and Malc almost passed out when he saw that when he was monkeying around sitting on a log in the dark, that if he'd moved backwards one inch he'd have somersaulted right back into the river.

We got the bacon and the eggs goin'. We began to plan on improving the sleeping arrangements when a little ole boy about five years old appeared and said his mother wanted to borrow some salt. After some questioning, we figured out the boy was the son of one of Malc and Harold's Macedonia classmates that had married when she was 'bout 14. She apparently had been living in a little lean-to there on the river for some months since her husband left her and her three kids to go look for work. The gal and the kids had been surviving on fish that they caught and water that they drank from the river, and of course she needed some salt.

We held a little conference, took all the food over to the young girl and her kids. We packed up and went back to the home place at Macedonia.

This little camping expedition was my first, last, and only one because this chicken has got more to do than spend the night on a piece of canvas snunched up to Carmen, tryin' to keep warm.

I came home often, and always remember how wonderful it was that Uncle Will Smith [Aunt Lilly's husband] and Uncle Maurice and Uncle Gregory always took the time to come visit, usually at Mom's, while I was on leave.

Uncle Maurice and Uncle Will especially liked to hunt, and Obion Bottom was a pretty good place to hunt duck. It would just plain ruin the whole day if Uncle Maurice found that somebody had shot more duck than he had. And of course, it used to do my heart good to beat him.

I recall once, on a blustery December day, huntin' ducks along the Obion. I decided to take my shotgun, and walk out on a log that extended over the river. Well, you guessed it, frost on the log. Had on hip boots.

Frost melted. Feet scooted off the log, and I went into the river, holdin' on to my shotgun. I disappeared into the water, come up, and Uncle Maurice helped pull me out. Uncle Will went over and set fire to a brush pile, had me remove my clothes, we wrung out the clothes, the wind blowin' nine hundred and twelve miles an hour, temperature well below freezin'.

I poured the water out of my boots and wrung out the socks. And I sloooowwwwly turned as I stood downwind from the brush pile while we tried to dry my clothes a little bit. But I soon found that to be a losin' proposition. I put on my clothes, jogged to my car, and turned up the heat. When my uncles arrived, we went down to Mom's and let her baby me for a while.

Uncle Gregory and Aunt Heddy would learn from Mom that Evaline and myself were coming home. They'd get in that Model 1930 car, drive over to the Mississippi, get on the ferry, come across and come up to Mom's to visit for a week. I recall when Uncle Gregory bought him a new car—a 1934 model. And he didn't know how to drive it. Scared Aunt Heddy to death!

As was the usual thing, we all were ready to shove off to Aunt Lilly's when Aunt Heddy eased outside and asked me if she could ride with Evaline while I tried to teach Gregory how to drive that car.

"Oh, yes," I said.

I soon found myself in the car with Uncle Gregory, but nobody but me.

We headed down the road and we came to the end of the levee, willows towering all over the place, and we couldn't see a thing. Uncle Gregory didn't as much as slow down. He come a-sweeping out on the levee, headin' up the road. We got up to Aunt Lilly's. He came into the driveway without hittin' the brake or slowin' down, came around Aunt Lily's house, and plopped into one of her peach trees. Fortunately, that killed the motor.

Aunt Lily says, "Gregory Johnson, haven't you got enough sense not to run over my peach tree?"

I took him out to the car, gave him an hour-long lecture on the use of the brake, the need of changin' gears, and other little niceties like occasionally tryin' to stop. I wonder to this day how he drove all the way from Arkansas without killin' himself, and apparently nobody else. I told poor Mom that I knew she had a sore knee, but for her to walk before she got in the car with Uncle Gregory.

Uncle Gregory had over $100,000 in cash, and he truly wanted his grandson, David, to go to college. He was so afraid that if he let David have the money to go to school, that he'd wind up being no count. And he listed a few examples in which this had occurred. And then he would always come back and point out what a rip-roarin' success that I had been, and I'd gone to school without money.

My eloquence was sadly deficient as I tried to get him to send David to school.

Earl Bryant, bless his heart, always gave me a job if he had anything to do. Well, when I was about 14, he had a patch of early roastin' ear corn, and he decided that his son, Roland, and his nephew, Buford, and ol' Dub would go pick a load of corn, and take it to Union City to sell it.

On arrival at Union City with Roland drivin' the car and Buford on one side of the street and me on the other, we began our house-to-house movement, giving the sales pitch that it was fresh corn pulled that mornin' and we were sellin' a dozen ears of corn, throwin' in one free to make it 13, for 25 cents.

Aside from a few interruptions like dogs tryin' to tear your legs off, the women were all about the same in that they would take a look at the corn, have you bring it in, they'd look it over and pick out 13 good ears, and pay you.

My surprise came when one of the houses had a door open, and there stood a young lady in a short-short negligee. There were no females over in our neck of the woods, so I had my mouth open, my tongue draggin' the ground as I looked up on this half-nude 23- or 24-year-old.

I gave her my pitch. She took an ear of corn in hand, and in so doing, the negligee fell off her shoulder. Of course, she didn't have any sign of a brassiere, and didn't pay the slightest bit of attention to the fact that I was lookin' her over the best I could.

She says, "Bring the sack on into the kitchen."

She took it and, one ear at a time, she pulled the shuck back, and took the ones that she selected out onto the table. That negligee didn't have any buttons, and it wouldn't stay on either shoulder, so most of the time, I not only had a chance to look at her boobs, but was also aware that she didn't have any panties on either.

She got her 13 ears, went back into another room, brought me my quarter, and stood there grinnin' at me while I stumbled out and back to the car. When I told ol' Buford and Roland, ol' Buford tol' me, "Get back in there. She was goin' to trade you out of the corn."

Whether she was or not, it was quite a day, seein' my first nude woman.

29

Evaline Conceives Walter

Once Evaline and myself moved into a little town called Beachwood, New Jersey. Most of the people went to the local post office to get mail. Evaline and myself had a beautiful white and buff collie dog, highly trained and very intelligent, named King. He required only that we show him the boundary of the yard when we moved into a new place. That done, without a leash, he would stay in his own yard.

Each day a Newark detective's wife would come by our house, headin' to the post office with their prize pit bulldog on a leash, tryin' to get loose to attack King. With never a budge from his yard, King would watch this dog as he came and went.

One day, as I sat on my front step, this monstrous dog jerked his leash out of the hand of the policeman's wife and bounded for King. King barely had a chance to turn when the dog sank his fangs into his neck in the bulldog death-grip. It scared King to death, but it didn't hurt him because the bulldog's mouth was full of the hair of King's massive ruff.

As he tried to twist, occasionally he could free his nose for a second, and the fangs that stick way out in a collie dog's mouth would slash the bulldog's face. Each slash went deep, but one took the bulldog's eyeball out. In seconds, the lady arrived and grabbed ahold of the leash. As she pulled, ol' King took the other eyeball out. She pulled him away and I commanded King to sit, and he growled. He didn't care for sittin'.

She headed for home on the run. In minutes, at high speed, down the road came the policeman's car, heading out of town.

Late that afternoon, who but the policeman appeared on my front lawn. He announced that it was going to take over $1,000 for the vet's fee, and he was goin' to sue me for $25,000 for that so-called prize bulldog.

I said, "Mister, my dog was in his own yard, stayed there, and was attacked by yours. And I am not going to pay you a cent."

He says, "You better get you a damn good lawyer, because I'll file suit immediately."

I said, "I'm on Admiral Rosendahl's staff at Lakehurst. He has two lawyers on his staff. One of them is A.J. Bernstein, Jr., from the Bernstein banking house." I said, "The other one's named Shumaker. He's from Philadelphia. And his dad heads up the legal firm." I said, "Those lawyers themselves and the dozens that they can call on haven't got a thing to do except handle this case, and it won't cost me a dime. If you want to waste your money suing me, be my guest. And if you get any more overgrown poodles that come smashing into my yard, recognize that I might be able to receive them the next time. Now mister, our conversation is finished."

It was, except for, maybe two days later, he careened into my yard in an attempt to run over King. He went on to the post office, and when he came back, I was standin' in the middle of the street, essentially forcing him to stop.

I said, "You maliciously attempted to hit my dog with your car." He says, "I don't like that word 'malicious.'"

I had my .45 in my back pocket. I patted it, and he could see what it was. I said, "The Navy has given me a medal to signify to everyone that I'm an expert in the use of this gun. Now," I said, "I'm from the hills of Tennessee, and that should signify to you that I don't mind usin' it."

Now, I never saw him after that.

For a considerable length of time we had wondered why Evaline hadn't become pregnant. Uncle Maurice decided to have a little heart-to-heart talk with Evaline, the tune of which was that it was about time we started a family. But we had never used any birth control, and Evaline explained to Uncle Maurice that so far neither she nor the doctors had been able to accomplish anything. But when we got back to Lakehurst, she was all charged up for starting again.

The doctors took me down for the sperm count to confirm that I had billions and billions of them. Then Evaline drug my butt off to be interviewed by her gynecologist. He asked me all kinds of stuff, including a question of how often we had sex. I told him two or three times a night. "Well," he says, "good God Almighty! That's too often! You're not likely to ever have pregnancy with that frequency."

I said, "Doctor, you know something. You're full of shit. You don't have the slightest idea of what you're talking about."

I asked the senior flight surgeon to get Evaline a gynecologist that knew a little something, and he came up with a conclusion that her vaginal tract was too acid, and killing the sperm. He prescribed some special douche powders, and she was pregnant within a few weeks.

King was protective of Evaline, and could back it up.

30

Post-Graduate School

About the same time that this bit of news arrived, Admiral Rosendahl got his orders to retire from the Navy. The admiral came down to my office and told me that I'd stuck with him through thick and thin and he wanted to help me to go wherever I wanted in the Navy. I told him I wanted to go to engineering graduate school, but that I couldn't because I had insufficient mathematics.

Walt Jr. arrived while I was in class at M.I.T. My classes included phys ed at noontime.

"Well," he says, "we'll just get a waiver on that."

I applied for post-graduate school in ordinance engineering. I was immediately selected for meteorological engineering, but the admiral called Washington to reiterate that I wanted ordinance engineering.

Shortly thereafter, July 1946, I received orders to proceed to naval post-graduate school in Annapolis, Maryland, for a three-year graduate study in aviation ordinance engineering.

On arrival in Annapolis, we moved into a himaja hut, which is half of a quanset hut. Now this wasn't so bad. We had two little cubby-holes called bedrooms, another little cubby-hole for our living room and dining room, and a spot, about as big as a table, for a kitchen. There was no bath, but we had a shower, and best of all, this place, fully furnished with heat and light thrown in, was for $30 a month. It didn't matter because all I did was study, study, study.

We were taking 27 hours, a whole year of the Naval Academy, in six weeks. It wasn't review for me. I hadn't had the math, the aeronautical engineering, or courses on the strength of materials, general dynamics, electricity, or electronics. I wished that I had never heard of the place. Yet I was doing my darnedest to pass.

About this time, A.J. began to receive what became 18 offers for scholarships for graduate schools from most of the top universities in the United States. I wrote Jake that if I passed, I'd get to go to M.l.T. and if l flunked, I would be sent to management school at Perdue University.

Old Jake waited a while to find out if I passed before deciding to go to his top choice, Cornell University. Otherwise, he planned to join me at Perdue.

Shortly after that, I was transferred to the postgraduate school as a student in ordinance engineering. Evaline had reached the point where daily walks were necessary, and we proceeded to follow the Doctor's orders after I got to the PG school. We had a routine where we walked up behind the homaja huts that we lived in at Annapolis. Time moved along, until one fair morning in November of '46, Eveline calmly announced that her water had broken. Far from calm, I got her into the car and headed for the Naval hospital. There after a short examination, her attending physician told me that it would probably be sometime that night when she delivered the baby.

I went back home, got ready and went to school. I had regular classes, including a phys ed class at noontime, following which I went by the hospital to see Eveline. Well lo and behold, Walt Jr. had already been born and Eveline almost put me to sleep kissing me with the ether that she still had on her breath. Now Walt Jr. had the world's biggest stomachache. He cried with the colic, from his birthday for about two months. One day, Evaline took a long delayed shopping trip and while she was away, I fed Walt Jr. a formula that the doc had prescribed. Well guess what. He went over, went to sleep, didn't hear a sound out of him for a couple of hours. Needless to say, we were off breast-feeding and onto the formula after that.

But my, my, my, this arriving at the postgraduate school had its toll. First off, the year at PG school was to have been a review, but for me it was acquainting myself with a lot of new engineering subjects for the first time. I won't belabor the subject again, except to say that we were taking 27 semester hours with a schedule that in 48 weeks covered four years of engineering school curriculum. This included college algebra, trig and differential calculus in the first 12 weeks, followed by the second 12 weeks of integral calculus and differential equations. Simultaneous with this, we also took first year direct current (DC) electricity for the first 12 weeks, and the second 12 weeks, we took alternating (AC) currents, while taking such side issues as dynamics, strength of material, chemistry, and vibrational analysis.

In fact, for the year at PG school I didn't know whether I was coming of going. Our social life was nil. Except on one occasion to celebrate the opening of the Severn River Officer's Club. The PG school turned out for the reception. Needless to say, the 12 aspiring scholars in our aviation ordinance school (the designation of which had recently been changed to the Navy's missile guidance school) attended the festivities. Likewise it is needless to say that we had 12 stinko drunk Navy aviators.

I hazily recall, as we were sitting on the porch of the club, it rained cats and dogs. With thunder and lighting. Half a dozen of us just sat there in our white uniforms and got soaking wet. One officer, not in our group, come a-heading up off of the porch looking for the restroom. He walked out through mud created by the new construction and suddenly he stepped off of the precipice and disappeared. We got up wondering what had happened to him, in time to see him crawling up the hill on his hands and knees in the muddiest, wettest white uniform you ever saw.

At the PG school, one doc Church was head of the math dept. Very early he reviewed my record and decided the PG school would be wastin' its time and my time to try to teach the course with my insufficient math background. The director of the PG school, Captain Singleton, had me and Dr. Church in for an interview, in which Dr. Church told him that it would be impossible to expect me to go ahead with this limited math background.

Captain Singleton says, "Doctor Church, our job is to train the ones that the Navy sends for the PG school. And for whatever reason the Navy has decided to send Mr. Ashe to school, and we'll keep him here as long as he can keep up with his grades."

We muddled through PG school. And by the time the 48 weeks were over, the 12 students had been reduced to eight. We graduated from the year at PG school at Annapolis, and the Navy sent us on eight weeks of field trips. In a sense, we were like a bunch of wild Indians let off of a reservation as we left the PG school. One incident I'm reminded of, on a trip to Chincoteague, Va., to the naval ordinance test station there, one afternoon some of us went fishing. Caught a bunch of fish.

While we fished, some of the others arranged for the use of a classmate's house for us to fry the fish. Armed with sufficient beer to float a battleship, we appeared at this officer's quarters. While some fried fish and others took care of the hush puppies, we went over the fence to the Captain of the Station's quarters and picked his tomatoes. We attempted to clean up the kitchen, needless to say, but we learned later that the classmate's wife came home and found her house smelling of fish. And found one tiny, weeny fish behind the stove.

One of our field trips was for two weeks at the naval proving grounds, Dahlgren, Va. There I was assigned as the test officer on some 50-caliber machine guns, to fire them to destruction with the air conditioner moving the temperature from the 100 degrees that were normal for Dahlgren in August down to 40 degrees in the cold room. After a few times up and down in the temperature, I made my report, which was incidentally well received. I also came down with the world's worst sinus infection.

How I was able to pass is something I don't know, but by the time I got to M.I.T., I sure wished I had flunked. My classmates at Annapolis were: one commander, one lieutenant, and nine lieutenant commanders. They were fighter pilots, dive bomber pilots, and torpedo plane jockeys. There were three Navy Crosses, six D.F.C.'s [Distinguished Flying Cross], nine Air Medals, and several Commendation Medals. The Navy soon decided that we were to become the first Navy guided missile post-graduate engineers. And since we were needed so badly, we were to leave Annapolis after one year and go to M.I.T. for two years.

Nine of the 12 passed at Annapolis.

M.I.T. called foul and pointed out that the deal required two years at the Naval Post-graduate school in Annapolis before going on to M.I.T. for a master's degree and, if selected, Ph.D. studies.

M.l.T. agreed to take us on probation. We must each individually make 3.5 or more on each subject. After our first semester at M.l.T., only three of the class, now reduced from 12 to 9, were able to pass the probation limits. M.I.T. asked the Navy to order the other six of us elsewhere. The Navy came up with a program for each of us that said we could go nine months to each of two Bureau of Ordinance facilities to finish our graduate work. I chose the Naval Gun Factory in Washington, D.C., and the Naval Ordinance Test Station, Chincoteague, Va.

We left Naval Post-graduate School with orders to go to the Bureau of Ordinance for two weeks, Naval Proving Grounds, Dahlgren for two weeks, Naval Ordinance Test Station at Chincoteague for two weeks, and to report to M.l.T. in Cambridge, Massachusetts, Sept. 19, 1947.

Everybody went their way and did their thing, but we managed to meet up at somebody's house each weekend to make up for all the parties we'd missed back at graduate school.

31

M.I.T.

Evaline and myself, with all of our earthly belongings packed into our Chevy, arrived in Cambridge, parked the car on the street for the night and checked into the hotel. The next morning, no car, no belongings. And what a mess, trying to get the five borough police forces to look for my car. In about a week they found it, over on the coast, with no tires, no radio, and the trunk prized open.

The big challenge in the Boston area was to find a decent place to live that one could afford.

I put an ad in the paper that stated, "Lieutenant Commander, wife and son desire a place to live while students at M.I.T.," and suggested that I didn't want to pay more than $150 a month. The next day my ad was answered and I made an appointment to go look at the apartment.

Because the owners seemed to like us, we lived in a mansion on Guadaloupe's Point with the ocean on three sides, while I was a student at M.I.T., 29 miles away.

I went to an address at Swamsquett Point, Massachussetts. I drove up a private drive to a mansion on Guadeloupe's Point. I visited at length with the lady that had called me. She finally asked would I like to see her home. Of course I did. But I was really interested in seeing this place that I was hoping to rent.

She gave me a tour of her house. What a mansion!! What a gorgeous place! What a large place!! I finally told her that her place was lovely, but I really needed to look at the rental property because I was in rather a hurry.

"Oh," she says, "this is it." She and her husband were going to be in Europe for a couple of years and were going to let me live there while they were gone. He was the owner of the Beau Brummell tie company.

I said, "Ma'am, $150 a month wouldn't even pay for the depreciation on the flowers that you have in this place."

She says, "If you like it, we would like for you to live in our home."

I won't expend the pages describing this gorgeous place, except to say that it was professionally decorated with deep carpets throughout, the most modern and complete utilities, every room a masterpiece. The living room alone was 40 x 40.

We moved into this place and put everything we owned in a utility room in part of what was the garage. The ocean was on three sides. The view was gorgeous. Among other things, there were curved windows in the corner of the living room. There were ebony statuettes in the dining room that formally seated 12 people at a large glass dining table.

Then, whoops, school started. It was 29 miles to M.I.T. Before long, it was snowing. As a matter of fact, in addition to a lot of small snows, we had 12 snows each more than 12 inches deep. If it hadn't been for our next-door neighbor that had purchased a new blowing snow removal machine, I would never have gotten through that private drive.

Down at M.I.T., a catastrophe was unfolding. Although I did well on vibrational analysis, electrical currents and electronics, no matter how hard I studied, I couldn't learn enough about servo-electricity to work the problems fast enough. On top of that, M.I.T., out of the kindness of their heart, decided to improve my math background by enrolling me in a class in advanced calculus. I wasn't even ready for beginning calculus. Down at Post-Graduate school we had had calculus and differential equations, and so forth, but anyhow ...

Comes the end of the semester, I had flunked that calculus. And as the Navy ordered me away, I went by to pay my respects to the professor. Only I was wearing a uniform. He blushed, for he certainly didn't know I was a lieutenant commander in the Navy, said he was sorry and wished me well.

I mention this because three years later, I was back in the Bureau of Ordinance on the admiral's staff where I went charging up to the office of an admiral that headed research. The admiral says, "Hey, Walt, I'm sure you know these fellas. They're professors from M.I.T. They're down here requesting the second digital computer."

He says, "This is Dr. whatever, head of the math department, and this is Dr. Erickson, deputy in the electronics department."

I said, "Yes, admiral, I know them. I should've sent you a memo. I've decided to send the second digital computer to Dahlgren. And I should've informed you before now."

He turned to these two birds and he says, "Well, I guess we're wasting our time."

But I still had flunked.

One thing for sure, the professors at M.I.T. were the best of their line in the world. My vibrational analysis professor was none other than that famous Ben Hartog who was constantly doing consulting work on vibrational problems. While I was there, he used the students of the class as slave labor in an attempt to prevent the destruction of a bridge on the west coast that was swaying in the wind and finally fell down before his suggested corrective action could be implemented.

Another interesting feature of our studies was that M.I.T. had a Chinese student studying under Dr. Draper, the head of the electrical department. This student went back to Red China to head up the Chinese guided missile program and he successfully launched Chinese ballistic missiles shortly after the United States, with the help of the German scientist, Werner von Braun, got our missiles into the air.

At M.I.T. there was no football, no basketball. A double armload of books and bifocal lenses were the order of the day. When my number one son later wanted to go to M.I.T. as an undergraduate student, I not only said no, but hell no. I told him he could go there as a graduate student later if he wished, but not as an undergraduate.

M.I.T. did have a fine Olympic swimming pool. The only unusual thing about that pool was that everybody was required to swim in the nude.

They set aside five days a week for the males and a couple of days a week for the females. It wasn't long before I learned that you could stand on the stairwells in the third floor and have a bird's eye view of the swimming goin' on next door. Didn't have much time to look because I was always off to another class.

But back to M.I.T., the courses were just going faster than I could keep up. We were right on the state of the art on electricity, electronics, and vibrational analysis. But my real nemesis was advanced calculus. As the semester came to a screeching end, we were informed that five of the eight were on probation and MIT had asked the Navy to order us to other duties. A battle issued between MIT and the Navy. This time the Navy agreed to send the five of us to five different naval ordinance installations where we would be continued in PG school, but our instruction would be more practical. I chose the Naval gun factory for nine months and the naval ordinance test station Chincoteague for nine months.

It was while at one of the field trips to Dahlgren that I prevailed on Pete Peters and Pete Parlett to fly with them to Boston to get some flight time. We flew SNJs. This is a single-engine, twin-seated, stick-controlled aircraft that was used in training at the time. At Boston, we went in to have a snack and came out to get into this plane. I encountered the hottest inferno that you could imagine, coming over to strap myself into the plane.

Shortly after take-off, flying south, I decided to disconnect the seat belt and shoulder harness and remove the parachute and, while I was rolling in stupidity, I pulled the canopy back. I got cool and was about to buckle myself in when Parlett signaled going into a dive. Peters, who was flying wing on him, banked to the left and came into a dive onto Coney Island. We were at 10,000 feet when we rolled over into the dive. I was floating around in the rear seat on zero gravity, putting my arms and my legs out to keep from being sucked out into the air stream. I was successful in holding myself aboard until we came out of the dive over Coney Island, at which time my head was down where my feet belonged, my feet up in the air, and me hanging on for dear life!

I got myself straightened up, hooked on the parachute, hooked on the seat belt and shoulder harness, closed that canopy, and I assure you this little boy never has been in an SNJ with the canopy open again, let alone without being buckled in with the shoulder harness and seat belt. Ho hum for stupidity!

But a few days later, I prevailed on another student, Jim Ward, to take me to Lakehurst to get some flight time. He managed to get a torpedo plane for this cross-country. The torpedo plane was leaking oil and the oil had come back on the torpedo compartment where I was buckled in. I couldn't see a thing.

A very uncomfortable flight, watching my time and wondering where we were because a fog was coming in and visibility was dropping. I was suddenly jarred by Jim on the intercom, saying, "Walt, we got zero-zero (visibility) up here. Do you know where we might be?" I quickly pointed out to him that I couldn't see anything. He says that he was flying at 500 feet when every once in a while he could see something.

I made a quick calculation. I asked him if he had seen a bridge off to the left. He said he was flying over one now. I said, "That must be the Delaware River Bridge at Camden. Directly ahead you should see a racetrack." He said, "The racetrack's coming into view."

I said, "Change course to zero-nine-zero."

He reported that he was socked in. I told him to stay on the course zero-nine-zero for 30 minutes, and if he hadn't seen the ground, come down because we would be over the ocean. But if the visibility improved any we should see the Lakehurst hangars in about 20 minutes.

Much to my relief, he shortly reported the hangar coming in and out of the clouds. I told him, come around and land. Fact is, when we got on the ground, I was so frightened that after I got my bearings I told him that I'd stay up to get my flight time—he could just go on back, cause I was going to get another way to get back home.

32

The Gun Factory

In 1948, the first stop for my post-graduate studies was the Naval Gun Factory, Washington, D.C. The gun factory was a sprawling industrial complex inside Washington that had 20,000 employees and custom made practically anything and everything that the Navy needed and used. On arrival I was ushered in to the assistant superintendent's office, whereupon he asked me, "I guess you know what you're down here for."

I said, "No, not really." I assumed it was to go into aviation ordinance.

He says, "You don't make any assumptions in the Navy. Admiral Schoffield has sent you down here with a reputation for solving our cartridge case problem."

He then proceeded to tell me that the gun factory was scheduled to build 1,400 three-inch shells a day at $4.32 per shell. To date, they were building 600 a day at over $14.00 a shell. Well, it had come. I was totally shocked that Admiral Schoffield would have stated that I could solve the cartridge shell problem, for in fact I had never had any production experience in my life.

After a bit more of welcoming me aboard took place, I was told that I was relieved of all other duties until I got the cartridge case plant on schedule at the correct price.

I went out of his office, found the production offices, found a girl that was one of the secretaries and asked her, "How do I get to the cartridge case shop?"

She says, "Simple. I'll call the chauffeur and the sedan will take you down there."

Needless to say, I became thoroughly acquainted with the sedan and the chauffeur for my travels around the gun factory.

I got out of the sedan, approached the cartridge case plant, and heard three distinct whistles. I later learned that this was warning the people in the plant that there was a three-striper approaching (but actually I was a two-and-a-half striper).

I went into the cartridge case plant, introduced myself to the civilian head of the plant. Told him I had been assigned responsibilities for getting the cartridge case shop on schedule and within the price provisions. He didn't seem to be particularly well-pleased to learn my assignment. But I went at the assignment with vigor. I took time and motion studies. I checked the flow of the material through the plant. Went from the process of where the brass came on the line, where it was rolled, cut, extruded, annealed.

At the end of the week I had concluded that the chief problem was an inadequate supply of brass coming from the brass foundry to the cartridge case plant. With this under my belt, I telephoned General Electric's chief executive officer, and made a deal with him. He was to supply me with two brass foundries on the basis that I would put it in the budget next year and the following year he'd get paid for it.

Needless to say, that action came back to haunt me at a later date. After a bit, General Electric rushed me two electric foundries and I installed them at the big steel foundry at the gun factory. I was ready to go on the line, seven days a week, 24-hour production. This information I passed on to Mr. Tucker, the plant manager. He and one quarterman (foreman) were to take the day shift, one quarterman was to take the midnight shift, and one quarterman to take the 8 to 12.

He looked me right straight in the eye and said he wasn't gonna go on three shifts a day, and if he did, he surely wasn't gonna put a quarterman on the night shifts. And that some young whippersnapper wasn't gonna come in there and tell him how to run his plant.

I said, "Mr. Tucker, this young whippersnapper is going to tell you exactly how to run your plant, and you will go on a seven-day shift, 24 hours a day. And you will comply immediately, or I'll relieve you as manager of the plant, and give you 30-day notice to show why you shouldn't be dismissed from civil service for failure to comply with an order."

Well, if I do boast a bit, within a month I was making 1,500 shells a day at $4.00 a shell. And being congratulated all over the place by the gun factory officers for my accomplishment.

Well, it was about this time that one of the officers there at the factory told me the next thing that I'd have to contend with would be the big gooseneck roller that rolled out brass sheets.

He said, "That gooseneck has been expected to break for a good 30 years, and if it breaks there's no way of fixing it."

I was going through a phase of my life in which my answer to anything was always to bet that I could do it. So I promptly said, "I bet I can fix it."

The research, learning to repair the gooseneck roller, took several days, but finally I found a book that showed me how to repair it, which I proudly presented to Commander Manning, and demanded my ice-cream cone, which was the extent of the bet.

The very next day I had the duty. This required being on call overnight, handling the messages and informing appropriate people if any particular emergency came up. But it also gave me an opportunity to go down and observe the cartridge case plant in operation on the night shift.

I drove up to the plant, heard the buzzer and moved inside. Down the line about 100 yards was Admiral Farion, superintendent of the gun factory, and Admiral Schoffield, chief of Bureau of Ordinance, and Mr. Tucker, the plant manager, all gathered around what, from my distance, I could see was the broken gooseneck.

I came up. Mind you, it's after hours. Lookin' like I'm really burnin' the night oil. I saluted the two admirals. Admiral Schoffield says, "Walt, Mr. Tucker says there's no way to repair this gooseneck. What do you suggest we do?"

All my two days of research came to mind and I says, "Oh, Admiral, we can repair it. I can have it back on the line within 15 to 18 hours." I said, "Mr. Tucker, get some people in to uncouple the gooseneck, bring a flatbed from over at the railroad track to lift the gooseneck up and deliver it over to the steel foundry. I'll call the manager of the steel foundry to tell him to put welders behind screens and for them to weld in 15-minute intervals until they get it welded. After it's welded it will take 12 hours for it to be annealed and we can bring it back on the line."

I heard Admiral Schoffield remark under his breath to Admiral Noble, "I told you he'd take care of this damn plant!"

The gun factory tour of duty was very pleasant, professionally and socially.

One of my duties after the cartridge case plant got on an even keel was to be in charge of the presidential yacht, the *Williamsburg*. Among other things, on an overhaul of the *Williamsburg* I wrote a work order to install gold-plated flush plumbing for the presidential commode. You can't imagine how dumfounded I was to learn that the president (Truman) was left-handed.

A quick re-work order had the plumbing installed for a man who was left-handed.

About this time, President Truman decided that he didn't have any use for the cabin cruiser *Katherine*, and he gave it to his daughter, Margaret, for her to use as she saw fit.

In a few weeks Margaret decided that she didn't care for it and gave it to us, the officers there in the gun factory, to schedule family excursions for those of us that were there.

Navy football games are played at Baltimore because Annapolis's stadium is too small. So it became routine for us at the gun factory to set up a special bus from the gun factory to the stadium in Baltimore. Likewise it became routine for the President's daughter, 25-year-old Margaret, and her friends to avail themselves of the use of this special bus.

Our Saturday trips evolved into quite a social hour, with people bringing different drinks to try out on the trip to Baltimore. One given Saturday I brought a jug of stingers, and with the jostling and juggling of the bus, showing Margaret how you drink from a jug back in the hills of Tennessee, she got soaked with the stingers with about as much going on her clothes as there was going inside.

But, we arrived in Baltimore, none the worse for the wear, except slightly stinko.

We went into the stadium, were seated in our reserved seats, and ready for the game to start. In due course, the national anthem was called and everybody stood with his left

Dub chats with Margaret Truman, left, daughter of the president.

hand over his right heart during the playing of the anthem. It just so happened that two knuckleheads just forward and below our position continued to gab with no indication of standing at attention, all during the playing of the anthem.

With the help of my stingers I inquired of these two birds, didn't they have sense enough to stand at attention while the national anthem was played? One of these jugheads inquired as to what it was to me? He was wearing a felt hat. I reached out with the full force of my weight, and pushed his head through the crown of that felt hat. And before you could say Scat!, there were three secret service men directly in front of Margaret, who was sitting right alongside me, and more coming.

Monday morning at the gun factory, the assistant superintendent opened the conference with, "There was a little horseplay at our Saturday football game. I want to caution you that we have distinguished guests, and we don't want any more horseplay."

I had some outstanding assignments while there. For one, I was officer in charge of the plant that built the Norden bomb sight. I also had occasion to go on the firing trials of a new automatic twin 50 that was being developed and produced at the gun factory.

33

We Learn to Drink

My nine months were quickly over, and I was off to Naval Ordinance Test Station, Chincoteague, Va.

Both Evaline and myself grew up as teetotalers, and really, we hadn't had the occasion to drink hard liquor. But once we went down to visit her brother Lark while he was at school at Annapolis. After a discussion of the subject, we decided that we should find out what it was like to get drunk.

Lark emptied his liquor cabinet of all the partially filled bottles and we sat down, we being Evaline, Mary, Lark and myself, to decide that we would, with malice aforethought, proceed to get polluted.

Lark would pour the contents of a few bottles into a glass and the four of us would proceed to drink it. After a few empty bottles were on our coffee table, I decided that everything that happened was the funniest thing that had ever happened, and all I could do was just laugh.

Lark, on the other hand, with a serious look on his face, would take the glass, rear back, and say, "For the good of science! For the good of science."

Evaline quickly decided that she was going to go on a crying jag, and Mary, bless her soul, was trying to help Evaline. She put Evaline on the bed, ran water in the bathtub, took a towel, put it in the water, and came out with the towel pouring water. Then she went over and smashed it down on Evaline's face, saying," Maybe that'll make her feel better."

Needless to say, that tickled me even more.

This went on well into the night until we all, in various forms, went to bed and went to sleep. The next morning, Evaline was feeling pretty good. Well into her crying jag she had vomited her drinks. I felt terrible. I casually picked up a magazine, opened it, and the first thing that I saw was a picture of some Four Roses bourbon whiskey, and I almost lost my socks.

The four of us never became much in the way of drinkers, but we knew what one experienced when they said they had a hangover.

Next stop on my ordinance training program was the Naval Ordinance Test Station, Chincoteague, Va. I arrived at Chincoteague the day after New Year's, 1949. I was exceptionally well received by the captain, who informed that he was looking forward to my assisting him in spit and polish. Also pointed out that he believed that the Officer's Club had someone picking up cash on the side. He asked me to make a point of spending some time in the evenings at the Officer's Club, to see what I could do about establishing the guilty party on our suspected rake-off.

This I did, keeping mental count of how many bottles were emptied, how much activity there was in the slot machines, and how much beer was being consumed. I then compared these statistics the next morning on the reported consumption at the club that was daily presented to the supply officer. After a bit it became apparent that more bottles were being emptied than reported. Additionally it seemed that there was underreporting of the slot machine take.

With a little training and more attention to detail, I soon confirmed that almost daily one or more bottles were emptied at the club than was reported through to the supply officer. By this time the supply officer had, of necessity, been rung in on the attempt to confirm that there was under-reporting and to determine the identity of the guilty party.

After about a month of meandering around the Officer's Club each evening, and probably establishing the reputation of being a sot, I reported to the captain that there was no question that the Officer's Club manager, a civilian, was raking off the club.

The captain set up a conference with the club manager and staked me out in the adjoining room. The club manager was calmly accused of taking funds from the club and we even estimated the amount of the take. Of course, the club manager, in a huff, began to deny all of these charges, until the captain called me in. He took one look at me, immediately pleaded guilty, stated how much he had fraudulently obtained, and agreed to pay it back. The captain fired him on the premise that he wouldn't press charges if the funds were returned.

Chincoteague was an active test station with planes of different sorts and pilots performing various tests each and every day. Since I was a non-pilot, I soon took the position of test coordinator. We were firing missiles from Wallops Island before NASA ever started their tests. It was fun, and very taxing duty, to schedule the various tests and have them run one after the other without interference.

Then, too, at Chincoteague, the captain of the station, Captain George Frasier, used the commanding officer's boat to go fishing. Frequently we would shove off early in the afternoon, head off-shore to a wreck, and pull in literally dozens of spot and trout.

I soon became aware that one of the reasons the captain took me along was so Mrs. Frasier wouldn't chew him out with me there, but she certainly later became outspoken in that she didn't want any more fish around that place.

Likewise at Chincoteague, the spring brought bay fishing. I soon learned to catch my own polliwogs by the use of a rat trap filled with bread. With these polliwogs on the hook, the procedure was: let the boat drift slowly until the fish commenced to strike, and throw over the anchor. Literally we used to catch flounder as big as door mats, and frequently we would take a G.I. can more than half full as we returned to the station.

Chincoteague was home of the oysters. I participated only in that I delivered gallons of oysters to the air station to be picked up by flights from Washington for various VIPs.

When some of our early tests at Chincoteague were ready, we notified people up and down the coast that we were about to fire a missile. When it would ignite, it would go like an unattended balloon in all directions. Each time we fired one of these early missiles we were safely in the blockhouse before we pulled the trigger.

34

Weeksville

All good things have to come to an end, and shortly I got orders to ZP-1 at the Naval Air Station, Weeksville, N.C. After three years in PG (post-graduate) school, I was glad to be rotating back to airship duty. On arrival at Weeksville, Evaline and myself had extreme difficulty locating quarters. We finally settled on a house that had the bathroom, commode and all, in the living room. Fortunately, we didn't live there but a couple of months. Then we got ordered to quarters on the station. These quarters were converted barracks and the number of rooms and size of your apartment was determined by rank.

The commanding officer of squadron one was a Lieutenant Commander Hosmer. He commanded the most slip-shod, non-regulation group of pilots that I ever had the experience of serving with. Right off the bat I tried to put the squadron on a basis of Navy regulations. I noted that daily the men put down chips and swept the hangar deck. I walked around, inspecting the area, wondering why it was necessary to sweep it every morning. I found that the three night-check crew maintenance chiefs sat in chairs, drank coffee, chewed chewing tobacco, and spit on the deck. I called these chiefs to task. I told them I wasn't going to have any more of this. That they could chew all the tobacco they wanted to as long as they swallowed the juice.

Can you imagine my shock when, that afternoon, I was called into the captain's office to be confronted with three maintenance night-check crew chiefs. The captain told me, "These

Those who may have thought my boyish good looks didn't match my rank learned better.

are the best maintenance chiefs in all the airship organization, and if they want to spit on the deck, they can do so. And if you don't like it, you can put your hat out on deck, and they'll spit in your hat."

I couldn't believe my ears. But I did know something that I didn't think he knew. That was that within a couple of weeks he was going to be relieved. There was nothing that I could do except have my belly churn at the insult.

Two weeks later Commander Herbert Graves relieved as commanding officer. A day later I called in the three maintenance chiefs. I said, "Well, chiefs, you went to the captain over my head. In my opinion, the captain was totally wrong in the way he handled the chewing tobacco situation. I've inquired a bit, and found that for the last ten years you men have moved from one squadron to the other, always together, always in night-check crew, and always spitting chewing tobacco on the hangar deck. I want to first let you know that that situation is now over. I'm going to have you transferred to three separate locations, each one as far from the other as I can manage. And you'll be outside the airship organization. You can listen in to the phone while I call the detailer and BuPers [Bureau of Personnel.]"

I called the detailer and told him I had these three chiefs. I wanted one of them to be sent to the Philippines, another to be sent to Iceland, and another to be sent to Italy. And as far as it was my concern, we didn't need them back in the airship organization.

Years later, at our first lighter-than-air reunion, Chief Tucker brought these three chiefs around, laughingly says, "Commander, I bet you don't know who these people are." I said, "I bet I do. They're the three tobacco-chewing chiefs from Weeksville."

Back at Weeksville I had known that they referred to me as the Boy Commander. Tucker asked the chiefs, "What did you learn from this little episode?" One said, "To never mess with the Boy Commander."

At Weeksville I proceeded to check out as command pilot and flew rather frequently as I proceeded up the grade. Because of a shortage of qualified command pilots, I put myself in one of the airship combat crews. The big thing that we had to do those days was checking out with airships on aircraft carrier landings. Preparations were made and finally the day arrived when ZP-1, 2, and 3 were to land on an aircraft carrier.

I took the first landing. The procedure called for each pilot to make three landings and three take-offs to qualify for carrier operations. After my first landing I proceeded with the second and the third. Then I got off the airship to report to the bridge of the aircraft carrier while the remaining ships were going through qualifications.

Needless to say, if the weather got slightly rough, airship-carrier landings were, to put it mildly, hazardous. I stayed on the bridge of the aircraft carrier *Mindora* as the afternoon wore on into evening and the weather got progressively rougher. At one time, I left the bridge to go back on the carrier deck to confer with the landing officer, Gene Lane, to tell him it looked like we were going to have to get ready to use the ax more frequently, as the blimps were pulled from side to side.

Just as I was halfway down, on the port side, the airship broke loose, and the pilot gunned it, coming up the catwalk with the propellers in the catwalk. Along with two overweight chief petty officers I jumped into an indentation in the catwalk, brought about by it being the firewall. I got there late and scrunched as far in as possible. The propeller of the airship cut the little half-belt in the back of my uniform. I wore that uniform without repair from then on.

As the night wore on, airships began to be damaged. One of them, commanded by Lieutenant Fahey, was sent to Lakehurst, and one of them, by Lieutenant Commander Norm Skoria, went to NAF Weeksville.

I asked for, and got, destroyer escort for the ship heading for Lakehurst because he was on one engine, the prop on the other one being bent, so it was difficult for him to even make headway. Needless to say, he had difficulty landing at Lakehurst.

I remained on the carrier overnight and experienced a very strange set of circumstances. The carrier was going to have night carrier qualifications.

At dinner you could hear a pin drop. These aviators were quiet as they contemplated the dangers of the night carrier landing. Still quiet, they manned their planes at about 8:00 p.m. and proceeded to do some of the most hazardous-looking landings and take-offs that I had ever seen. And I've always stated that if an aviation cadet could start his training watching night carrier quals, there would be a lot fewer aviators.

Amazingly enough, the pilots all gathered into the wardroom after the carrier quals were finished. The conversation was a bedlam. Each pilot, with his hands explaining to the other pilot, "Did you see me do thus-and-such?" Of course, it's a well-known fact that aviators can't talk without using their hands.

Back at Weeksville, the wing commander had decided to form his staff, made up of key officers from squadron 1. The operations officer became the wing chief of staff, two communications officers became the wing communications officers, and so it went. But we, in ZP-1, were having to compete with the other squadrons without key personnel, including the captain, because the captain had additional duties as wing commander. So I felt well-mistreated in that I was acting captain without my key officers and having to compete with the other two squadrons.

About this time we had a hurricane evacuation alert. Squadron 2 and ZX-11 squadron from Glenco had been moved into Weeksville, and for a couple of days we hourly discussed what our actions should be. One day, out of the blue, the wing commander asked me what I would do with the airships. I told him I would locate the hurricane and fly away from it. He says, "Do it." He says, "ZP-1 will be acting wing commander and we'll fly the ships wherever he sees fit."

I took off from Weeksville, heading southeast with nine airships, with instructions that I would fly until I located the hurricane, and then I would turn right, directly away from it. That I would locate the hurricane by locating the point where at 60 knots the airship had a 90 degree drift. I knew that this would be very close to the center of the hurricane.

As we proceeded southeast, about midnight some pilot from ZP-2 that I later learned was Lieutenant Gordon Burke, spoke over the intercom stating, "Mr. Wing Commander, my tired old eyes believe I see 90 degrees."

I says, "You do? Then come to course 235 degrees. We're heading for Glenco (Georgia)."

On arrival in Glenco a ground fog covered the lower 200 feet of the atmosphere. I decided to land. I came around and did so, but it was absolutely zero-zero visibility. I ordered the airships to remain aloft until the fog cleared. One enterprising pilot says, "You've landed now and you're not the wing commander any more, and I'm going to land my airship.

The voice I recognized as that of Lieutenant Levitt. I stated, "Mr. Levitt, I strongly recommend against it." He proceeded to land, went into the trees, damaged his aircraft. When he got on the ground, he called up to the other ships, telling them to remain in the air, and this the rest of the squadron did.

One day in October the wing commander came in and said, "I'm sending you to Key West to keep 'em from crackin' up the airships."

It just so happened that Lieutenant Commander Wiggins on a hur-evac (hurricane evacuation) out of Key West had gotten lost and cracked up an airship just short of Glenco, Ga. Amazingly enough, in a 200-acre field, there wasn't but one stump in the whole field, and Wiggins hit it dead center. (More about this later.)

I learned later the real reason for my transfer was that Lieutenant Commander Louis Strum from the class of '40 was being ordered into ZP-1. Strum outranked me. That would have retrograded me back to operations officer, and I guess the wing commander didn't want that to happen to me.

With bells a-jinging I arrived in Key West in November. Now I like Key West as a place to live, and as a place to operate airships. But it hit me with a wham to find that I was going to be the maintenance officer.

Captain Doug Cordner welcomed me on arrival and told me that I was the new maintenance officer. With Howard Smollen as Executive Officer (XO), and Buck Newsome as operations, my natural seniority meant I was maintenance officer.

I'd never been the maintenance officer, and didn't know too much about it. And I welcomed the news four or five months later that Buck Newsome was being transferred to Lakehurst. I fleeted up to operations officer where I felt quite at home and quite capable of running the squadron.

My first order of business was to establish seven combat crews and I promulgated immediately that on any flight, especially a hurricane evacuation, the designated airship crew would fly as a crew in its own particularly assigned airship. I had learned that when Wiggins crashed he was flying a make-up crew of volunteers that, for one reason or another, wanted to go to Glenco.

Throughout the rest of the year there were no more hurricanes, but in the spring of the following year the frequency of hurricanes more than made up for the lull. It seemed that every few weeks we were off on a hurricane evacuation.

I recount my memories of one such evacuation. After anxiously watching the reported movements of the on-coming hurricane, it was decided that we would fly out to Glenco. Quickly, take-off preparations were completed and ZX-ll's seven airships were en route. The weather was bad. As is always the case when you're caught on the downwind leg of a hurricane, the air is rough, the wind is strong, and the weather is bad.

About time my flight reached Lake Okochobee, we were contacted by FAA and directed to take altitudes 500 feet apart starting at 2,000 feet. I immediately came back to my flight stating, "This is the flight commander. Do not carry out those orders. FAA, the weather conditions are too rough for airships to operate at those altitudes."

FAA said, "Comply immediately. We have 50 airplanes flying VFR to destinations in north Florida."

I told my flight, "Continue to ignore those orders. Three airships (I called them by name and number) take the west coast of Florida. Two airships take central Florida, and two airships the east coast of Florida. All airships take altitude, maintain 100 feet apart, with maximum altitude 500 feet.

I then told FAA that they didn't control us at 500 feet and below. We proceeded on to Glenco without further difficulties. Landed, made preparations for take-off for further north, but on checking the situation, decided to hold, and two days later flew back to Key West.

This was the night, early morning in fact, that Valentine opened the bar at Glenco. And I was having iced tea when somebody slipped me an iced tea glass full of Drambuie. I swallowed a big swig of the Drambuie, thinking it was iced tea, and literally lost my breath.

The tour of duty at Key West was especially good for me in that we had continuous photographic missions covering ordinance tests from various ships and submarines in the Key West harbor. Among our missions were dropping the Mark-24 and Mark-34 torpedoes. I recall one day as I was about to take off, Captain Cordner came out and said he would take the ship. Normally I would have been quite concerned, but Captain Cordner was an outstanding pilot.

We flew out to the mission area, dropped our torpedoes and returned to base. Captain Cordner says to me, "You ever do any flat-hattin'?"

And I says, "Quite a bit, Cap'n."

He says, "You fly the coast with the rudder and I'll maintain altitude above the trees."

Needless to say, we had a wonderful afternoon flat-hattin' the beaches of Key West.

A tour of Key West can't be described without discussing fishing. It so happened that Gordon Burke was stationed at Key West the same time I was. Our schedule included fishing three times a week from the bridges and one or two times a week from the squadron fishing boat.

We purchased a partnership seine, literally pulled it apart more than once, each of us demanding that we follow that particular person with the seine. We also found a place to buy live shrimp, three dozen for $1. And we established the famous betting routine, Ashe, Burke, and Eckert, $1 for the first fish, $1 for the biggest fish, and $1 for the most fish.

We had the pleasure of catching from 28 to 38 fish for each of us per day. We gave the fish to everybody, and kept for ourselves three fish to skin and grill on the electric stove at home. The fish couldn't be too big, nor too little, Walter would eat about half of a side of his fish, Evaline would eat three-quarters of her fish, I'd eat both sides of mine, and we'd daily throw the rest away. How we kept from becoming thoroughly saturated with fish, I don't know.

Along about this time another hurricane evacuation came up. In an orderly fashion, we took off with the seven airships heading for Glenco. On arriving at Glenco, I told the ZX-11 officer in charge at Glenco to keep me informed about the movement of the hurricane because I was going to the BOQ to get some sleep.

He said, "Well, just a minute. We've got a problem. I have this letter from the commanding officer of ZX-11 that says I am the one, and the only one, to determine ZX-11 hurricane evacuation. And here's another letter from the admiral down at Jacksonville that delegates the hurricane evacuations of airships at Glenco to the commanding officer of the air station." And he says, "And here's a letter from the commander of the fleet air detachment that says that he and only he will determine time and destination of airships at Glenco."

Just at this time, the watch officer says, "Mr. Reagan, captain of ZP-2 wants to see you and Mr. Ashe in aerology right away."

We went to aerology, I still with my flight suit on. We went walking in and Captain Kline of ZP-2 was bawlin' out one of his pilots and turned to me and says, "And I'm not gonna have any trouble out of you, either!"

He says he had flight plans for each of the ZX-11 airships, one to go to Knoxville, one to go to Huntsville, two to go to Weeksville, and three to go to Akron. The flight plan was made out and he would tell us when to take off.

I said, "You can't land an M ship at Huntsville in this kind of weather."

He says, "I told you I wasn't gonna have any trouble out of you."

I went on back to the hangar and I told Mr. Reagan, "Keep me informed on the weather, and I will still determine when ZX-11 airships evacuate Glenco."

He says, "I'm sorry, Walt. I can't let you do that. I have this letter which directs that I have the responsibility for it."

I went up to the BOQ, tried to get a little sleep, couldn't, went down to breakfast, went back up to try to sleep, and still couldn't. I was racking my mind as to how I was going to get out of flying the airships to Huntsville and Knoxville. Finally, after lunch, I decided that what I would do is take the flight plan that commander fleet air detachment had prepared and

I would take off to the designation that he had listed, and I would change my flight plan in air and go direct to Key West.

I called Mr. Reagan's office for a sedan. I arrived in the hangar and said, "Larry, who's your command duty officer? I hate to put you and him in the position that I'm going to put you in, but I intend to take off now, so if you would ask Mr. Levitt to come in, I'd appreciate it."

Well, Levitt happened to come in at that time.

I said, "Ben, send the carry-all, pick up my crews, send a truck to get chow." I said, "I'm going to take off for Key West."

He says, "Walt, when I saw you come in the hangar, I knew you'd do that. I've already sent for the crews and I already have the chow on the way down."

Mr. Reagan says, "Walt, I can't let you do it."

I said, "I'm doing it anyway. Mr. Levitt, I hate to put you in this position for ground-handling."

He says to Mr. Reagan, "Mr. Reagan, Walt's the operations officer of the squadron, and I believe that letter from the captain was meant for people outside the squadron."

Then he said, "Walt, I'll take you off."

Shortly thereafter we had seven ZX-11 airships circling the air station at Glenco. I thought it was the nice thing to do to let Captain Kline know that I decided to not comply with his instructions. Knowing where he lived at the beach, I flew over and dived on his house and pulled away toward Key West. I was highly mortified to look and see my other six airships did the same thing.

Captain Cordner at Key West was contacted by Captain Kline, who notified him that he was pressing court-martial charges against me for failure to comply with his dispersal. But that threat was nipped in the bud when Captain Cordner told him, "If he had of complied with your orders, I'd have court-martialed him."

35

We Have Susan

When Walter was two years old, Evaline took him to the doctor for a checkup. Walter was used to having his way and was somewhat difficult for the doctor. The doctor disgustingly stated to Evaline, "What this kid needs is a brother or sister!"

Evaline says, "I wish you would tell me how!"

His tone immediately changed, and he gave Evaline the name of a gynecologist at Duke, and Evaline made an appointment and went over to visit him. Well, needless to say, in such things the first thing is to check and see if all's well with the male. So the next thing I know, I find myself up at Portsmouth, getting a sperm count.

You can't imagine my exasperation when I walked into this lab and the nurse pointed to the bathroom, said, "Give me a specimen."

Between being embarrassed, disgusted, and just plain sore, with three or four nurses outside the door, I proceeded to get a specimen. She handed the specimen to the doctor, and his only comments were, "No problem here-billions of 'em."

Again, by a combination of various douches, in the course of a few months Evaline was pregnant with Susan.

About this time, December 1951 rolled around, and Evaline and the pediatrician decided that our expected baby should be born and Evaline make it home before Christmas. With this little bit of information, they plotted that Susan would be born on the 19th of December, making certain that Christmas would be spent at home.

On the appointed day I took off in the morning, took Evaline and Walter by the hospital, dropped off Evaline, proceeded up the Keys for Walter and myself to do a little fishing. About three hours later we came back and checked in at the hospital and found we'd had a little girl about an hour before.

Walter had already been promised that he could name a sister after one of his friends, a little girl named Susan Shorter. The only thing left was to wait the prescribed four days, and I picked up Evaline and our new daughter Susan, and brought them home.

Susan's first few months were fraught with problems that were soon alleviated by a special kind of evaporated milk for her diet. Even so, Roy Perriman and his wife, Edna, visited us in April, and Edna reported back to my mother that Susan hadn't been able to gain any weight and didn't look like she had a chance of making it.

Evaline looks on as Walt Jr. holds the sister he named Susan at Key West, Florida.

It goes without saying that Evaline's mother, Mrs. Paseur, rushed down to the Keys to make sure that her new granddaughter was well cared for. I must note that, while they were visiting us, I took Mr. and Mrs. Paseur fishing on the squadron boat. Deep sea fishing was a new experience for both of them, but it changed into a fiasco when Mrs. Paseur wore herself out hauling in large barracuda, and Mr. Paseur couldn't even get a strike. I was using mullet for bait, made certain that both had identical-looking baits on their line, but come what may, Mr. Paseur, standing four feet from Mrs. Paseur, didn't catch a one and Mrs. Paseur caught six big ones.

Needless to say, she didn't let that old man forget that fishin' trip the rest of his life!

Late in April we were transferred to the Bureau of Ordinance in Washington, D.C. We reported in, found us a house in Annandale, moved in, and were ready for duty except that a check-up indicated that Susan apparently had tuberculosis of the lymph nodes.

Inquiries at the Naval Hospital, Bethesda, located a drug, nicotinic acid, that was needed for treatment. The drug was controlled by the hospital, but required private purchases for its use on dependents. We quickly moved again from Annandale to Bethesda so we could be near the hospital during the period of treatment. As quickly as it could be arranged, Susan was scheduled for surgery to remove the infected lymph node.

On the day of operation the surgeon demanded proof of a live bacillus before he would operate. They took Susan back up to the ward and began running tests to locate a live bacillus. During this time of this unsuccessful search, the surgeons decided that Susan had a badly infected lymph node and began to treat it by injections of penicillin directly into the infected node.

With this treatment, in a few days we brought Susan home, and I have always been in favor of the Navy's medical checks and balances between general practitioners and the surgeons.

By this time Susan was a year old and hell on wheels. She was into everything, and if she couldn't reach it, she climbed for it, including going to the top shelves in the kitchen to locate the sugar that Evaline had tried to keep away from her.

With all these moves under our belt, it seemed rather strange, but factual, that we bought a house in Annandale and moved back there.

Now, my tour down at the Bureau of Ordinance had started with a bang, with my being assigned to aviation research and given the job of supervising the contract to develop a 60-caliber machine gun. For some reason I was dissatisfied with aviation ordinance research and asked to be transferred to missile production.

While digesting the emphatic "no" to my request to be transferred, I was asked to report to Captain Robinson in anti-submarine plans. The interview was short and quick and I was told to report to planning the next day. In the Bureau of Ordinance, planning was a staff position and had more horsepower than research. But Captain Robinson's reputation throughout the Bureau was that of a hard-driving, strict disciplinarian.

So, amid pats on the back for sympathy, I was transferred to anti-submarine planning. But reporting to Captain Robinson I quickly learned that he was one of the finest gentlemen I ever worked for. I found him to be a dear friend and a highly qualified teacher.

My duties consisted of maintaining purchase plans for all anti-submarine aviation ordinance, submarine and destroyer fire control, all torpedoes and mines, as well as atomic depth charges. Captain Robinson gave me one bit of advice and that was, "When you write a letter, say what you mean so the recipient will know what you mean. You have too many letters to write for you to write any the second time, so don't worry about your split infinitives and other descriptive language."

He says, "The other thing is, when we need some information we need it for the admiral, and we must have it immediately, even if it ruffles some of the feathers of the other branches of the Bureau."

Armed to the teeth with these directives, I moved from place to place in the Bureau. After a bit of familiarization, I learned where to go to get the necessary information quickly.

Once I was sitting at my desk and received a phone call from a Captain Suddith on the staff of Admiral Burke, who was chairman of the joint staffs. Captain Suddith told me that he had checked and found that Admiral Schoffield was in New York, Admiral Parsons was in Chicago, and Captain

Robinson was in Spain. Admiral Burke wanted me in his office immediately. I said, "Yes, sir!"

I caught a taxi to the Pentagon and appeared at the Chairman of the Joint Chief s conference room. Two Marine sergeants stood outside the door with fixed bayonets. One asked me what he could do for me. I said, "Tell Captain Suddith that Commander Walter Ashe is here."

This he did, and I was ushered into the Chairman of the Joint Staff's conference room. Here were the Chief of Staffs and assistants of the Army, Navy, Air Force, and Marines, along with Admiral Burke's staff and numerous civilians.

Admiral Burke said, "State your name and code."

I said, "I'm Walter Dee Ashe, PLA-1, Bu-Ord."

He says, "Is there anyone here that can confirm the identity of this officer?"

Captain Suddith stepped forth and says, "I can, Admiral. I meet with Commander Ashe rather frequently in the Bureau of Ordinances."

He says, "State your security clearances." I says, "Top secret, crypto."

He again repeated the question, "Anyone here who can confirm the security clearance of this officer?"

Captain Suddith again stated that, "Yes," that he exchanged comments and letters in the Bureau with these security clearances with Commander Ashe.

He says, "Do you have any other security clearances?"

I says, "Yes, sir. I'm Q cleared." [Q clearance referred to atomic weapons production.]

He repeated the questions with Captain Suddith, and Suddith again confirmed that he discussed and reviewed Q clearance matters in the Bureau with Commander Ashe.

The Admiral then said that things had reached a point in Taiwan where it was necessary to take covert action to prevent an invasion by the Chinese Army. He said that at present more than 100,000 Chinese troops were massed across the Formosa

Straits, and they were expected shortly to be ready to invade Formosa.

He says, "I want the Bureau of Ordinance to design, prototype, test and develop anti-junk mines to be installed along the coast of Formosa."

He says, "I want this done in 120 days."

I said, "Aye-aye, sir," knowing full well that it couldn't be done.

I came back to Bu-Ord, called RE-7, the mine warfare people in the bureau, and asked for a design engineer named Dick Plank to report to my office.

I related the admiral's instructions and asked him, "When can I have a design for an appropriate mine?"

He says, as he unfolded some papers, "I thought that that was what you'd want. Here is my latest design."

With this, I called the admiral in command of the Naval Ordinance Lab, White Oaks, Maryland, and told him that I was sending an engineer to White Oaks right then, and that I wanted within three days a mine design. I gave him a number and told him I'd follow him with a letter authorizing the expenditure of the funds.

I then called Yorktown, Va., and talked with the admiral in command of Mine Warfare, Yorktown, and told him he would be getting a new test vehicle in three days. I wanted prototypes built and tested.

So it went. I called research in the Bureau of Ordinance and told Captain Eli Rich that he would be at Key West 60 days hence, on a floating lab, to test the mines.

He says, "And where will you be?"

I said, "I'll be in an airship directly above you, witnessing the tests. On the basis of what we witness, we'll put the mines into production."

So it went. The next morning I was in the admiral's office, telling his secretary, Jean Childes, that I gotta see the admiral the minute he comes in, no matter about his appointment schedule.

Admiral Schoffield came in. I related in detail Admiral Burke's comments and what I had done. And I shook my head and said, "Admiral, we can't do it in 120 days."

Admiral Schoffield says, "Walt, Admiral Burke was just bulk-heading the Air Force. Remember, he used to do this before you and I ever did, and he knows we can't do it in 120 days. I'm supposed to see him tonight at a cocktail party. I'll tell him what the situation is, and what you've done. You've laid out a good program here."

36

Sharing Equipment

Amid my primary duties, and I had many, early in '52 I was assigned a responsibility under the Military Assistance and Development Program (IMDAP).

The powers that be had prevailed upon Congress, and in order to assist the defense of various nations Congress had agreed to appropriate funds replacing with new equipment any equipment that the Defense Dept. found that they could spare for the various nations.

The Secretary of Defense directed the Pentagon to take care of the Navy requirements. Incidentally, by quick letter, Admiral Schoffield was directed the responsibility.

At a meeting called shortly thereafter, Admiral Schoffield directed Captain Robinson to perform this responsibility. As we left the admiral's office, I delayed to go into the head. On arrival in the captain's office I found him dictating a letter to his secretary directing that I take all ImDap responsibilities. Mainly on account of I didn't have anybody to delegate to, I was stuck with the job.

The way it worked is, naval attachés from each of the world's capitals sent letters to the Pentagon requesting certain equipment, ranging from out and out naval ordinance and guns to shipboard fire control. Of course, the Pentagon could countermand any order promulgated, and in one instance did reverse my directive.

I formed a committee of several senior officers in the Bureau and we reviewed these naval attaché requests to determine if the Navy could spare the items requested. I just couldn't see giving material to France with Mr. De Gaulle's attitude. I couldn't see a justification for the Arab nations when at the same time we were supplying Israel. Fact is, the recipients under my regime were Britain, Canada, and Australia, along with an occasional approval to Italy and Spain.

Egypt was in the forefront of requesting various supplies, and I just couldn't see my way clear to approve weapons or weapon systems for transfer to Egypt. After several such requests were turned down, a good friend, Captain Norm Scuria, who then was the naval attaché to Egypt, appeared in our office one morning and presented himself to Captain Robinson. He asked in what way was he failing to substantiate and justify Egypt's need for the weapons.

Captain Robinson said, "Captain Scuria, Commander Ashe has full control of that program and I suggest you discuss your requests with him."

Captain Scuria turned around and says, "Well, hi, Dub! I didn't know you were here in the Bureau."

I said, "C'mon, Norm. Let's go have a cup of coffee."

Over coffee I told him that there were not justifications enough to cause me to make available arms for Egypt.

He says, "Dub, I know your position regarding Egypt and Israel, but I want to tell you, you're dead wrong."

I said, "Norm, I didn't ask for this job, and I wish I didn't have it. But as long as I do, Egypt and Syria and Jordan are not going to have anything available for them."

I might add that of the hundreds of requests that were approved the only denial that was overridden was a request by France for three 105 fire control systems. I knew an ol' boy that had worked with me in the Gun Factory's Norden bomb site production. By then he commanded the warehouse facilities in Norfolk where the 105 system was stowed. I reached him on the phone, and explained the situation. I suggested that the little ball that made up the computer system be removed from the fire control system. I don't know how many years it took the French to get the thing to work.

In my final days in the Bureau of Ordinance I was urgently engaged in making a decision about which aerial torpedo would be best suited for blimps and airplanes. It had narrowed down to a General Electric Mark 43-0 and another manufacturer's Mark 43-1. As part of expediting this program I sat down with a delegation of officers from Britain, Canada, and Australia and reached an agreement with them. I would supply the torpedoes and, paralleling the testing in our ranges, would let them perform the tests on their ranges if they, in turn, would supply the test data back to me.

Although this was highly classified, there was a leak of some sort that resulted in a claim in the *Washington Post* that the U.S. Navy was supplying foreign governments with new, secret torpedoes before they were made available to our forces.

This dissertation, covering a couple of columns in the *Washington Post*, came out on a Sunday. Monday morning, at about 9:00 the British captain, a Canadian commander, and an Australian commander came into my office. The British captain shook hands with me and says, "I say now, old boy. It was a good try."

I said, "What do you mean, 'good try" captain?"

He unfolded the newspaper. Pentagon Public Relations had stated that this would be looked into and, rest assured, stopped. I said, "Captain, I intend to go ahead with our agreement."

He says, "How can you, with this newspaper article?"

Captain Robinson leaned forward and says, "Commander Ashe makes an agreement with you, he'll carry out the agreement. Doesn't make a good goddamn what the *Washington Post* or the Pentagon has to say."

Along about this time I wrote a letter that had far-reaching effects on my career. It seems that one Vice Admiral Perry had decided to require all airship pilots to take heavier than air training. One notable exception would be that four-stripers would be allowed to go to surface ships.

I thought then, and I think now, that that was another one of Admiral Perry's asinine decisions. At any rate, I wrote a letter from me via the chief of the Bureau of Ordinance, stating in four paragraphs that we didn't need any heavier-than-air pilots, that they were being released to inactive duty, and that commanders who did take the training would never have an opportunity to gain sufficient proficiency to be useful in the aviation program, and that I strongly recommended cancellation of the program.

I was advised by Captain Robinson not to send that letter, and I guess it was a mistake to have done so.

Due to some tests that were expected to go on at Key West, I was ordered back to ZX-11, where I became the executive officer. As is always the case, getting adequate housing in Key West was quite a job. The skipper's wife, Ann Cruise, knew and ran around with a crowd at the Casa Marina Hotel. One couple among them was actress Rita Hayworth and Dick Ames. Ann Cruise arranged for us to move into Rita Hayworth's cottage while we looked for a house.

Commander Cruise, the commanding officer of ZX-11, had fleeted up from exec to C.O., and I had relieved him as executive officer. It was easy to fall back into the routine of fishing three times a week because Commander Burke and Commander Eckert had reported in for their second tour about the same time that I had.

It didn't take long under Captain Cruise to get the squadron back on an even keel. Our duties consisted primarily of photographic coverage.

One day with a K ship in flight, photographing the experimental hedgehogs that were forward-firing depth charges from destroyers, several submarines were submerged out in the operating area, carrying on exercises with their ship counterparts. Such was the case with the airship and the destroyer *Sarsfield*.

As the day wore along, there was an equipment malfunction on the *Sarsfield* requiring delay in the program. During this delay, I had an ensign on board that I was instructing in antisubmarine warfare. We simulated making runs on submarines until, lo and behold, we got MAD (magnetic anomaly detection) contact on a submerged unidentified object. I looked around and noted that we were several miles from the sub that was working with the *Sarsfield*.

I went into action, sounded general quarters on the airship, relieved Ensign Wharton, took the airship down to about 20 feet, and commenced tracking this submerged object. I was getting positive MAD contacts, dropping the smoke floats, coming around in a tight circle. I called the *Sarsfield* to confirm that she still had contact with her target submarine. Then I called the submarine base stating that I had an unidentified contact, and requested that all of our submarines be surfaced.

Shortly, you could see the submarines out in the operating area popping up in various spots, but none in the vicinity of the sub that I was tracking. I then called airplanes in the area to come over and assist working the contact, and notified the *Sarsfield*, which turned and at maximum speed approached our position.

I flicked through the confidential instructions that required an unidentified target in the operating area to be challenged, and notified Washington, stating, "Unidentified submerged contact. What are your instructions?"

All I got from Washington was, "Received your message."

The *Sarsfield* sent me a message stating that he would relieve me as scene of action commander. I asked him, "Do you have contact?"

He said, "No."

I said, "I'll retain scene of action command."

By this time, the submerged unidentified target was approaching the submarine sanctuary. (If anything entered submarine sanctuary it was supposed to be sunk.) I again sent off to Washington a message that said, "Unidentified target five miles from submarine sanctuary. If he enters sanctuary, I will bomb him."

I noted that the target commenced to speed up and turn slowly to port.

I believe this was due to the *Sarsfield* approaching at top speed. The next contact indicated that the target was swinging back to the south and picking up speed, at which time I lost contact.

On arrival back at Key West, Boca Chica, there was a captain of VX-1 and an anti-submarine MAD officer. They came stomping aboard the airship to confirm that my contacts were honest to God MAD. Other than a few letters that were exchanged, this unidentified target was forgotten. I still don't know what I had. I think I had a very high-speed submarine. I don't think it was ours. I think it was a Russian contact.

37

The NAN Ship Exercise

The NAN ship was new, bigger and better, but in a pinch we used an older K-ship to save the day for airship anti-submarine warfare, for a time at least.

As part of ComOpDef 4, my unit, ZX-11 participated in the operational development forces anti-submarine warfare programs. The Nan ship, 1,000,000 cubic feet in volume, had arrived in Key West and had been equipped with some of our new, highly classified, anti-submarine detection gear. Plans were made for a large fleet exercise in which the air admirals were on the defensive because the submarine admirals claimed that the new Nautilus would sink the fleet.

ZX-11 was all prepared to take this new ship and equipment to Roosevelt Roads to compete in the exercises. The only thing, the day that it was planned for the NAN ship to fly to Roosevelt Roads, Puerto Rico, a NAN ship at Lakehurst split apart, and all NAN ships were grounded. I overheard Captain Cruise talking with ComOpDef 4's chief of staff, Captain

Steffan, passing on this information and stating that it looked like we wouldn't be able to participate. I went running into the captain's office and said, "Just a minute, Captain. If we have to, we can do it with a K ship."

He says, "Naw, the K ship would be overloaded with the equipment." I said, "Well, we can fly it overloaded."

Captain Cruise, still on the phone with Captain Steffan, said, "I'll have to call you back. My exec believes that we can do it."

Over the phone I could hear Captain Steffan say, "Who's your exec?" Captain Cruise says, "Commander Walter Ashe."

Captain Steffan says, "You mean ol' Dub Ashe? If he says he can do it, he can do it. He used to be one of my officers on the *Raleigh*."

We got one of the K ships and transferred the detection gear from the NAN ship to the K ship, and continued our preparations to take off that evening.

As night wore on, we kept waiting for the temperature to drop so that we could get the maximum lift from the airship. Just before dawn, I took off with Lieutenant Lewis and Lieutenant Commander Valentine as co-pilots. Using the long runway at Key West, and with engines wide open, I succeeded in lifting off a few feet from the end of the runway. It took 50 miles up the Keys to reach an altitude of 100 feet.

All day we flew into a strong headwind, reaching Guantanamo, Cuba, about 10:00 o'clock at night. There was a detachment of ZP-2 at Guantanamo. I asked them to inspect the ship for leaks and top it up with helium because I couldn't imagine why it was so heavy. In fact, I estimated that we were flying 6,000 lbs. heavy.

Their inspection uncovered approximately 800 lbs. of electronic spare parts that my electronics officer, Ed Verberg, had put on board up in the air tunnels.

I went on up to operations to file a flight plan to continue on to Roosevelt Roads. The operations duty officer wouldn't clear me because of extensive thunderstorm activity. I asked the wave duty officer to get the operations officer down to the flight office. He came down and established that we couldn't take off because of the bad weather, and stated that the commanding officer of the air station had closed the station to all air traffic.

I told the operations officer, "Well, I'll have to clear myself. I'm on a very important fleet exercise."

He says, "I recommend against it." And they made up another map showing thunderstorms all the way to Puerto Rico, with towering thunderheads reaching above 60,000 feet.

I cleared myself and took off about 6 in the morning. All went well at first, but by the time we reached the Tortuga Islands, headwinds were ranging from 55-65 mph. In fact, position report for 9 o'clock showed us at the western end of Tortuga Island, and the 10 o'clock report showed that we had advanced only 12 miles to the eastern end of the island. I was flying at 61 knots, keeping the altitude about 50 feet above the surface of the water.

By the time the 11 o'clock report was due, I had lost my trailing antenna and was unable to transmit Morse code. We could readily read messages that were being sent, but were unable to, in any way, send our position report. After a bit we read a message from ZX-11 stating, K-116 is overdue position report, presumed down at sea, request air-sea rescue assistance.

Fairwings Atlantic sent this message to ComAirLant (Commander, Air Operations, Atlantic Fleet), stating our last known position and we were presumed down at sea. ComAir Lant sent the message to Air Force air-sea rescue in Bermuda, stating the K-116 was overdue and presumed down at sea. After about a 30-minute delay, air-sea rescue Bermuda sent a message to ComAir Lant. It stated, "Weather extremely severe in area. Unable to comply air-sea rescue for 24 hours."

While these messages were flowing back and forth, we were plodding on our course, making a ground speed of 5 or 6 miles an hour. After a bit, the powerful low frequency station at Annapolis came through with a booming voice that stated, "This is Overseas Annapolis. Come in K-116."

They repeated this message for 15 minutes and then Oversea Panama came in with the same message repeating for 15 minutes, followed by Oversea Miami repeating the same procedure. Then they started over again.

I was helpless to—in any way—inform them that I was still airborne, and was actually picking up an extra knot or two of ground speed.

The storms were so vicious that, in addition to having difficulty maintaining altitude, it was so dark inside the airship that I had difficulty reading the charts. As night came on our ground speed began to pick up a little bit more, and by 11 o'clock that night we raised Ramey Air Force base on voice.

I told Ramey, "This is the King-116, unable to transmit. Please send message to Key West stating our position 30 miles north of Ramey, on course, ETA 4 a.m."

Ramey says, "King-116, you're supposed to be down at sea."

I says, "Well, as Mark Twain stated, the situation has been greatly exaggerated."

Shortly the message came back from Ramey saying, "The commanding general has never seen an airship. He requests that you fly over."

I come back, "Respects to the commanding general. Unable to comply his request. I am extremely low on fuel."

Back came the message, "The commanding general suggests it won't take but a few minutes to overfly Ramey."

I said again, "Respects to the commanding general. I may need that little bit of extra fuel."

We proceeded on to a point northeast of San Juan, where we flew out into a beautiful, moonlit night, with clear skies. What a relief after having flown 18 hours in terrible weather.

We came in and landed at Roosevelt Roads. All hands, including the wives, were out on the field to witness our landing. Lieutenant Ashford came on board and says, "Commander, you need a check. We'll perform the check to get you in the air as soon as we can."

I said, "Bob, I've been running the ship leaned out to the max for 20 hours. I think you can forego the check and take off immediately after you fuel."

Lieutenant Commander Majors was the officer in charge on deck and he drove me up to the BOQ a little while before daylight. He says, "The bar is closed. The only thing I have to drink is this bottle of Canadian Club, and I don't have anything to go with it."

I sat there and drank that fifth of Canadian Club, went up to my room to go to bed. I could smell bacon cooking, and instead I went down to breakfast. I got to rest that day while Bob flew the ship. Needless to say, our ship got off, contacted the Nautilus, reported position, and the air admirals were successful in "sinking" the Nautilus.

'The Devil's Triangle'

At 7 o'clock the next morning I took off for Key West, 1,100 miles to the west. It was a beautiful day, a bit windy, and a forecast of easterly winds to remain all day. We came around the point at San Juan and took our course heading westerly.

A routine flight developed. The cook told me to come on back and have steak and eggs for breakfast. After seating myself and getting ready to dig into the steak and eggs, Lieutenant Commander Valentine came running back saying, "Commander, our compasses are spinning!"

For those of us that had spent many hours flying in what was called The Devil's Triangle, the phrase "compasses are spinning" immediately put us on the alert. Forgetting my steak and eggs I charged forward, sounded general quarters, and told Lieutenant Lewis to take it down to 50 feet and hold the airship downwind.

Make no mistake about it, the compasses were spinning. The magnetic compass, mounted horizontally, was turning in unison with the gyroscopic compass that was mounted vertically. The spin was a slow circle that took about a half a minute to go 360 degrees.

On the loudspeaker I commanded all hands, "Check the CO_2 bottles and the life jackets. And check to be sure your knives are at ready."

I called the crew chief forward, told him to tie his arm to the life raft that was back aft, and instructed him, should we go into the water, to inflate that life raft and proceed to pick up the crew.

Lieutenant Commander Valentine suggested that we head back to San Juan. I suggested to him, "That's well and good, but which direction is it?"

The compasses continued to spin.

We had a discussion as to how long we could fly with the compasses spinning. I pointed out that we could fly as long as it was daylight, and that I could plot my positions by noting the color of the water. If by darkness we hadn't determined where we were, rest assured with the downwind, we could fly onto the coast of Mexico without a problem with fuel.

We sat and waited, minute after long minute for about a half hour before the compasses, without further ado, stopped their spinning and came back to their original course.

I could check this course by comparing it with the wind that had been steadily blowing the entire time.

After a discussion with the officers and crew I decided not to report this incident because it was a repetition of many other such reports that had come in from airplanes and surface ships. We also knew the crew likely would be detained and interrogated for a lengthy stay.

38

Assigned to the Tulare

About this time, I requested transfer to heavier-than-air training and received the shock of my life when I was informed that heavier-than-air training was denied. It so happened that all of the airship pilots had been going to heavier-than-air training. I went to the captain and said, "I need to fly to Washington to check on my dad-blame orders."

I got on a plane and went to Washington to BuPers to see if there was anything I could do to get orders issued, and it seemed that the office of one Vice Admiral Perry had decided, in view of my recommendations against the program, that I would not be permitted to go to heavier-than-air training. Vice Admiral Stroop, chief of BuWeaps, and Vice Admiral Flaherty, chief of BuPers, both attempted to get Admiral Perry to change his mind.

After the workings had run their course it was determined that I would rotate to sea for a tour of duty on surface ships. I learned that I was to be ordered to serve Force Atlantic as executive officer of a tanker plowing back and forth to the Mideast. With this information I again flew to Washington, went into the Command Detailer, a captain in BuPers, and told him that I didn't want to go as the exec of a tanker.

He gritted his teeth and looked across the desk at me and says, "You are a *prima donna*, and have always gotten your orders changed to suit you. But this time there will be no changes. You will go as the exec of the tanker."

I said, "Captain, request permission to see the Chief of BuPers."

He says, "Permission not granted. Understand? Not granted."

I got up, left his office, and headed straight to the Chief of BuPers office. On walking in, I saw that the chief had his door open, and two rear admirals were with him. Just outside his door were three other rear admirals waiting to see him. I went over to his receptionist and told her I didn't have an appointment, but I would like to wait in the chief's office in case he had a few minutes that I could see him.

She says, "What is your name, sir?"

I said, "Commander Walter D. Ashe."

It so happened that just at that instant the chief of BuPers had come to the door to apologize to the three rear admirals for keeping them delayed so long. When he heard my name, he recognized it from the discussion that had gone on about my heavier-than-air training.

He says, "What's your trouble, Walter?"

I said, "Admiral, your detailers want to send me as the exec of a tanker and I don't want to go."

He says, "Well, I don't blame ya."

He turned and introduced me to the two admirals that were in his office and said, "He's the lighter-than-air officer that Perry prohibited from going to flight training."

He says, "I agree with your letter, incidentally. What would you like to do?"

I said, "I'd like to take command of a destroyer but realize that it's been 13 years since I've been to sea, so what I would prefer to do is go to amphibious forces, qualify for command of a destroyer, and proceed with that command."

By this time he had reached his desk. He turned and pushed the button down to the captain that I had talked with previously, and says, "I have a Commander Walter Ashe in my office."

He paused, and says, "Where do you want to go?"

I says, "Pacific."

He says, "Long Beach or San Diego?"

I says, "San Diego."

He says, "I want him sent to the biggest ship in San Diego as the exec."

The detailer came back saying, "The biggest ship we have is the new aircraft carrier *Enterprise*."

The admiral said, "Obviously I didn't mean the aircraft carrier. Make that the biggest amphibious ship in San Diego."

He said, "I have a commander of class of '42 that's the exec of the biggest ship, the new *Tulare*."

Chief BuPers says, "Transfer him."

He then turned to me and said, "I'll guarantee you that when your sea duty tour is over you'll come back to aviation."

I began to gain a little confidence and said, "Admiral, that guarantee is no good."

He says, "Why so?"

I said, "Your tour will be up by the time that my sea duty tour is over."

He says, "I'll put it in writing."

He then wished me the best of luck and said I'd be getting orders as the exec of the *USS Tulare*. I took a circuitous route away from the detail offices as I left the bureau. I got what I wanted by just plain dumb luck!

39

On the Tulare

I went back to Key West and impatiently waited for the receipt of my orders. They came one Tuesday morning for me to be in Coronado, California, the following Monday for a course in amphibious warfare.

Walter was at school and Evaline was at the Officer's Club at a wives' bridge party. By the time I got word to her to go by and pick up Walter and to come home so we could pack that night, I had arranged for the supply department to come over and start packing.

The packing was completed Wednesday afternoon. I'd previously sold our house (before receiving the orders), and I packed our personal belongings in the car and we shoved off for Atlanta. It was a long, hard rush, but we made it into San Diego Sunday evening, and I was at class the next morning.

They had included in my orders a course of instruction at several places: sonar school, air defense school, ABC defense school, such that, by the time the courses were completed and I was ready to report to the *Tulare* I was very well equipped to assume my duties.

A few weeks before reporting aboard, I went by to meet the captain and pay a visit. Of course, he anxiously inquired as to what my background consisted of, and when I told him that I had been an airship pilot and hadn't been to sea for 13 years, the poor man looked as deflated as a blimp with a hole in it.

A few weeks later I reported aboard, just prior to an operations evaluation and inspection. The captain suggested that I delay relieving for the couple of days required for the inspection. This I was glad to do because everything was totally foreign to me.

The inspection went badly in that all departments of the ship were either poor or unsatisfactory except for the medical and supply departments. I certainly keenly observed every operation as it unfolded during the inspection. By the time two days had passed I had formed some pretty concrete decisions on some changes that I would make.

After I walked the former exec down to the quarter deck and said, "I relieve you, sir," my first stop was the ward room. I called the wardroom steward, a big fat black fellow, into the wardroom and told him that he was fired. "Report to the supply officer for other duties."

There was a tall, good-looking colored boy, James, a first class petty officer. I asked the wardroom steward on duty to have James report to the wardroom. I told James he was the new wardroom steward and what I wanted done in the wardroom to bring it up to my standards.

I told him the wardroom would buy new uniforms for the steward's mates, embroidered with *USS Tulare* above the pocket on one side and the wardroom steward's name above the pocket on the other side. The stewards would wear a complete freshly laundered uniform from the evening meal to the next evening meal. We wouldn't have any more curry in anything, and if I even smelled curry powders in the wardroom I'd bust him one rate. And I suggested he go make a search of the wardroom pantry and deep-six any curry powder he found aboard. I told him the wardroom would be quiet, and if I heard any horseplay among the stewards back in the pantry I would restrict all stewards on board. I said to him, "I expect you to maintain complete control of the steward's mates."

He says, "Commander, could I say something, sir?" I said, "Yes, go ahead."

He says, "Some of them fella's, you tell them to do something', and they don't do it."

I said, "James, you're the biggest fella on board, aren't you?" He says, "Yaaah, sir!"

I saw a few busted lips, but never anything serious.

My next move was to call an all-officers conference. I stated that the wardroom would be open from 7 to 8 for regular breakfast, 12 to 1 for lunch, and 6 to 7 for dinner. That for lunch and dinner we would sit down exactly on the hour, and if I was more than 30 seconds late, the next senior officer would have the wardroom be seated. I stated that every lunch and dinner would consist of a bowl of soup, a salad, two vegetables, one meat, and a dessert. That breakfast would be a choice from pancakes, waffles, cereal, and a meat and eggs. Where feasible, we would have fresh milk, and we'd always have a watch with fresh coffee.

I then appointed a committee with instructions for them to make out the menu one month ahead for my approval. I told them *Tulare* had just completed an inspection in which most departments were unsat. That we would commence a series of drills until we reached the point where all departments were outstanding. If necessary, we'd have drills every night until we reached this goal. I told them the first drill we'd call right away, now, to simulate repairs to rudder control.

After we finished this drill, back to the wardroom, and I critiqued the things that needed to be changed. One of them was that I stated we'd operate the rudders with live power. The warrant electrician says, "Commander, you're going to get somebody killed."

I said, "No, we'll go at it slow until we know how to do it, and then work up speed until we can do it quickly with live power."

He says, "I'm not going to use live power without direct orders from the captain."

I said, "And that's another thing we might as well go over just now. Any officer on board that objects to any order that I promulgate has permission to see the captain. But, whichever way the captain decides, within 48 hours either this exec or that officer will be transferred."

Needless to say, I never had an officer that questioned one of my commands again.

About a week later an ensign appeared at my stateroom with his hat full of money and five sailors in tow. He says, "Commander, I have some money for the recreation fund."

I says, "What you talkin' about?"

He says, "The ship's organization calls for taking custody of the money and putting the men on report any time men are caught gambling. I caught these five men gambling in the bilges."

I said to the men, "Take this money and divide it up among you. I've got a report to make from the bridge."

I went to the bridge, turned on the powerful ship broadcasting system, and stated, "Now hear this! This is the exec speaking. It's come to my attention that some *Tulare* men have been observed playing poker in the bilges. Henceforth, poker playing will be permitted in the compartments under the following conditions: The senior first class of each compartment will be responsible that there's no cheating, that there's no playing on the credit, and that there's no playing during working hours. That's all."

I went back down to my stateroom. Within a minute the flag's (admiral's) chaplain, who happened to be visiting on board, came hustling into my room, where he stated, "I'm not going to stand idly by while you change this beautiful ship into a floating casino."

I said, "Chaplain, I'll tell you when to have church services and where to have church services, and if and when the men can play poker."

About this time the captain's steward knocked on my door and said, "Commander, the captain say he see you right away!"

I went over to the captain's cabin. He came to the door and said, "About this announcement that you just made."

The chaplain says, "Yes, captain, that's what I want to talk with you about, too."

The captain says, "Have all the department heads report to my cabin in 15 minutes."

I met them down in the wardroom and they were commiserating with me, stating, "I know they do this in aviation, but they won't permit this on surface ships."

We went up to the captain's cabin, filed in, and sat down at his conference table. He said to his cabin boy, "Give me that deck of cards there in that top drawer."

He turned, and commenced dealing the cards, and says, "The first jack deals."

We played for about 15 minutes, and then he excused us. But he had made his point.

How fortunate I was to get the tour of duty on *Tulare* with the skipper that I had. Captain Colin Jack McKenzie was a fine officer, a fine teacher, an outstanding seaman, and an outstanding ship handler. Many things occurred, but he was always right there, ready to assist.

The chief thing creating the unsatisfactory situation in the deck department was the inability to get "away all boats" completed in the prescribed time. *Tulare*, with her big booms and heavy mike boats, required 42 minutes against an allotted time of 30 minutes.

I commenced a program of drilling on "away all boats," and by announcing the length of time that it required for each of the holds to complete the job, I formed somewhat of a competition. After a few weeks, I'd worked it up to where the individual holds were completing the "away all boats" drill in from 22 to 28 minutes.

The first lieutenant, Mr. McGuire, said, "I'll have to hand it to you, commander. Your system worked."

Another problem we had in gunnery. We couldn't hit the target. The guns were automatic 3-inch 50s, with the best fire control that the Navy had. That, plus my background at the

Gun Factory where I had personally worked on these guns, created for me an interest far above the normal.

The first day drilling with the guns, the target came over the ship, we commenced firing, and with my ability to see the shells go out I quickly noticed that we had fire control difficulties. I sent all the fire controlmen down to the doctor for a check on the eye chart. I uncovered no flaws in this area, so I decided that we were going to be unsat until such time as I could get some qualified duck hunters on the controls.

On my loudspeaker, which by this time was overworked, I stated that I wanted all Tennessee and Arkansas duck hunters up to the bridge. As you would expect, some half a dozen boys, including the disciplinary problems on board, appeared for interview. I told them that each was assigned to a separate fire control, but during daylight they were relieved of all other duties except to be on duty an hour at a time on the fire control following a plane or a star or a bird, or if there were no targets, the horizon, for the next four days before our next firing.

"When ah says turn to, son, it behooves y'all to turn to!"

Four days later the tow plane came over. Captain gave the orders to commence firing. Within seconds the target was blasted out of the sky. The plane unfurled a second target. It was blasted out of the sky. Third target, same results. I went over and reported to the captain, "I think we've found the difficulties with our gunnery system."

Another interesting development concerned the engine room. I told the chief engineer, "Clean up that engine room! When we have an admiral come on board, I want to be able to invite him into the engine room for an inspection without any advance notice."

He looked at me pitifully and said, "Commander, I don't have enough men to keep it clean."

I said, "Issue a big rag and have each man on watch, at all times he's on watch, have this rag in his hand and be cleaning up the area in the immediate vicinity of his watch."

He said, "Aye, aye, sir!"

A few weeks later, in Japan, one of my ordinance postgrad friends that had recently been promoted to admiral came on board and I invited him to stay for lunch. Before lunch I invited him to take a tour of the ship, including the engine room. Rear Admiral Vince DuBaugh congratulated the chief engineer, stating that he had the finest looking engine room that he had ever seen. And, with the captain as our guest, along with the admiral, we served dinner in the wardroom and the admiral was fluent with his accolades on what a wonderful job the wardroom steward's mates were doing, and what an outstanding lunch we had.

Shortly after getting on board, the ship set sail for Japan via Honolulu and Sydney, Australia. An incident in Hawaii proved very interesting. The ship was all set to get under way at 1500 hours. At 1430 I called, "All ashore, going ashore! Underway in 30 minutes."

The captain had a procedure that worked well for the *Tulare* in that he had liberty expire and underway occur simultaneously. As time moved on up, at 10 minutes before the hour, I passed the word, "All ashore, going ashore! Underway in 10 minutes." Two men who had been reported as AWOL had been observed on a bicycle coming down the dock. One was pedaling, the other was steering, and both of them thoroughly inebriated. I can see the two men now. They were rolling from side to side on the dock.

As they got close to one side, the men on the ship would hold their breath, sure they were about to go over. They straightened up, and there was a united exhalation, before they almost went off the other side, and everyone held their breath again.

The bicycle, the two men, and the yard police arrived at *Tulare's* gangway at the same time. The yard police were going to arrest the two men for stealing a bicycle. Lieutenant Commander McGuire went down to the dock, got the men back on board, but along with them came four yard police.

The police were insisting that the men be turned over to the police and McGuire got the men loose on the ship. The word was passed for two fictitious names to lay up to the quarterdeck. By this time, I said, "All ashore, going ashore. Under way in one minute. Single up all lines and haul in the gangway."

The yard police were still on board. They commenced to frantically look. Finally, as the gangway reached four or five feet above the dock, they went running out and jumped off. The captain came on the bridge and I told him, "In all respects, ready to get under way, sir."

He says, "Cast off line one."

We gave the horn a blast, and backed out.

It was with mixed feelings that I went around Ford Island and headed out into the sunset. I hated being gone for eight months, but I was deeply excited and exhilarated about the experiences that were facing me on this wonderful cruise.

En route to Sydney, Australia, we had a gay old time initiating polliwogs into the rights of shellbacks and became golden shellbacks at the same time. We crossed the equator at the same time as we crossed the international date line.

Away to Australia at 25 knots. An old trick when entering a foreign port was to notify the naval attaché and ask him to invite 40 couples representing the financial, political and military people of the port you're visiting. This we did in Sydney. On the day of arrival the wardroom hosted a party of people that the naval attaché had invited. The ladies of Sydney tried to outdo themselves as they reciprocated by having a party practically every day that we were there. Sydney was a gay old place, everything it was cracked up to be. Its reputation as the best liberty port in the world still rang true.

After two weeks in Sydney we proceeded to Guam and were introduced to 16-ounce beer cans. A couple of days at Guam was enough for *Tulare's* sailors to seek out, fight, and become smeared by both the local Marines and Seabees. But still intact, and all hands aboard, we shoved off for Yokosuka, Japan.

It so happened that the *Tulare* had obtained permission to travel singly to Australia while the squadron went as a group at a slower speed to Japan. The skipper was intent on arriving in Yokosuka before the ships of the squadron.

We entered Tokyo Bay in a driving snowstorm, continued at 25-knot ground speed right up to Yokosuka harbor. We swung in and tied up and, along with the skipper, I got in a taxi and raced to the officer's club. We quickly ordered a drink and barely had sat down when the commodore came in with the skippers and officers of the squadron. My Captain McKinzie slowly asked, "What kept you?"

While en route from Australia to Japan, the *Tulare* stopped over in Guam. I went ashore, and offered the services of *Tulare's* shore patrol to help the shore establishment maintain law and order. He thanked me, but pointed out that we weren't needed. Right off the bat, our men went to the ship's service recreation facility. It was the first time that I had ever seen 16 oz. beer cans, and apparently, the *Tulare* crewmen decided that they could drink as many of the 16-ouncers as they could 12-ouncers. They learned where the local nightspot was, proceeded to go in, in force, introduced themselves to the SeaBees and promptly beat the dickens out of the SeaBees and kicked them out of the nightspot.

The word spread rapidly, and SeaBees that weren't at the nightspot hurried there on the double. They, in force, literally stomped the *Tulare* crewmen. But word again spread rapidly back to the *Tulare*, and another 100 crewmen proceeded to the nightspot. With sufficient force at hand, they promptly maimed and mutilated the SeaBees.

Well, on Guam, there was another base that had a few thousand men, and as the word leaked down to them that *Tulare* had taken over the local nightspot, those Marines proceeded to the nightspot and literally kicked the *Tulare* crewmen out of the place. This caused several casualties, none fatal. But one sailor with his throat cut where a broken beer bottle was pushed in with force, was delivered to the Naval Hospital for treatment.

Through the night the doctor and the corpsman treated numerous lesser casualties. It so happened that the captain, myself, and several of the department heads were high on the mountain at Guam's lovely officer's club.

We were sitting around drinking with a dozen or so nurses. The captain invited the nurses back to *Tulare* for coffee and cake, and, believe it or not, four of them accepted. We came on board and started up to the captain's cabin. Mr. Crosby, the command duty officer, pulled me aside and told me that there had been riots in town and the men back aboard ship had continued the riot, and we had the deck force and the black gang (engineering) that were fighting each other centered in the mess hall.

I said, "Call out all first class petty officers and arm them with blackjacks and quell this riot!"

He says, "Commander, I've already done so, and the fighting goes on in the mess hall as the petty officers try to stop the riot."

I lit out running, went back to the main deck entrance to the mess hall, and as I ran down the ladder in civilian clothes, what a mess came into view! The petty officers with blackjacks were trying to drive the engineering force back, but the deck force was coming in from the starboard side and joining into the free-for-all. As I arrived on deck, I could hear from several sections, "It's the exec! It's the exec!"

They stopped fighting and lit out running up the ship into the sleeping quarters. Just ahead of me, I could see men with their clothes on jump into bed and pull the blanket up and over their head.

I went on up to the bow, turned to the starboard side, came back down, and the same thing that had occurred on the deck force side of the ship was happening on the engineering side. I came back into the mess hall. Mr. Crosby looked at me and said, "How, how, how did you do that, commander?"

And about that time, my chief master-at-arms showed up and he lambasted me with the statement, "Commander, don't you ever do that again! You're liable to get killed! Let me go in!"

The next morning, after a bit of investigating, I learned the details of the riots in town, and further ascertained that only one man had been sent to the hospital. I reported this to the captain, and he exploded. He says, "Get the doctor and the Marine captain."

This I did. He told them to get out to the Naval Hospital, get that man and return him to the ship, that we were getting under way at 10:00 a.m., and if they weren't back with the man by 10:00 a.m., that he'd leave all three of them in Guam. The doctor commenced offering sensible reasons why it might be difficult to get the man. The Marine captain grabbed him by the arm and says, "Come on!"

They didn't have any transportation. They ran out and there was a jeep on the dock. Marine Captain Slater quickly wired it to start without a key and headed off to the hospital. On arrival there, he told the doctor to go about getting the man released and he'd go up and get the man, and they'd be back down to that jeep in 15 minutes, ready to go to the ship.

Well, sure enough, back on the ship bridge, I soon saw them coming. They left the jeep on the dock and came running up the gangway with the injured man dressed in his hospital gown.

I walked down to the captain's cabin and told him, "Captain, ship in all respects ready to get under way."

We went out and singled up all the lines, cast off, and commenced backing down at exactly 10:00 o'clock. The doctor treated the man with his throat punctured on board ship as we proceeded on to Japan.

40

Japan

The first stop out of Yokosuka we arrived at Okinawa to pick up a load of Marines heading for the Philippines. It seemed that the civilian ship pilots of Okinawa had a procedure that required every Navy ship coming alongside the dock to have one of the pilots at the con of the ship. The captain told me of this situation as we were approaching the docks and said for me to take care of the pilot when he arrived.

I went down, met the pilot as he came aboard amidships via a rope ladder, took him on up to the bridge, introduced him to the captain and got a cup of coffee. In a bit he says to the captain, "Well, captain, I'll relieve you of the con."

Captain says, "No, I keep the con of my ship." And he kept heading for the dock.

The pilot, rather red-faced, asked permission to use his ship-to-shore telephone. The captain says, "Fine. The exec will show you."

On the phone the pilot said, "This bird insists on holding the con for himself."

The voice on the other end of the line says, "Tell him to lie off! Lie off!"

The pilot said to me, "You heard him. Aren't you going to tell the skipper?"

The skipper was coming into the dock at the time, and so I says, "The skipper's pretty busy right now."

With no further event we came alongside the dock and tied up to wait for our Marines. As the gangway went down, the pilot, obviously in a huff, went down to the dock and headed across to some building. In a few minutes the commodore of the squadron, by ship-to-shore telephone, asked the captain about this retaining of the con. And when the captain told him, "Yes, I retained the con," the commodore ordered him to the flagship and told him to report on the double.

I ordered the gig lowered. With the operations officer, I sat on the quarterdeck with the captain, waiting for the gig to come around to the stern of the ship. The captain says to me, "Do you know Admiral Stroop?"

At that time Vice Admiral P.D. Stroop was commander-in-chief of the seventh fleet on station somewhere in the South China Sea. I had served on Admiral Stroop's staff in the Bureau of Ordinance. I says, "Sure, I know him."

He says, "What kind of a man is he?"

I said, "He's the kind that'll give you a straightforward answer to any problem at any time, without delay." He looked wistfully out to the flagship and said, "The commodore will relieve me of my command. You'll be in command of the ship. Do what you wish, but as you get underway, I advise you to take the con."

The boat came around and he walked out on the gangway, looked up at me, and says, "As commanding officer, I direct that you do not contact Admiral Stroop on this matter."

I saluted him and said, "Aye, aye, sir!"

As the gig went around the stern I yelled, "Communications Officer! I have a message I want to send to commander seventh fleet, priority, plain language."

My operations officer, Commander Harriman, said, "Commander, I heard the captain tell you not to send that message." I looked at Commander Harriman and shouted in his face, "Harold!"

I went on to send the message: "Ashe sends. Information, flagship. Under what conditions is the commander of a naval vessel required to give up his con?"

With the binoculars, I anxiously followed the progress of the gig as it made its way out across four or five miles of Buckner Bay. I was anxious that the message I knew would be forthcoming from Admiral Stroop arrive at the flagship.

As the captain started up the gangway in the distance, my communications officer says, "Priority, plain language coming in. *USS Tulare,* Ashe sends: As you well know, the only place that the commanding officer is required to give up his con is the Panama Canal."

A talented cartoonist aboard the Tulare used a popular "Pogo" figure and also one of Dub's favorite words in the ship's cruise book.

After a bit, the captain returned to the *Tulare,* all smiles, and said that Admiral Stroop's message must have arrived seconds before he did, because the commodore said, "You've done it again, Jack."

The captain says, "What's that, commodore?"

"This message from the commander, seventh fleet!"

The captain says, "Oh, I told my exec not to send that message! He's a good friend of Admiral Stroop, and he apparently sent it anyway!"

The commodore, through clenched teeth, says, "I'll get you yet, Jack."

(Transcriptionist's note: Dad put his head back and chuckled here.) I don't know the nature of the bad blood between the captain and the commodore, but every time the captain tried to do something, the commodore tried to trip him up.

We loaded the Marines. We had a headquarters group that included 75 to 100 Marine officers. That night, after 8 o'clock reports, I strolled into the wardroom after a hard day, ready to relax, and six Marine officers were shuffling the cards, about to play poker. Three colonels, two lieutenant colonels, and one major. I came over, gleefully rubbing my hands, stating, "I sure could use a good poker game."

They exchanged glances among themselves, and finally the major stated, "Commander, we have a general rule in the headquarters group that nobody outside the group will play in our poker games."

"Well," I said, "I'll make a general rule for the *Tulare* wardroom. No poker game unless the exec's in the game."

Surprisingly enough, they got up and walked out.

The USS Tulare, among other duties, carried equipment and supplies needed for amphibious operations.

41

The Philippines

On to the Philippines. One evening as the ship's in the harbor at the gulf, we received orders to move. The captain started pulling in the anchor as four or five other ships in our group commenced to get under way.

I said, "Captain, something's wrong here. Was that message properly authenticated?"

He says, "Yes. Do it again."

I, with my easily recognizable voice, came over for authentication.

Back came the message, "Will the man with the keys to the ice machine lay down to the same?"

I said, "Captain, that's the lieutenant in charge of the disruption team that came over with us from the states." I explained that I became furious in the wardroom after a couple of times of passing the word for the man with the keys to the ice machine to lay down the same. I said, "He's telling me that this is an erroneous message."

The captain stopped hauling in the anchor, and we stayed put while the other ships made their move. In the critique of this attempted disruption as part of a war game, the captain says, "The message wasn't properly authenticated was the reason why we didn't move."

In due time, we got underway and returned our Marines to Okinawa. A general came out from the Marine camp at Okinawa to pick up the colonel on board *Tulare*, and the captain left with them as they shoved off to Kadena Air Force Base for a night of revelry.

A Marine lieutenant colonel came up to me on the bridge and says that if we had some transportation, we could go, too.

I says, "We've got plenty of transportation. We've got our holds full of your 6-bys," a term for three-axle trucks.

So I unloaded a 6-by, designated one of the sailors as a driver, and the Marine colonel and myself shoved off to Kadena Air Force Base also. We went into the officer's club and they were having a big dance on completion of an inspection at the Air Force base that day. A band was playin' and champagne was flowin'.

There in the corner, near the entrance, was an Air Force captain and his date and a Marine first lieutenant and his date. The lieutenant-colonel says to this tall blond in a white evening dress, "Ma'am, may I have this dance?"

The Marine lieutenant says, "She's with me."

The lieutenant-colonel says, "Now I didn't ask you to dance. Ma'am, may I have this dance?"

She just giggled, and the Marine lieutenant stood up and says, "I said she was with me.

That Lieutenant Colonel popped that Marine in the mouth with sufficient force that it sent him scooting into two or three chairs out on the dance floor, and he says again, "Ma'am, may I have this dance?"

She got up and they went dancing off.

To the brunette in a red evening dress, I calmly said, "Ma'am, may I have this dance?"

Her date, the Air Force captain, didn't say doodly-squat.

We danced out, and the very first thing introduced the girls to the colonel, my captain, and we all were introduced to the general. And they all danced with the girls. We never did come back to join their dates at the table where the Marine got knocked down.

About midnight I couldn't find the colonel, so I shoved off to the *Tulare* without him.

Out of Okinawa, on the way back to Yokosuka, we had a required drill of refueling at sea at night. This seemed like a tricky sort of business to me and I watched the captain as he approached the tanker for refueling. As we neared the tanker, the tanker's stern was swinging out toward *Tulare* and the captain gave the order, "Left rudder!" to come in closer to the tanker.

I yelled, "Captain! Rudder midship, the tanker's tail's comin' in!"

After the exercise was over, he called me off the side of the bridge, and said, "If you ever see that I've done something that you believe to be wrong, be sure to call it out. But remember, ships have bows and stems, not tails."

Eventually *Tulare* was scheduled to go on an R&R trip to Hong Kong. The squadron, sailing in company, received a message stating, "Fastest ship your group proceed top speed. Take over duties as station ship, Hong Kong." Even before the commodore designated *Tulare* to proceed on this mission, we'd already set course for Hong Kong and were moving up to top speed.

We arrived in Hong Kong after the departure of the seaplane tender that had duties as station ship. The seaplane tender had been ordered away to shadow three Russian cruisers that were proceeding through Malacca Straits. Without any guidelines as to a station ship's duties and responsibilities I proceeded to establish boat schedules and busily occupied my time attempting to resolve some of the problems in the harbor.

A couple of days after arriving at Hong Kong, the captain and myself went ashore across Hong Kong harbor on the mainland in Kowloon. After a bit of sight-seeing, we went into a British country club. After reviewing the scenery and thoroughly enjoying the British hospitality, the captain, who was sitting directly across from me, looked over my shoulder to my back and says, "Oooh, no!"

He then said to me, "Yonder comes the commodore's wife with some other woman."

They spotted the captain and came over to our table, and we invited them to join us. The commodore's wife introduced us to the other woman, who proved to be the wife of an airline pilot flying out of Hong Kong. She explained that she'd come to Hong Kong to join the commodore, who was expected in tomorrow.

We visited, drank several martinis, and then had dinner. After dinner, the airline pilot's wife invited us to join them back at her house. We bungled into their little ole car and proceeded to her apartment there in Kowloon. After a few more martinis, which we sorely needed, it was determined that we'd go on a drive along the beach and Crespian Bay.

On arrival at the beach, there wasn't a light in sight, and it was literally as dark as the inside of a tunnel. They got a blanket and some towels out of the car, and we went out on this dark beach. It wasn't long until someone suggested we go swimming.

I hadn't had enough martinis for that to sound like a good idea, but I went along. We pulled our clothes off on this deserted beach, and went down to the water swimming. That commodore's wife took a liking to me and she was all over me like a coat of paint. Before long, that airline pilot's wife went back to the car and got a camera, and on occasion she would snap a picture. And three or four times the commodore's wife at random made a few snapshots. Once, when she was indicating she was about to snap a picture, I jerked up a towel between me and the camera and so the night went. Eventually, they took us to the dock and we went on boat back to the ship.

The next day was uneventful except for the captain calling me in and stating we were stupid to go out on the beach with those women, and he hoped to heck the commodore's wife had sense enough not to tell him.

During the day, the ships of our squadron arrived in Hong Kong harbor. The next morning, there was a message received from the flagship that said, "*Tulare,* get all hands topside in the uniform of the day."

The captain said to me, "What do you suppose this is all about?" I said, "I can't imagine, since we're about six miles from shore."

But we complied anyway. About noon a messenger arrived at the *Tulare* and gave the captain a large manila envelop. In a bit, the captain asked me into his stateroom and showed me several pictures that had been taken two nights before and a note from the commodore's wife that said that she was sorry, but she showed the pictures to the commodore and he became very disturbed.

I looked at the pictures and said to the captain, "I can't blame him a bit, but that dumb woman, what does she mean, showing him these pictures?"

In the spring, the commodore got his orders and, as was customary, the squadron had a big going-away party. Well, it was customary for the commanding officers of each of the ships in the squadron, along with their wives, to go to this party. You can imagine my surprise when I got an invitation for Evaline and myself to attend. Although I had rather been six other places playing pool, I did attend the party.

The only other commander there was a Baptist preacher who was the chaplain on the commodore's staff. The seating arrangement consisted of three tables lined vertically and one head table across the top. I made my way to the foot of the third table, and along with the chaplain, enjoyed dinner.

In the course of events the commodore was presented with a big silver platter on which was engraved the fact that he had commanded the squadron between a couple of dates. He handed this platter to his wife, and it was passed from one person to another around the tables. Well, as it came by our location, the chaplain says to the people around us that he could never let a collection plate come by without putting something in it. And so he put three nickels in the plate.

It continued on around until it came back to the commodore's wife's position. She jumped up, yelled something, and with high heels a-clickety-clickety-click, came around to the end of my table, and took that platter and popped me on the head, exclaiming that not but one person would have the nerve to put three nickels in her gift. And clickety-clickty-click with the high heels she took the platter back to her seat, and I never had the pleasure of seeing her again.

In my duties as station ship commander, first thing I did was send a message to Mary Sue who was recognized as the underworld queen of Hong Kong docks, as well as the purchaser of garbage from the various U.S. ships in the harbor. A few hours later I saw a boat approaching with a big Chinese woman and two tremendous bodyguards. I met her at the gangway and escorted her to the wardroom.

Rather funny, I offered her a cup of coffee. As she reached to take it, her body guards grabbed the cup of coffee to protect her from being poisoned.

She asked, "Station ship commander wants to see Mary Sue?"

I says, "Yes, I want Mary Sue to guarantee that her girls won't roll the American sailors while in her taxicabs. I also want Mary Sue to tell the bumboats (trading boats) to stay away from *Tulare* so I won't have to man the high pressure fire hoses."

I then asked, "What can the station ship commander do for Mary Sue?"

She requested 60 feet of a very large rope and requested the garbage from *Tulare*. She stated that she'd have her girls paint the ship outside if I'd supply the paint.

I further agreed to let her put two girls aboard ship to rake the trays of the garbage as the sailors came through the line. I had to give my personal assurance that nothing would happen to the girls while they were carrying out this duty.

Mary Sue gave me her card with a note on it in Chinese. I never knew what the note stated, but a few days later used the note to give to a fisherman to bring me and the operations officer back to the Tulare one night when we were lost over in the Kowloon area.

The very same day that Mary Sue had arrived I had occasion to ask one of the sailors what was the percentage commission that the money exchangers were charging to convert U.S. money to Hong Kong money.

The sailor told me, "Five percent in, five percent out."

I literally exploded, recognizing that such exorbitant rates were terribly expensive. After some inquiries I learned that the money exchange function over at the pier was controlled and operated by three missionaries—one Catholic, two Protestant. I sent Lieutenant Commander McGuire some four or five miles across the harbor to the dock with a message requesting that the senior missionary come out to see me.

About an hour after departure McGuire returned to *Tulare* with a message from the Catholic missionary that he didn't have time to be running around calling on station ship commanders.

I took the same boat and proceeded back to the pier. Once there I walked down the pier to the missionary's office, went in and demanded, "Since when you haven't the time to call on the station ship commander?"

I said, "I've learned that you are charging 5 percent each way, as commission on exchanging Hong Kong monies for U.S. monies. I consider that exorbitant and am not going to put up with it."

Well, he looked me in the eye and told me he'd charge what he saw fit and I didn't have anything to do with it.

I told him, "Cut those percentages in half, effective this minute. And if you don't do it, I'll close your pier down, and all those overpriced souvenirs for mom and who have you will rot on your pier."

This missionary says, "You can't do that!"

I said, "I can, and I will. I'll divert the boats of my ship and all the ships in the harbor to another pier and all the taxis will come down to this designated pier, and you'll essentially be closed down."

I left him in a huff but periodically checked and found, at least for the duration of my stay, the commission was reduced to 2.5 percent each way.

There was a typhoon bearing down on Hong Kong the day that we were about to leave. The British admiral sent us a message asking what our intentions were. The captain was waiting for me to get dressed to go ashore to shop for mink stoles for our wives. The captain told him that we would check the 3 o'clock weather report.

When we arrived back from a successful shopping tour, the English ships had already vacated the harbor and the large, ocean-going Chinese junks were coming into the harbor. I checked the weather and it looked like the typhoon would be hitting Hong Kong the next day. So, at about 1600 we up-anchored and headed for Singapore, about 1,500 miles away.

In accordance with our normal routine, we fired off a message to the naval attaché in Singapore notifying him of our planned visit and suggesting that he invite some 40 couples on board *Tulare* for a luncheon on the day of arrival.

We came into Singapore, anchored about five miles out in the stream and made preparations for our guests to arrive. Interestingly enough, the new naval attaché had married the beauty queen, Miss Singapore of 1941.

Almost without exception, the guests attended the luncheon and we set about participating in the parties that they organized in return.

One interesting feature, I had been invited to an exclusive country club as guest of a British commander's wife and the chairman of the Bank of England's wife. After an afternoon of touring the Straits of Lohor with the girls as chauffeurs, the commander's wife invited me to a dance that night at this same Dingland Club. I met her husband, the British commander, and had a very lovely evening. But the next day the naval attaché came out to my ship to inform me that I had best not to be in company with this commander's wife because, a few weeks before, Prince Phillip of England, en route back from Australia, had stopped over in Singapore and set up housekeeping with this commander's wife until some of his own wife's loyal ministers reported him to the queen, and they put him on a plane out of Singapore and flew him off to London. I remember when Admiral Judith (he was a captain at the time, but he was the naval attaché) came over and reported that they had her under surveillance, and that's why they knew of my fraternization. He wanted to tell me about it for my information. I can assure you that I didn't accept any more of the commander's or his wife's invitations.

As we were arriving in Hong Kong, Captain McKenzie mentioned to me that we would be going on to Singapore shortly, and the British were keen on entertaining and also keen on formal dress. He thought it would be a good idea while at Hong Kong for us to go shopping and get tuxedos and other party-type dress. This sounded like a good idea to me because I had long since outgrown the tuxedos that I once bought in Key West.

As soon as we could arrange it, we went over and bought a white tuxedo jacket, dark blue formal trousers, a tuxedo shirt, a cummerbund, the whole ball of wax for a young naval officer to come calling. And, later when we arrived in Singapore, the first cracker out of the box was that we were invited to a big British operational command cocktail and dinner party.

We got all spruced up in our new duds and away we went to the party. On arrival we quickly observed that the British men were wearing long coats and pointed white collars, and to our consternation and embarrassment, we were dressed exactly like the British mess boys.

We withstood our problems of dress and went back to the ship. The next day, we were invited to be the guests of the admiral, Lord and Lady Scotts-McCree. We dressed up in our white uniform and never tried again to compete with the British on this business of clothes and dress.

But interesting enough, the party with the admiral was for his family, his aide, and the two of us. Very exclusive! On arrival at the admiral's quarters we were ushered into a large drawing room and served the most delicious wine that I have ever tasted. I noticed that occasionally the admiral would talk to his aide and the aide would disappear upstairs and come back shortly, shaking his head. Once, the admiral disappeared upstairs, and when he came down he had a young lady on his arm that he presented to us as his daughter, the Lady Margaret.

With too much wine under my belt, I put two and two together and decided that she didn't want to come down to her dad's party and associate with two lowly Yanks. In a few seconds after her arrival downstairs, Lady Scotts-McCree took my captain by the arm and led him into the dining room. Behind them walked the admiral. The Lady Margaret put out her arm and walked me into the dining room as the aide walked behind us. We sat down in this graciously appointed dining room as only the British seem to know how to arrange. But, by this time, I was furious at this Lady Margaret for her seeming audacity to flaunt socializing with us. I dare say I took it personally, and the first thing that I said to her was, "Ma'am, you are a spoiled brat."

She says, "I have never been addressed in such a manner!"

I said, "You've been giving your father a hard time, refusing to come down to have lunch with me."

She was angry, her eyes were flashing, and she said she was the Lady Margaret, and I was certainly being rude to her! I said, "You are the daughter of the Lord and Lady Scotts-McCree, a British lord whose ancestry dates from when?"

She explained that her forebears were given the lordship back in the 16th century, and the title was associated with one of Britain's colonial wars.

I said, "In the states we don't recognize heraldry, or any of the monarchy's personal designations. For instance, my own forebears date back to the Black Prince of England."

Well, you know that gal took a liking to me right off the bat! We discussed how the revolutionary General Ashe's ancestry had been traced to the Black Prince. We discussed Mark Twain, and she just dearly loved *Tom Sawyer*. She expressed doubt concerning the size of catfish in the Mississippi, but I assured her that the little tributaries of the Mississippi had catfish over 100 pounds. And other discussions went on at length, and the next thing that I knew, we were the only two left in the dining room, the others having proceeded to one of the many drawing rooms.

After we left, the captain said to me, "How did you hit it off with the Lady Margaret?"

And I told him that I pointed out to her that I personally was a descendent of the King of England dating 500 years before her forebears ever received their lordship. I said, "Further, that was after I told her she was a spoiled brat."

The captain's only comment was, "Oh, no!"

42

Singapore

One evening, while at Singapore, I went ashore to just look around. I came back to the dock just in time to barely miss the 11:00 o'clock boat. I had boats running from the *Tulare* to the Singapore dock, leaving every hour on the hour.

So I had almost an hour to kill waiting there at the dock. It was completely dark except for one electric light bulb that hung a couple of feet above your head. The Singapore waterfront is not exactly Sunday school at Macedonia. As I looked out at the passing bodies that included sailors from the Malay states, China, and the East Indies, I automatically got closer to the light.

I was wearing a white uniform, and thus stood out among the people like a sore thumb. Shortly, an East Indian waltzed up to me with a sad story that he was going to have to sell his ruby for $1,000. He insisted that I look at it. The ruby looked gorgeous to me, but as time moved on and I shook my head "no," he came down in price, first to $500, then to $100, then to $10.

Of course, I recognized the old con game, but paid careful attention, and when I got a chance, I grasped that ruby firmly between my thumb and forefinger, and, with my left hand, went into the pocket to get him his money.

And he wouldn't think of taking the $10. Well, you never heard such screaming and yelling, but I held his ruby. Quite a ruckus attracted a good crowd, and as I held my ground the Singapore police arrived. A very nice English police captain explained to me, "Commander, I know exactly what he's trying to do. But he has the law on his side because he didn't take your money. You'll have to give back his ruby."

This I did and had a very pleasant conversation with the police captain until my boat arrived. An uneventful trip back to *Tulare* and I went to bed.

About the time that I was going to bed the *Tulare* liberty section came to the boat dock after leaving a party where they were the guests of some component of the British Navy. They, having missed the boat, went down the street a couple of blocks and went into a bar and restaurant owned by a Chinaman.

Of course, to a man, the *Tulare* crew had a few too many. In a bit, a young water tender came into the bar and sat down at a table occupied by two boatswain's mates. One boatswain's mate said to the other, did he smell something? The young water tender was not aware of any difficulties, but, in a bit, one of the boatswain's mates stood up and socked him in the jaw, knocking him partway across the room.

Well, immediately, the engine men came to his aid, knocking down the boatswain's mates. The melee soon reached the proportions of a full-fledged riot with *Tulare* sailors breaking bottles on the bar and running into one of their shipmates of the opposite deck and engineering force.

There was a very large and long mirror back of the bar that was broken in several places. Glasses were strewn everywhere. Metal chairs were bent and warped.

I had sent the Singapore police a force of eight shore patrolmen, even though the police had suggested that they didn't need them. The Singapore police (they don't carry guns) arrived with their nightsticks but were promptly thrown out of the restaurant by my fighting sailors. The shore patrol that I had sent them came in and, in time, got the situation under control, and put the men on boats going back to the *Tulare*.

The next morning, bright and early, the chief master-at-arms and the command duty officer came up to make a report of the difficulties. I immediately feared an international incident.

I got a boat to go ashore. (The captain wasn't on board. He had stayed overnight with friends in Singapore.)

I arrived at the waterfront and immediately got a taxi to police headquarters. There was the police captain that I had seen only a few hours before, and he took me down to the Chinese bar to look it over. Well, as I've just explained, it was a mess. Around the bar and restaurant there were several Chinese with these little abacuses. They were computing the damage. I asked the police captain to find out from the owner what the damages amounted to. He had a conversation with the owner who smiled at me, with gold teeth a'shining that hadn't seen daylight in many a moon. After a bit he told the police captain that there was $1,800 damages. I told the police captain, "There's more damage than that here in American dollars, and he's quoting Malay dollars!"

The captain told me that they had a procedure that, if it can be repaired it's not considered damaged, and they don't count the cost of labor.

I said, "Well, that doesn't seem fair to me." He said, "Yes, but that's the system."

I said, "Tell him that I'll give him $500 American dollars (about $4,500 Malay dollars) if he'll sign me a release relinquishing claim for damages.

He told the Chinaman this and the smile showed me gold teeth that I hadn't even seen before. I went back to the ship, went up to the bridge, and over the loudspeaker announced, "All hands hear this. This is the exec speaking. You should feel proud of yourself. I just inspected the devastation created by you men as you rioted last night. I was very fortunate to get all charges dropped by paying the restaurant owner $500 American dollars. Now, until such time as you return $500 dollars to me, all liberty is canceled."

I looked out on deck, and all the chiefs were taking off their hats and starting around, collecting money. In about an hour, the chief master-at-arms came up to my stateroom with dollars, quarters, you name it, and counted out a little over

$650. I took $500 of it and put the rest in the ship's recreation fund. I got on the loudspeaker and said, "That was a rapid recovery. Liberty will continue as scheduled, but all hands are cautioned to try your damnedest not to have any more riots!"

After an uneventful trip back to Yokosuka we made preparation for an operation evaluation. Customarily, the ship-handling portion of the evaluation is done with four different people—one a department head and the other three being officers of the decks. The ship-handling operation we had for this date was for our ship in a column to come up and come alongside of a ship of the squadron to hook up for a fueling exercise. Everything was timed, such as how long required to get into position, hook up, start pumping. While this was going on, the ship had to remain between 90 and 120 feet from the ship that was supplying the refueling.

The chief of staff of the commodore, when ready to start the exercises, came out and said to the captain, "Your exec will have the first operation run."

I had never handled the ship in this exercise. We'd been drilling the OOD's (junior officers who stood watches as officer of the deck) so they would know how to do it. The captain's jaw jarred loose about a foot, and he figured that we'd had it. I said, "Captain, I have the con. All engines make 125 turns, right 10 degrees rudder."

Having noticed the same exercise many times as the OOD's were being trained, as well as relative motion, I knew where to ask for 115 turns. We came alongside the target ship, fired the line over, hooked on the first pass, and commenced refueling the minute the ship had slowed down to where it was making the same speed as the target ship. I carefully watched. They had a line over from our ship to the target ship, and I kept that line between 100 and 110 feet. On disconnecting, I smartly sounded, "Engines ahead 125 turns. Come around to position."

The chief of staff had a lieutenant of the inspection party over on the port side of the bridge watching the time expiration and distance from the ship. The chief of staff asked him, "How did he do?"

The lieutenant says, "Perfect."

Only then did my captain get his jaw back up to where it was normal.

You know how much he must have wondered. Of course the commodore was set to get him and to get me.

I well remember an exercise in which the skipper was in command of the *Tulare*, four LST's and three LSD's when we went up the Ahsung Man River in Korea to simulate supplying the 8th Army over the beach. We gathered together a SEAL team of underwater specialists and had them move ahead of the *Tulare* as we went up the river. We proceeded until the water depth changed from 32 feet to 28 feet, and there we anchored.

To complicate matters, a typhoon was moving close to Guam and expected to reach our area in about five days. The team for locating the point along the river for going ashore was dispatched on the double, and we prepared to go ashore at a little village about eight miles up the river from where we anchored.

Soon I noted that no boats were coming back. I requested from the captain permission to go ashore to see what the delay was. Along with my master-at-arms, I took the next boat in and came up alongside the little village and saw that they had used the bulldozer to open a path up out of the river into the town, and another path out of the town, back down to the river. In the town, they had one-way traffic.

I walked ashore and asked who was in charge and an army colonel stepped forward.

I said, "What's the delay here?"

He says, "It is going rather slowly."

I said, "You're going to have to open up a street for two-way traffic through the village."

He said, "I'm trying to resolve it without knocking the houses down in the village."

I said, "Man, we gotta speed this up. We've got a typhoon approaching."

As beachmaster, I took charge, waved a boat in with two more bulldozers, directed them up to the top of the river cliff, swung my arm in an arc and told the bulldozer operators, "We're going to have to knock these houses down."

Moans and crying filled the air as the village population realized I was about to knock their houses down. In a few minutes, the moans and cries changed to shouts of anger and they began to throw bricks, rocks, and bottles at me. When the first barrage of rocks hit, an army sergeant with a submachine gun stepped in front of me saying, "What are your orders, sir?"

My master-at-arms had likewise stepped in front of me, and he says, "Keep your shirt on, sergeant.'"

I said, "Hold your fire unless they knock me down, in which case, we'll open fire on the front ranks. But I believe that the disruption will expire as soon as we start tearing the houses down."

It was indeed a sad feeling in the pit of my stomach to watch the houses being bulldozed over and heard the house owners cry and moan and wail. But we established two-way traffic through the village, coming in and going out, and commenced to unload the ship as rapidly as possible. [The homeowners got reparations.]

After about three days of unloading we were aware that the typhoon was about six hours away. Through the night the typhoon arrived and the wind the next morning at about 10 o'clock was laying at about a 45-degree angle as the rain pounded our operation. I was busily engaged in expediting unloading such that by about 3 o'clock I notified the captain, "There goes the last four boatloads. I suggest that we haul in the anchor and get underway and pick up those four boats on the move."

He said, "That's a worthwhile consideration."

I looked at the river current, the wind coming off the side of the mountain, noted our anchor position and I just couldn't imagine how in the world the captain was going to get us out of there.

This I voiced to Commander Harriman, my operations officer. I said, "Harold, how would you get this ship out of here?"

He says, "I don't know. But I have all the confidence in the world the captain can get it out."

I said, "Well, so do I, but I especially wonder how, if I was stuck with the job, how I'd do it!"

About this time the captain appeared on the bridge to ask me if I'd like to get the ship underway. I had decided as I looked at the location, that the way I would do it would be to hold the anchor (leave it in place on the bottom), give the ship hard left rudder and start backing up the river, then give it hard right rudder, go ahead one-third down the river, and repeat these maneuvers until such time as I had the ship pointing downriver.

Well, I announced that I had the con. "Prepare to get under way. All engines back one third."

I commenced backing down and the navigator came running over and whispered in my ear, "Commander, your anchor is still out."

I said, "I know it."

After about three shifts of going forward, backing down, going forward, backing down, I stopped the engine, hauled in the anchor, and started down the river.

You could hardly see because of the rain reducing visibility, but shortly we got sight of two of the boats coming up. We expeditiously hooked on and hauled them aboard, soon followed by the next two boats.

When you're in a river, orders are to go ahead with barely sufficient speed for steering, to keep from knocking water up on the villages alongside the river. The captain said nothing about my relieving of the con, so I decided I would show him how aviators handle ships. I said, "All engines ahead. Make turns for 5 knots."

Down ahead of us were a bunch of fishing boats. The navigator says, "Commander, there's about 10 fishing boats directly ahead of you."

I said, "I see them. Helmsman, steer a course directly to the center of the group of fishing boats."

I knew the fishing boats would be sure that they went just barely ahead of the bow of our boat, so that the evil spirits could be cut off from the stern of their boat. This they did.

After some little bit, I decided to test the captain further. I said, "All engines ahead. Make turns eight knots."

And I was twisting from side to side, running back and forth, taking bearings as we ran down the river.

He still said nothing. So I decided to test him further, and commanded, "All engines ahead. Make turns at 12 knots."

The typhoon was coming in from the southeast, which was on our port bow, and the ship was beginning to list from the force of the wind. I said, "All engines ahead. Make turns 15 knots."

The wake from our ship was knocking the water well up on the shore of the river, and I saw that the captain was trying to test me out. But he came over after a bit and says, "Commander, I thought you said you didn't like Korea."

I said, "Captain, I despise the place from one end to the other."

He says, "What you hangin' around here for? Let's get the hell out of here."

I said, "All engines ahead, top speed."

We commenced to pick up speed and were going about 22 knots when we hit the breakwater. The foaming waves were climbing in from the ocean to the river and the bow of the ship hit the waves, shot into the air and came slapping down. The captain said he'd take the con, and he set course for Shimonesake Straits in the Sea of Japan.

He told me that he was going to cross the Sea of Japan and go through the Straits into the inland sea for the night. American destroyers get pilots to go through Shimonesake

Straits in the daytime, and here we were going through at about midnight in a typhoon with no pilot.

I kept a close look on the wind and held the captain's belt as he was taking bearings. Out on deck a few times I shouted at him that we were going to have to get some bricks to put in his pocket to hold him down.

We had a wind across our bow of 89 knots as we went into Shimonesake Straits but the inland sea was calm. I told the captain, "We'll heave to and go fishing tomorrow."

We rolled on through the night while the typhoon was a-howling just over the mountain. We spent two days calmly going down the inland sea toward Yokosuka.

43

No More Big T

As we were preparing for the squadron to get under way returning to the states, the commodore decided to have a party. I had all the *Tulare* officers take a fluorescent T and put it over their white shirt under their uniform. When the party was in full swing, I had one of the officers go turn off the lights. As he did, the only lights that could be made out were the 40 or so Big Ts that the light had fluoresced, shining there in the big party.

I could see that the commodore was terribly displeased. He made no bones about it that he didn't appreciate that Big T.

Occasionally, wives and families of crew members would be invited aboard for a day. Here Dub shows Evaline the command center.

Shortly before heading for Pearl Harbor the captain's relief came on board and they made plans for the captain to be relieved in Pearl Harbor and he would leave the ship and go to his new duty station in Washington.

Somewhere north of Midway Island, with the squadron cruising along on a Sunday afternoon, perfect weather, we got a message saying the Commodore would high-line transfer from the flagship to the *Tulare*. As he came on board, the two captains greeted him and asked what they could do for him.

The commodore said, "I'd like to see the exec for a bit."

He said to me, "Let's take a walk back to the helicopter deck."

As we moved along, he says, "I've got a squadron to run and you are making it very difficult. Everywhere I turn, the Big T shows up winning the exercise. The only way, it seems, that the other ships can have a chance at winning any of the exercises is for the Big T not to win."

And he turned around, pointed his finger in my face, and said, "I don't want you to win another exercise!"

I says, "Well, commodore, the same as you've got a squadron to run, we've got a ship to run."

He says, "Not another exercise are you to win!"

We turned and went on back up to the bridge. He didn't say boo to the two captains, got on the highline, and transferred back to the flagship.

The captain says, "What was that all about?"

As best I could I related to him exactly what had happened. A little while later, down in my stateroom, the prospective captain came down and says, "You know, we've got to comply with what he said."

And I said, "Captain, I just want to remark that you've got a ship to run the same way that he has a squadron to run."

My prospective captain says, "Well, let's don't let him see the Big T anymore on any exercises."

I had had painted a sign for when we arrived in San Diego that said, "The Big T is proud to be home!"

I hung that on the port side, away from the flagship, and my skipper never said anything pro or con about it. Likewise, we continued to win all the exercises, and he never said pro or con, good or bad, about that.

We arrived in San Diego after having been in the Far East for eight and a half months. As I mentioned before, I had a sign that said "The Big T Is Proud to Be Home."

My duties as the exec of a ship without a chaplain included trying to placate the divorce cases that had come up and get agreement for others who were pending to be settled out of court. Routine training exercises included yard time in Long Beach and "repair ship time" off shore from Long Beach.

Rather interesting, the captain, myself, and four department heads appeared on the repair ship. The captain had in hand a long list of repair items including putting a glass cover on the

outer deck of the bridge. I had tried to get the captain not to include that as a repair item, but he had done so anyway.

In the repair ship's wardroom, after a conference with the repair ship exec, he had reduced our list to a very few items. When the captain of the repair ship came into the wardroom, he looked up and saw me, and said, pointing at me, "Give him any repair items he wants." The captain of the repair ship was Captain Coulter, a long-time airship pilot.

After he left the wardroom, the exec says, "Well, let's start down the list again." When we reached the glass cover for the bridge, our captain said to me, "I don't guess there's any use in asking for that item, is there?"

I laughed, and said, "Not a chance."

After several successful exercises, the *Tulare* was sent on R&R to San Francisco. En route to 'Frisco, and especially the early morning hours as we approached Treasure Island, the radio was hammering away at news indicating that President Eisenhower was ordering an attack on Lebanon.

After many other incidences of carefully watching the scene as military action was taken, I concluded, about 5 o'clock in the morning, that, indeed, an attack was imminent. I went to the bridge and told the captain I thought an attack was imminent and that we'd get very little R&R.

He turned and disgustedly looked at me and said, "You gun clubbers are all alike. All you want's a war!"

We went on into and anchored at Treasure Island. The captain hurried over to tell me, as soon as I could get tied up and squared away, to let as many men as I could go on shore leave.

I said, "Captain, I still believe that we're about to invade Lebanon. And my recommendation is to top up the ship with fuel and ammunition and fill the Marine reefers with supplies."

With disgust on his face, he said, again, "We didn't come up here to work. As soon as you can get ready, let the men go ashore."

He left the ship, and I called a conference of all department heads. I told them that we were going to top up with fuel, top up with ammunition, and load the ship with supplies. I told the personnel officer, "There's an aircraft carrier in port under considerable yard overhaul. Go over to Treasure Island and don't come back without having these 69 men for our full war complement."

I turned then to the chief engineer and the first lieutenant and says, "Now we'll commence loading ship."

The first lieutenant says, "Commander, we can't load ammunition and fuel at the same time. I suggest that the black gang (engineering) load fuel and we'll load ammunition the next day."

I said, "No, I feel that we need to be ready to go, because if we're going to Lebanon, the *Tulare* and the *Alamo* are our only fast ships on the West Coast, and if there's resistance in Lebanon, reinforcements will have to be sent through the Panama Canal."

We could simultaneously load the reefers and refuel, and that's what we proceeded to do. Late in the afternoon, with the reefers bulging and maximum fuel, we shifted to loading ammunition. As the night wore on, the first lieutenant and the boatswain came up to the bridge to see me and asked that the ammunition reloading be postponed until the next day. I says, "No, we'll do it now."

He says, "These men have been working all day and all night. They're going to start passing out."

I says, "Messenger, go get the doctor."

When the doctor arrived on the bridge I told him, "It's rumored that we may have some people passing out on the line. Put a few corpsmen out on watch, and any man that passes out, give him a shot [that is, an IV infusion] of saline solution, and put him back on the line."

Through the night the loading operation continued. We finished the next morning a little before 7 o'clock. As we were finishing, a classified priority message arrived on board requesting "all ships Pacific fleet" to report the number of miles they could travel without refueling, number of days of supplies on board with marine load and with only ship's complement (crew). Report ammunition on board and the number of men required for full war complement.

About this time I looked out the window of the bridge and saw the personnel officer coming back with what looked to be 100 men. I wrote the message to CINCPAC (Commander in Chief, Pacific) stating: "*Tulare* all respects ready to get under way immediately. Can travel 10,000 miles without refueling. Eight weeks supply food on board loaded with Marines. Twelve weeks supply with ship's complement. Fully topped up with ammunition."

Just as I was about to send this, down the dock came a taxi. The captain jumped out of the taxi and told me about a message about to come in.

"We need to be prepared to answer it on the double."

I handed him the message and turned and walked slowly away. I was disgusted with him. We could not have been other than first because we were trigger ready to fire. I'm sure it had a lot to do with the captain being selected for admiral. But he never thanked me for doing it.

44

Lakehurst NAS

I dreamed that I got my orders and I reported in to Lakehurst, New Jersey. In my dream, Evaline and I had gone house hunting and rented a place that had a beautiful lot overlooking the beach and we had a boathouse there at the beach. A couple of weeks later I got my orders.

It was with considerable anticipation that I reported in to Lakehurst and saw the house and lawn and boathouse just like it was in my dream. I had never been to this location before.

Before being detached we scurried, getting our San Diego house ready for sale. When a colored doctor came to buy the house, I made the mistake of telling him that I couldn't sell the house to him because of his color. After a few weeks of not being able to sell it, I was surely sorry of that mistake and I've never made it again.

Finally one day, Evaline was talking to one couple in the dining room while I was talking to another couple in the kitchen and each of us sold the house. I went into the dining room and Evaline says, "Well, these people have just bought the house." I stated, "Well, the same thing has happened with these people."

I said, "Folks, I don't know how to resolve this, but the way I'm going to do it is, the first one of you that arrives with a $2,000 down payment will get the house."

One fellow said, "Well, just a minute, I'll go to the house and get the money."

The other fellow said, "What about a check?"

I said, "No, I'd have to take a check from two of you. Like I said, the first one with $2,000 cash."

He went home and came back in about an hour and we sold the house.

We decided to make a 30-day cross-country vacation on our leave before reporting into Lakehurst. First we went to Boulder Dam, on to Bryce Canyon and the Grand Canyon, then on to Yellowstone National Park. After about a week in Yellowstone, Susan and Walter, both at the same time, commenced to say that they'd had enough of Yellowstone. They wanted to go visit Uncle Jake. As a matter of fact, I was ready myself.

We left Yellowstone, stayed at Cody, Wyoming, that night and arrived at Uncle Jake's in Missouri the next evening. From there we went to visit my mother and Evaline's mother, then swung on down into Atlanta to visit Gladys. From Gladys' we went on to Lakehurst where we rented the house that I had dreamed about.

My arrival at Naval Air Station Lakehurst became complicated by plans of Captain Kline, from the office of Chief of Naval Operations, to make airship test and development (AT&D) a separate command. The captain of the station, Captain Van Evra, called me over to his office and let me know in no uncertain terms that he was against it becoming a separate command, and if it was done over his objections, AT&D would be the last on the list for getting any support from the naval air station.

My orders read that I would have additional duties as chief test pilot and senior member of the BIS trial board for four new 3W airships.

Incidentally, these airships were the largest non-rigid airships ever constructed and were being built at the Akron air docks. Rather ironical, I got back into the good graces of the captain by impressing his wife with ghost stories from our stay at Newport, R.I.

The captain's procedure for calls was that he would notify three officers and their wives on Friday to come over and make their social call. It so happened that the chaplain and his wife, a public works officer and his wife, and Evaline and myself were chosen for the same day. I had learned that Mrs. Van Evra was sold on ghost stories, so I brought up the subject.

Instead of leaving at 5 o'clock, the normal time, we were still there at 11 p.m., telling ghost stories.

One of my first actions was to get rid of the pigeon problem in dock (hangar) one.

I called in Chief Brady and asked him how long he had needed for the men clean up the hangars from pigeon droppings each morning. He said that had been needed ever since he'd been there. But we had a problem. Both Mrs. Gollilogy and Mrs. Van Evra spent lots of time admiring the pigeons. And Commander Gollilogy, the officer in charge of AT&D, did everything to protect the pigeons.

I told Chief Brady we were going to get rid of the things. I would get shotgun shells and a .410 shotgun. He could strap flashlights to the shotgun barrel, climb out on the steel rails of the hangar, and kill two or three G.I. cans (large garbage cans) full of pigeons each night. I told him to announce to the men that we were doing this to get rid of the irksome problem of cleaning up the hangar decks from pigeon droppings.

Operation Pigeon Disposal proceeded quite satisfactorily. One day Mrs. Gollilogy and Mrs. Van Evra appeared down at dock I to admire the pigeons in flight. And Mrs. Van Evra says, "Walt, it seems to me that there's fewer pigeons than there used to be."

With a blank face I agreed with her. There did seem to be fewer of them around.

Before I relieved as AT&D department head I had to wait about nine months until Commander Gollilogy received his orders. During this time I went to Akron to participate in a test flight of the new 3W airship. Since, among other things, we were required to record how the airship acted in a heavy snowstorm, we set up housekeeping at Akron, waiting for a forecast of a big snow.

One day an airship was ready for the Navy's acceptance flight and we took off going north into Canada, where there was a big front with heavy snowfall forecast. We flew out of Akron, across Cleveland International Airport, where I circled the home of George Allen (one of the 3W pilots) at the approach area of Cleveland International. I had no problem because all I had to do was tell the airport that an experimental airship was crossing their station and the control towers held all air traffic in abeyance until we cleared the area.

We crossed Lake Erie, proceeded northward along the Canadian side.

It was very interesting to see school children from town to town outside schools, waiting as we proceeded on our flight path. The airship was one and a half million cubic feet in volume and over 300 feet long, and it was an impressive sight for the kids. As the day turned into night, snow began to fall. As the night wore on I experienced the biggest snowstorm that I ever witnessed.

I asked one of the chiefs to climb to the height-finding radar and give me a report of how the snow looked. We had two spotlights back on the tail, shining down between the tail fins, and markers along the tail to see how much snow we did accumulate. After a bit, he called down to say, "You're not going to believe it, Commander, but there's 29 feet of snow between the airship fins."

I said, "I believe it, because I'm carrying four degrees down, flying at 50 knots. Watch while I try to shake off some of the snow."

Well, I climbed, I dived, I rolled, I twisted, but to no avail—the same amount of snow continued to remain on board the ship. We flew out through the front. The next morning the snow had abated and the sky was clear and had a beautiful purple haze. I noted that the temperature just outside the Plexiglass of the pilot's compartment was 40 below zero. One of the provisions of the Navy acceptance of the 3W was that you could kill one engine, let it stay idle for an hour in temperatures below zero, and then restart it and do the same with the other engine.

As we were swiftly going over the ship, checking off the required items, we gave the allowed time of an hour for the engine to be idle. But then we couldn't start it. I notified Goodyear Aircraft that we were unable to start the engine. They supplied additional instructions, but the engine still wouldn't start. Flying on one engine, we turned and headed for Akron, having to fly back through that front before landing.

As we crossed Cleveland we came out of the front and decided, one more time, to see if we could start the engine. With the increase in temperature, the engine started like a top.

We landed at Akron easily, having the use of both engines after a 29-hour flight. I scheduled a conference for the next morning with the Goodyear Aircraft Corp. engineers. The net result: they were required to make some modifications so the engine would pass.

The night before, as we were flying through this heavy snowstorm in the vicinity of Battleaxe, Michigan, Lieutenant Commander Dave Hayes came forward and said, "Commander, we have contact on many jets up to 50,000 feet, coming in from the north."

Well, that was back in the days when our airborne early warning systems were at the peak in preparing to notify of any unidentified aircraft coming over the poles from the north. I said, "Dave, energize the circuit with Colorado Springs."

He says, "I've already done so."

At about this time Colorado Springs came in with a message, stating that there was a drill on the Canadian-American DEW (distant early warning) Line. They would appreciate it if we would remain silent on the report.

We learned that the airship radar would pick up jets 200 miles further out than our DEW Line radars.

Flying Wind Tunnel

The airship had a tunnel amidship that went 105 feet straight up to the height-finding radars. You could walk out on the top of the airship, which the crewmen did on many instances.

It was indeed wonderful to be back at Lakehurst, back with many of my old friends that I had served with before, some of them three and four times. I liked Lakehurst because I was doing work that was useful and that I knew how to do well. I was sorry that I hadn't been able to take command of the destroyer that I'd been recommended for, but at least I knew the projects and programs of airship research.

As I've mentioned before, it was almost nine months after I arrived on board before Commander Gollilogy was detached, thereby allowing me to become head of airship research. I say airship research because I was making an attempt to change the old AT&D (Airship Test and Development) to a research organization.

Prior to my relieving Commander Gollilogy, I was assigned as coordinator of activities for Armed Forces Day. This proved to be quite a large undertaking, as I gathered together such organizations as the Blue Angels, the Army Parachute Team, Tank Platoons, and even tethered free balloon rides in Dock One. We had over 100,000 guests that came aboard for Armed Forces Day.

Airship research had some 25 active projects underway. We were adequately manned, adequately funded, and quite capable of performing our duties. But always the handwriting was on the wall of expectations that the Navy was going to phase out airships. The Bureau of Weapons increasingly assigned us tasks that were in no way associated with airships. For instance, investigating the cause of commercial airline crashes over the Alps, and countless other small research programs.

Almost weekly some crackpot claiming to be somebody that he wasn't would appear at our door with some far-fetched research idea. Such a setting existed when one day, a gentleman came calling, claiming to be Professor Hazen, head of Forrestal Laboratories at Princeton University.

After introductions, his opening remark was, "I guess you are aware that the wind tunnels at Langley are in error."

I tried to placate him by saying that, "Yes, I've heard about it." I excused myself, went in and handed a note to my receptionist asking her to see if there was a Forrestal Laboratory at Princeton, and if so, ask to speak to Professor Hazen. After a bit, during which time this gentleman had attempted to acquaint me with the problems of the wind tunnel at Langley, she came in with a note. It said, "Dr. Hazen is out of his office. He's gone to Lakehurst for the day."

It seemed logical to assume that my visitor was from Forrestal Labs and was David Hazen. As the day wore on, I pulled in the chief engineer, Mr. Herring; the Navy aeronautical engineering officer, Frank Carter; and many of the AT&D engineers while we discussed this problem. I was anxious to get into research programs involving other than airships, and was ready to try to solve the problems of the wind tunnel. I did not have an assigned project from the Bureau of Weapons, and thereby didn't have funding to do airship modification. But I solved these problems by doing it anyway, using monies from other programs.

We went on a crash modification program, readying one of our NAN ships with a long tube about 25 feet in length and two and a half feet in diameter that moved up into the airship. When the flying models were attached, the airship out flying, this tube could be extended out beyond the airship airflow, creating a lab, if you will, without the wall effect found in a wind tunnel.

Over a period of a few months, the airship modification was completed and we began to fly Dave Hazen and his Princeton graduate students to collect these data. At different airspeeds the air pressure and flow over the wings was detected and recorded.

As time wore on, Dr. Hazen wrote an article, published in one of the aviation magazines, praising highly the success of this airship flying wind tunnel. As I've mentioned before, Vice Admiral Perry in the Pentagon was redoubling his efforts to phase the airships out of the Navy. When he became aware of this article in one of the aviation magazines, he called Rear Admiral Les Chambers, the head of research in the Bureau of Weapons to ask about the program.

I had kept the Bureau of Weapons informed through conversations and visits with Vice Admiral Stroop, the head of BuWeaps. I was in error not to have informed Admiral Chambers. I received a phone call from Admiral Chambers, and he questioned me about the flying wind tunnel. He became quite angry, and told me to be in his office the next morning at 9:00. I knew that I was in trouble, but as I drove to Washington, I decided I had better see Admiral Stroop to explain this situation and get some guidance.

The next morning at 8:00 sharp I walked into Admiral Stroop's office, but his secretary, Jean Childes, told me the admiral was out of town and wouldn't be back until the next day. Jean, an old friend from back in my Bureau of Ordinance days, asked me, "Walt, what's the trouble?"

I told her the story, and stated that Admiral Chambers was going to skin me alive. I told her that Admiral Chambers would probably have me cool my heels outside his office for at least 15 minutes, but if she would, to please give me a call at Admiral Chambers' office and tell them that Admiral Stroop would like to see me.

She agreed to do this, and I went on over to Admiral Chambers' office and waited outside his office. And it so happened that at about 12 minutes after 9 he asked me into his office. He was still angry. He says, "How much did it cost to modify that airship?"

I said, "About a million dollars."

He said, "How much would it cost to put it back to its original configuration?"

I said, "About a million and a half dollars."

He says, "Who assigned that program to you?"

I says, "Well, nobody. I'm the chief of research at Lakehurst, and upon investigation I decided that something needed to be done and I did it."

He pointed his finger at me and said, "You get back up there and stop this program." And about that time his secretary says, "Admiral Chambers, Admiral Stroop would like to see Commander Ashe."

Admiral Chambers was terribly agitated, and said, "Don't you tell Admiral Stroop about this wind tunnel."

I said, "Admiral, Admiral Stroop knows all about it. I've briefed him several times, and he's been up to Lakehurst and looked at the airship with the tunnel on board."

I went over to Admiral Stroop's office to see Jean Childes, continuing my bluff to kill time until Admiral Stroop got back. I walked in and almost passed out when, there in front of me, stood Admiral Stroop.

He says, "What's your problem, Walt?"

I briefed him as best I could in 15 or 20 minutes. On finishing he asked me, "How much money would you need to expedite that program?"

I said, "No more this year, but I'd probably need about two million dollars for next year."

He says, "You go over and tell Les Chambers that I said to give you two million dollars to expedite the flying wind tunnel."

I grinned, and says, "Thank you, Admiral."

I went back to Admiral Chambers, went into his office. I said, "Admiral, Admiral Stroop told me to tell you to give me an additional two million dollars to expedite the flying wind tunnel." Needless to say, I had one angry, exasperated Rear Admiral. [This would be about 1961.]

The wall effect was creating erroneous data in the wind tunnel [at Langley] and the bad data was causing the V-stalls [vertical take-off] and the S-stall [short take-off] aircraft to crash.

Some months after my visit to Admiral Chambers and following Admiral Perry's directive that all airships would be phased out of the Navy and deflated by the end of May, 1961, I got a phone call from the assistant Secretary of the Navy for Research, Dr. Wakeland, who incidentally was an old friend of Dr. Dave Hazen from Princeton days. Dr. Wakeland said, "I'm having a meeting in my office at 9:00. I'd appreciate it if you would attend."

I said, "Mr. Secretary, it's 8:00 now. I'll get a plane and get there as soon as I can, but I'll be late. I can't make it there in an hour."

He says, "Come as soon as you can."

Lieutenant Commander Carter was the duty officer. I called him and asked him to get the SNJ ready. I'd meet him at station operations. I wanted him to fly me to Washington immediately. We took off shortly thereafter, flew direct to Anacostia. I got a taxi to the Pentagon and made my way to Assistant Secretary of the Navy Wakeland's office.

A chicken colonel [full colonel], Marine Corps, who was the Secretary's aide, ushered me into the Secretary's office. There before me were three vice admirals, the Secretary, Dr. Hazen, and an empty chair for me. I went over and sat down. The Secretary says, "Commander, we're discussing continuing the airship research program for another year. He says to Vice Admiral Perry, who was Deputy Chief of Naval Operations (DCNO) Air for the Navy, to proceed.

Admiral Perry spoke fluently and incorrectly for about 30 minutes, during which time he claimed that the research program at Lakehurst could be done more efficiently, as well as more cheaply, with fixed-wing aircraft. He said it would take 3,000 men and 30 million dollars for the support of the Naval Air Station, Lakehurst, to continue the program.

The Secretary then turned to Vice Admiral Halloway, the chief of Naval Research, who spoke very quickly for a few minutes, in which he stated that he didn't know whether this research could be done with fixed wing aircraft or not, but that we certainly had to get the data.

He turned then to the Vice Admiral who was the chief of the CIA, and he spoke very directly, saying, "Mr. Secretary, we've got to have these data, and it doesn't matter what it costs." He looked directly at Admiral Perry and he says, "I don't believe that it can be done with fixed-wing aircraft."

The Secretary turned to Dr. Hazen and says, "Dave?"

Dave went through about 15 minutes, during which time he stated that he got more data in one night with Commander Ashe's research airships than they got with telemetering at Cornell for a whole year. He says, "I don't know anything about the other program that you're discussing, the infrared detection, but I don't believe that anybody knows how many people or the cost of running the program is." He says, "Commander Ashe has been running it, and I believe that Commander Ashe can make the best estimate of how much it would cost."

I looked down at my feet, wiggled my toes, and thought, "You dumbbell, you ain't never going to be nothin' but a commander."

At about that time the Secretary says, "What about it, Commander Ashe?"

I said, "Mr. Secretary, I've been running both of these projects on a budget of $6.5 million dollars annually. I don't pay for the military that is provided by the Navy and supported by Lakehurst that is above and beyond the cost of the projects. I have been doing this with 41 Naval officers, 42 civilian engineers, and 96 Navy technicians." I looked over at Admiral Perry, and he's looking icicles through me, red in the face, and short of breath.

The Secretary thanked us, and we got up and walked out of his office.

Well, I knew well enough not to go down the passageway with three angry admirals, so I waited in the Secretary's outer office. Shortly, the squawk box sounded, and the Secretary says, "Colonel, there's three vice admirals and a commander left my office a few minutes ago. See if you can find the commander and ask him to come to my office.

The colonel said, "Mr. Secretary, he's in my office now."

I went in to the Secretary's office, and there he and Dr. Hazen both had their feet up on the Secretary's desk. The Secretary says, "Well, we're going to stomp on the beard and we're going to keep these two research airships for another year." He says, "You sure that you can do it with the people you have?"

I says, "Yes, sir, I can do it with the people I have, but I can't do it with warm bodies. As soon as your decision becomes known they will be transferring replacements in for the people that I have." I said, "I can do it with the individuals that I have, but not with the same number of warm bodies."

He says, "I'll take care of that." And he called the chief of BuPers and told BuPers that my people were frozen, that replacements would occur only if I agreed, and he says, "And Commander Ashe will be authorized to travel as he sees fit in carrying out these projects."

I got a set of orders that said, "Commander Walter Ashe, in performing AAA highly classified projects for the Secretary of Navy for Research, is authorized to travel to such places at such times as he sees fit in performing these duties."

Can you imagine such orders! I had the authority to steal! In fact, a few months afterwards, I went over to brief Captain Kline on my intention to take the wind tunnel airship to Key West for a month's operation. Captain Kline told me, "You're not going to take any station officers, or station airships, or station airplanes anywhere."

It made me angry, and I told Captain Kline, "You stick around and see."

He exploded. "Commander Sparr, Commander Sparr!" Herman Sparr came in and he says, "Mr. Sparr, I want you to make out court-martial proceedings against Commander Ashe."

I walked out and back over to my office, disgusted with myself for making the captain mad. In about an hour, Herman Sparr called me to say, "Commander, I wish you wouldn't get the captain all riled up. It's taken me an hour to get him simmered down enough not to continue with court-martial proceedings."

I had thought that I could get along without ever having to reveal that I had such authority from the Secretary of Navy. And I never did reveal it, but Virg Eckert knew that I had something.

By the way, I went down to Key West and spent two months.

45

Key West

We took off for Key West on a Monday morning. Uneventful flight to Glynco except for headwinds that caused us to decide to remain overnight. The next day, after taking off from Glynco and going down the bay for about 50 miles, there was suddenly a terrible vibration and a lot of noise. I knew we had blown an engine.

At the time, Lieutenant Allen was on the controls, and like a good Navy pilot, he headed for the sea. The airship was pretty heavily loaded, and at first it was difficult to hold altitude on one engine. But after a bit it was noted that we were automatically dumping fuel. Due to some crossover valves, we were running on the service tanks and simultaneously dumping fuel from those same tanks. The single engine began to cut out and come back on intermittently as we continued to lose altitude.

After a bit, the mechanic got the crossover valves straightened out, but we were still dumping fuel. He soon determined that the fuel dump valve was stuck open and the electric motor on the valve was keeping it open.

As we were proceeding across the bay toward the ocean, Lieutenant Commander Sparr happened to be on board, getting some flight time. A few days prior to this, he had had difficulties in an SNJ aircraft, and had to parachute out into that same bay. While waiting to be rescued, the tide came in and he had to climb one of the little dead trees to keep out of the water. But with time, some of the snakes in the bay determined to share Mr. Sparr's perch above the water.

So he, in deep thought, looking out the window of this slowly descending airship, kept repeating to himself, "Mater wocasins down there, Mater wocasins down there!"

Very slowly we proceeded back to Glynco, went into the hangar, and sent the R4D that we had back to Lakehurst to pick up an engine. The crew, working around the clock, spent most of three days replacing the engine. I decided that they deserved a big beer party. I ordered food from the general mess, but at my expense I purchased two kegs of beer. I took a busload of the sailors off watch out to Jekyll Island for the beer bust.

Some knowledge, and the confidence to put it to use, only come with experience.

After a couple of hours of eating, drinking and making merry, two state policemen came up. One of the chiefs met them, and he says, "Commander, these officers would like to see you."

They told me that they were sorry, but someone had made a complaint, and it was illegal for us to drink alcoholic beverages in the state park. I asked one of the chiefs to see how much beer we had left. He said, "About a half of a keg."

I had made motions for them to bring the two officers a plate, and of course, they brought them a glass of beer. One of the officers said, "I appreciate it commander, but I can't have any of the beer because I am on duty."

The other one said, "Well, I'm about to go off duty, and I'm mighty thirsty."

The two officers sat there with us for about an hour and a half while we finished the beer, and continued to enjoy the hotdogs and hamburgers.

The next day we proceeded to Key West. We got down there and organized night flights in order to make the best possible platform for conducting flying wind tunnel tests. (The airship flew more stably at night.)

We were getting phenomenal data, thoroughly appreciated by Dr. Hazen and his graduate students. We continued to make these flights until we and Dr. Hazen found that we just absolutely had to return to Lakehurst, which we did.

While at Key West, one morning I came out to quarters for muster and some of the men came up from the little spars of the bay where they were catching snappers. At quarters I remarked, "It's come to my attention that fishin's goin' on down here." After a little squirming on the part of members of the crew, I said, "I'll challenge the three best fisherman among you men to a fishing duel. We'll go out on the keys and fish for two hours, and if I don't catch more fish than all three of your selectees put together, I'll furnish the beer."

Well, there was a whoopee up and down the ranks, and I for one surely thought that that was a bet that I would lose, and I certainly planned to. A few days later, with food ordered from the general mess, we went to one of Key West's beaches to be ready for the fish fry. We took a bus up to Bow Channel, and with a lot of pomp and ceremony we began fishing, with plans to fish from 2 to 4 o'clock.

Well, with my long-time experience fishing with Commander Burke and Commander Eckert, it was no trouble for me to reel in the fish. As a matter of fact, the fish seemed to be biting better than normal. Our two hours expired just as the water hit high tide. We went down along the ridge picking out 20 or 30 of the bigger snapper, and we threw the rest of the fish over into the water. It was rather sickening to see all of those dead fish in the water. And about that time a squad car of the state police pulled up and stopped.

They came over and announced it was illegal to catch more fish than you were going to eat, and there was a $5 fine for every dead fish you threw back into the water. One of the chiefs says, "Officer, something you ought to know. The Commander caught most of these fish!"

After a long, tedious discussion on conservation measures, the officers decided to permit us to go free with a warning, but they were going to write a letter from the Florida Fish and Game Commissioner to our commanding officer. I told the officer that the commanding officer was director of research, Naval Air Station, Lakehurst. Of course that was me, and a few weeks later I got a letter listing the fact that we fisherman, listing our names, had been warned for illegally killing fish on the Florida Keys.

I had the men from R&D Lakehurst at quarters and read the letter to them. I stated that I didn't want any more breaking of Florida laws on the part of AT&D personnel.

While at Lakehurst, I became involved in a very interesting and dangerous argument with the commanding officer of the War Reserve. It so happened that at various places throughout the Navy they had these big supply depots of often-used spare parts housed in warehouses ready for use in the event of war.

After the airships had been removed from the Navy, except for my two research airships, we had no place to go within the Navy supply system to get spare parts. And as luck would have it, we had to replace another engine.

I had my supply officer, Lieutenant Commander Harrison, send a request to the War Reserve to "borry" an engine until we could get it replaced through the Navy supply system, a period we estimated to be two to three months.

The commanding officer of the War Reserve turned down our request, stating that we damn well have to wait the two to three months. I called him and said, "Captain, I have triple-A priority, highly classified projects with the Secretary of the Navy, and I'd certainly appreciate borrowing an engine until we can replace it."

He told me not only no, but hell no! "You're not going to get one of the War Reserve engines."

I thought all night, slept little, thinking of what I could do to alleviate the situation. I finally decided, against all rules, I would just take the engine. The next morning, I called the commanding officer of the War Reserve again, and asked him to reconsider his refusal and let me have that engine.

He exploded. He let me know in no uncertain terms that I damn well wasn't going to get an engine from the War Reserve. I said, "Captain, don't be too sure about that!"

I held an all-officers conference each morning anyway, and I went into that conference and told someone to get Chief Eye from the hangar. I told Commander Shannon that I wanted him to take 100 men, and to put them in formation, ten columns of ten each, and to personally march them to the War Reserve, arriving at the War Reserve warehouse at exactly one minute after 9. I told him I wanted him to give left-face parade rest in front of the War Reserve and to be ready for any eventuality.

I told Lieutenant Commander Carter that I wanted him to get on the low-boy with eight men and to arrive at the War Reserve at exactly 9:01. I told Mr. Harrison to prepare a request for an engine with the statement on the bottom of the request that we would replace it as soon as the Navy supply system would ship us an engine.

About this time, Chief Eye came through the door of the conference room, and I says, "Chief, I would like you to get one of those big cutters used to cut cables on airships. Join me here in my office and we will walk over to the War Reserve, and when I tell you, I want you to cut the lock on the door to the War Reserve."

Lieutenant Commander Hayes says, "Chief, you know if you do that you're going to be court-martialed, and so is Mr. Carter."

Mr. Carter says, "I figure that I'll get court-martialed if I do or I'll get court-martialed if I don't."

Chief Eye says, "That goes for me, too."

We waited the few minutes necessary for our timing to be right. And all of us headed to the War Reserve. I walked with Chief Eye and Lieutenant Commander Harrison, and when we arrived at the War Reserve, the captain of the War Reserve, along with Lakehurst supply officers and most of the men of the supply department were waiting for us. I saluted the War Reserve captain and said, "Captain, I'd like to ask you again to borrow an engine."

His face red, he could hardly talk. He said, "I told you you're not going to get an engine," when, just at that instant, some distance away, you could hear Commander Shannon establish the cadence of "Hup, two, three, four, hup, two, three, four."

We didn't say anything else until Commander Shannon, with his 100 men, arrived at the War Reserve, and gave the order, "Halt, left-face, parade rest!"

I said to Chief Eye, "Chief, cut the lock on the door to the War Reserve warehouse."

Just about the time he cut it, Lieutenant Commander Carter with the low-boy and eight first-class petty officers drove up. I says, "Mr. Carter, take an engine from the War Reserve, and take it over to Dock One. Mr. Harrison, give the request for an engine to the captain. Captain, as soon as I can get that engine through the supply system, I'll return it to you."

We turned, and along with the men under Commander Shannon, walked back to my big airship Dock One. We went into my office and were drinking coffee. Every once in a while Dave Hayes would say, "Commander, I can't believe you did this! You're going to be court-martialed!"

I said, "I know it, Dave, but out of the court martial there will be an establishment of a spare parts supply system for us."

Some minutes and a few cups of coffee later, Captain Epps, the commanding officer of the air station, called me on the phone and says, "Walt, what have you done?"

I says, "Captain, I needed the engine and I took it."

He says, "The commanding officer of the War Reserve is here in my office and he is sending a letter to the Secretary of Navy requesting your court martial! He wants to know what your chain of command is."

I said, "Captain, tell him I've got three chains of command. Operationally, it's the Admiral at Johnsville down to the Secretary of the Navy. Administratively, it's through you to the Admiral at Philadelphia to the Secretary of the Navy. If it's technical, it's to the Secretary of the Navy via the Chief of Bureau of Weapons. I don't know if all those chains of command or any one of them apply."

We continued to drink coffee there in my office. In about an hour and a half, my secretary, Fran Jacoby, says, "Vice Admiral Stroop is on the telephone."

I picked up the phone and said, "Good morning, Admiral."

He says, "Walt, I understand you're having a little trouble with the pork-choppers."

I said, "Yessir."

He said, "If you bump into anything you can't handle, let me know."

Admiral Stroop had nipped that court martial request in the bud before it ever got off of the ground.

A NAN ship, somewhere above (we believe) the New Jersey coast.

46

Back at Lakehurst

The Naval Air Station, Lakehurst, was a large station that was home base for several commands. In addition to the air station complement, there was the large Bureau of Aeronautics test facility with many pilots and civilian engineers. There were four helicopter squadrons, a fleet air wing, and two airship squadrons. There was a parachute school and several smaller schools. It was the custom that a daily aerological report and weather forecast was conducted from 8 to 10 a.m. The attendees at these aerological reviews varied with prospective weather conditions. That is, good weather conditions would find lower-ranking representatives from each of the several commands.

Nan ships stored at Hanger one at Lakehurst NAS.

One day, along with Commander Shannon, my operations officer, I went to the briefing. There I noticed that the airship squadrons were represented by the captains and operations officers, and, likewise, so were several of the other commands.

The aerological officer and her chief presented a detailed weather summary and forecast. The forecast stated that winds would be light from the southeast and we would have light snow with accumulations of less than half an inch. On completion of the forecast presentation, Commander Belew, the captain of airship squadron 3, told his operations officer, Lieutenant Commander Sparr, to go take off the next airship scheduled to fly out to its station in the Atlantic. As he was getting up to leave, I spoke to Commander Shannon and said, "Bob, notify all research airships to return to base. Dock 'em and as soon as they're in the hangar, close the hangar doors and chain them."

Commander Belew says, "Wait a minute, Mr. Sparr!! Come back!" He said, "Walt, are you expecting bad weather?"

I said, "I surely am. I expect we will get a blizzard from the northeast this afternoon and tonight, and I expect the snow to accumulate 10 to 12 inches."

The wing operations officer was sitting there and said, "Captain Belew, you better get that airship out on station or the wing commander will skin you alive. Walt Ashe doesn't know anything about the weather."

Commander Belew says, "That's what you think. I know better. I flew in his crew for a couple of years."

There was further discussion of the weather before I proceeded on back to my office up next to Dock One. After a bit, maybe a couple of hours, the exec of the air station called me and said, "You keep your opinions on the weather to yourself. The aerological officer is over here in my office. She complained that you not only disagreed with her forecast, but suggested to Belew and others that we were going to have a blizzard."

I said, "Max, I take the aerological officer's forecast as an item of advice. And I make my own decisions. I happened to disagree with the forecast and told Commander Shannon to notify all my airships to return to base. Seven of them are tucked into Dock One now and the big hangar doors are chained shut. We'll have a blizzard."

Shortly after talking to Commander Cawley, the head of the public works department called me to say, "Walt, I understand that you don't agree with the weather forecast."

I says, "I don't, but I'm getting sick and tired of being reminded of it."

He says, "Well, I've got a problem. I'm low on money, and if I call in the public works snow crews and it doesn't snow, I'm going to be up against it."

And I said, "Captain, if you don't call them in, you're going to be up against it. I predict that by 3 o'clock we'll have a blizzard from the northeast and, even with your special crews, you'll have trouble keeping the main roads open, let alone the runways."

Well, in due course, it began to snow and the wind picked up, and by 3 that afternoon, the roads were clogging and snow was covering the ready airships that were on the field. I had a special high-pressure water tower mounted on the top of an airship mast, and I sent my crew down to Captain Belew's airship and began to pump water to keep the snow off the airship.

After a bit, with the help of the snowplows, he was able to take that airship off for Bermuda. Needless to say, I had no further criticism of my weather forecasting ability.

While at Lakehurst, Evaline, bless her heart, was asked to teach school. This she seemed to enjoy, and one day she asked that her principal and another teacher be permitted to come visit my facility in Hangar One. We were heavily involved in running top-secret tests in infra-red detection with one airship and we were, as mentioned before, involved in state-of-the-art efforts on wind-tunnel wall effect with the other airship. In addition, we had other assignments, including a request from David Taylor Model Basin to construct a ground-effect vehicle.

I assigned Commander Barnes as the guide for Evaline and her school teachers. He showed them enough for them to know what we were doing, but was careful enough not to supply any classified information. One of the tasks that we had was very highly classified radar development. Barnes told the teachers that, when they went to school and studied electricity and physics, they were fully acquainted with the formula that voltage equals amperage times resistance (E=IR).

"Well," he says, "it's not exactly true. As you increase frequency that formula gets further and further from the fact."

And many other comments were presented. Finally, Barnes brought the teachers into my office. The many exclamations of praise and bewilderment were best summed up by Evaline's principal's statement, when he said that we were so far above what he learned in school that he found it difficult to even comprehend what we were doing.

Whereas Lakehurst grammar school's principal was conversant with electricity moving in milliseconds, he was totally floored when you commenced dealing with nanoseconds.

And that calls to mind an incident in Dock One after about three months of night and day activity to get the flying wind tunnel rigged for flight. The generators were on board, the airplane model attached to the tunnel, the airship tethered about 50 feet in the air when, with all of airship research and the Princeton crew as witnesses, we gave the signal to commence operations.

As the rpm of the four-motored model aircraft increased along with the roar of the engines on the airship turning at high speed with the propellers at flat pitch, suddenly the whole thing just "rrrr, rrr, rrr," ground to a halt.

In disappointment and bewilderment, everyone looked at each other with question marks across their faces. I pulled my hair and yelled, "I'm surrounded with large quantities of stupidity! Now, Dave, you and your people meet with mine in my office."

We went into the office and I said, "Hasn't anybody in here ever heard of power factor?"

Dave says, "Yeah, I'm familiar with power factor." (Editor's note: In this usage, power factor refers to a mismatch between voltage and current, which need to be in perfect sync in order for electricity to perform real work.)

Commander Barnes says, "I don't know what you mean by power factor, boss."

I said, "Bill, as a propeller turns, inductance moves up the faster it goes. And if that's not compensated for with capacitance, the power will come over to the edge of the sine curve and you'll get very little or no power."

I said, "What we must do is put into the circuit variable capacitance so that it will increase as the speed of the propellers increases."

I said, "I suggest that this can be done by using banks of light bulbs and a Variac (transformer) to switch on more capacitance."

This we set about doing, and a couple of weeks later we were ready to successfully test the wind tunnel airship. Dave Hazen remarked to me, after all the people had left my office, "I don't know why I didn't think of that power factor." I says, "Dave, just between us girls, I didn't think of it, either."

While at Lakehurst I was a member of their conservation club. This included our building an enclosure and growing quail and pheasants to meet a corresponding input from the state of New Jersey. One day, Commander Burke, the president of the club, arrived at our house and told me that our dog had killed a bunch of quail. This didn't sound like something that Susan's collie, Lady, would do, but he brought the quail on up to my house and we proceeded to dress them.

Susan was very disturbed that anyone would even suggest that her dog even *bothered* the quail. And I must say that I agreed with her. But as we were cleaning the quail in our basement, Commander Burke was saying that I was gonna have to do something about the dog. Susan came down the steps and sat with all of her eight years of indignity and asked, "Commander Burke, did anybody see Lady kill any quail?"

Burke sighed and says, "No, Susan, they didn't."

She then said, "Commander Burke, did anybody see any feathers on Lady's mouth?"

Burke says, "No, Susan, they didn't."

Susan says, "Commander Burke, you don't know anything. All you know is you got a bunch of dead quail." And she turned and went stompin' up the stairs.

Commander Burke looked at me, fully resigned, and stated, "Walt, if that girl becomes a lawyer, I'm gonna make a point of bein' good."

As part of my duties at Lakehurst, I was chief test pilot and head of the Navy acceptance trials for the 3-W airship. There were four of these airships built. They were a million and a half cubic feet in volume and approximately 330 feet in length. They had the height of a 12-story building and we had installed a 40-foot-diameter radar. Over the test period of the 3-W, I separated the crew into two parts for the BIS [Bureau of Inspection and Survey] trials.

One group, headed by Lieutenant Commander Wittcomb, would conduct the bureau acceptance trials. The other group, operations evaluation, was headed by Lieutenant Commander Dave Hayes.

The first ship was used for the acceptance trials. Numerous data, numerous flights, proved that the 3-W was well capable of performing its missions. In due time the airship was accepted. Normally, after an aircraft has gone through the rigorous exercises (such things as V-max speed, entry and dive, determining maximum take-offs, and numerous other tests in the heavier-than-air field), that test aircraft is put out to pasture. But we didn't have but four 3-Ws, and it was decided that the 3-W would be transferred to airborne early warning squadron 1 at Lakehurst.

After a few months of successful flights, suddenly one day, the 3-W airship crashed into the ocean off Barnegat, killing the entire crew of 24 people. A board of enquiry was appointed. It was made up of four captains that included Captain Kline of airship wing 1. Captain Kline set about trying to cast doubt on the thoroughness of the BIS trial tests. Thanks to the irrefutable testimony from inspectors from my AT&D crews, these allegations were dropped.

There were lawsuits brought against Goodyear by the next-of-kin of several of the crew members, charging that Goodyear hadn't designed the airship correctly.

I want to state simply, and I believe, factually, that that 3-W loss was due to pilot error. It was customary to run on one engine at a time on the airborne early warning flights, and when they changed engines, they would start one before stopping the one in use. From the testimony of eyewitnesses that saw the airship go down, it's quite apparent that the airship was losing altitude without maintaining pressure. A simple twist of the switch would have increased the pressure and prevented the weight of the big radars on top of the ship from falling through and tearing the ship.

At the time of this crash, the second 3-W was undergoing operational evaluation. Dave Hayes and his crew flew the airship from Lakehurst to South Weymouth. I was on board with Captain Epps, the commanding officer of the air station, and Vice Admiral Stroop, chief of BuWeps, as guest. En route to South Weymouth, while going throughout the ship, showing Admiral Stroop the size and other capabilities of the airship, he turned and asked me, "Are you going to set a world's endurance record with this airship?"

I said, "Admiral, I have been notified by word of mouth and phone conversations not to attempt an endurance record."

He was going up the ladder from first deck into the wardroom and he stopped, turned, and looked at me. He says, "That wasn't what I asked you. I asked you, Are you going to do it?"

I says, "Yes, Admiral, I plan to, and you will be the first notified when we break the record. He nodded and grinned.

One week later, as Dave Hayes attempted to put the airship in the hangar at South Weymouth, the ship kited, hit the hangar, and deflated.

With the deflation went my dream of breaking the world endurance record for aircraft.

I had planned to fly for two weeks up and down the Atlantic, from Argentina to Bermuda to Roosevelt Roads, back and forth, and claim it as part of the operational evaluation. I was sure I was going to get in trouble for doing it.

The airship crash against the hangar at South Weymouth was due to locking the brake on the ground-handling mule's cable. The sudden locking of the brake broke the cable, and as the ship kited, it went into the hangar and was torn.

47

Wind Tunnel Research

I was rather pleased one day to learn that the under-Secretary of the Navy for Research, Dr. Wakeland, had accepted my invitation to come up and take a look at the flying wind tunnel airship. That night, my research outfit had a big cocktail party. We invited Captain and Mrs. Epps to attend. As they arrived, I proceeded to present each of them with a martini. As I handed Captain Epps his drink, I leaned forward and passed out.

The people at the party knew that I hadn't had much to drink, so they called the ambulance that immediately came down from the dispensary to take me up for a check with the doctors. Instead, I went home and called Dr. Fruin, the chief flight surgeon. He asked me what my pulse was, and told me that if it reached 90, I should come up to the dispensary.

Commander Ashe worked with a team led by Princeton physicist Dr. Dave Hazen to develop a "flying wind tunnel" in the tail section of a NAN ship. The device provided better information than land-based wind tunnels.

Commander James remained there with me, and he occasionally tried to take my pulse. After a while, he told me, "I can't take it. It's stopping every once in a while."

After a bit, he decided to take me up to the dispensary. I went in and told the young lieutenant (a doctor) what my symptoms were and he decided to check me over. The first thing after he started the physical examination, he jumped back and says, "Don't move! Just lie down. Remain still. Your life may depend on it."

They went running around for a bit, gave me a shot of something, then he told me that he believed that I had had a heart attack and he was going to transfer me to the hospital in Philadelphia. Angie called the club and told Evaline, who, in turn told Captain Epps and others, and she came on up to the dispensary. By this time, they had me ready to go into the ambulance, and the doctor told the corpsman in my ambulance to remain with me until I was on the 11th floor of the Philadelphia Navy Hospital and not to leave me with any of the other hospital corpsmen.

I told Evaline to remain at home and they would keep her informed as away we went with the siren going for the 50 miles to the Philadelphia Naval Hospital.

En route to the hospital, I would pass out occasionally, but would shortly thereafter come to. On arrival at the hospital, I noted that the commanding officer of the hospital, along with several of his doctors, were there to meet me.

The hospital corpsmen tried to take over to take me to the 11th floor, but my Lakehurst corpsmen insisted that they had orders to stay with me until I was on the 11th floor. There the doctors examined me, confirmed that I'd had a heart attack, and began giving me various injections to help handle the heart and thin my blood.

During the night I continued to pass out occasionally. At about 3 o'clock in the morning I looked up and there was Evaline and the Lakehurst chaplain. I told Evaline, "I told you to stay home," and then passed out again.

The next morning around 9:30, I was aroused as the three doctors that had been attending me during the night came in with another doctor to examine me. This other doctor, a Dr. McFadden, was a heart specialist. He looked at my chart and said, "Commander, it's a good thing you have an excellent heart, or these doctors would've killed you."

He said to the doctors, "This patient has internal bleeding."

They went running around giving me shots to counteract the blood thinner. Made my legs stiffen and my toes turn up. After a bit, he decided that I had a bleeding ulcer, and they began the treatment for this ulcer. It was: drink half-and-half every other hour, and Amphigel every other hour.

This continued for the next four days, during which time I continued to pass out occasionally. Finally, on the fourth day, they brought me a piece of toast. That piece of toast tasted better than any steak that I'd ever had!

Now. Back at Lakehurst, things had been popping. Captain Epps shortly after my attack back at the Officer's Club at Lakehurst, had called Captain Fruin to see how I was doing. Captain Fruin wasn't at the dispensary. He'd gone to pick up his daughter, who was at a school dance. After a bit, when he learned that the doctors at the dispensary were sending me to the hospital at Philadelphia Naval Yard, they called the commanding officer of the Naval hospital. That's why he and the other doctors were there, waiting to greet me on arrival.

Captain Epps didn't like the way I'd been treated at the dispensary, and had Dr. Fruin transferred the next day.

Back at Philadelphia, I wasn't doing so hot. They had established belladonna sensitivity in me, and I was just lying in a stupor most of the day and night. They moved me into a room right behind the nurse's station, and the nurses, day and night, checked on me every few minutes. Each four hours, the oncoming duty surgeon and anesthesiologist would come up to check me, and were ready for an emergency operation at all times.

I refused to have surgery to remove most of my stomach and told the doctors that they could do it only if I was unconscious and dying.

Throughout the next couple of weeks I improved a bit, and got to where I could get up and walk around the hospital, where I demonstrated that I was my momma's son because daily I went to visit everybody on the 11th floor.

Even after I began to improve, I had occasions of hallucinations. One day I buzzed the nurse and she came running in. I said, "I am lucid enough to know we don't have monkeys in the hospital. But I thought I'd better tell you that I'm seeing monkeys."

She asked me, "Describe what you're seeing."

I said, "Well, now there comes a big black one right now. A monkey came through that door, jumped up on that chest of drawers, and he jumped on me just then."

After a bit, they decided to give me a blood transfusion. They hooked me up, started the blood flowing, and the nurse told the corpsman to stay right beside the bed and watch me. In a little bit I said to him, "They got bedbugs in this hospital."

He said, "Why do you think so, commander?"

I said, "They're just biting me, biting my stomach and legs." He pulled the blanket down, grabbed the needle out of my arm that was giving the blood transfusion, and called the nurse. I had big splotches on my chest and legs, and this was what I thought were my bedbug bites.

In a few minutes the doctor arrived. He says, "What's your trouble, commander?"

I said, "They gave me some blood from somebody been eatin' garlic!"

He says, "You're stabilized now."

I said, "What's my blood pressure?"

He told me, and I recall saying, "There's [folks] in the graveyard with better blood pressure than that," and I passed out.

My room, just behind the nurses' station, gave me a position to be privy to the conversations that went on between the nurses and the ward corpsmen. We had one nurse, a Lieutenant Commander Rossacar, and when she had the watch, she would ride those corpsmen to do field day, cleaning the utensils, waxing the floors, and do otherwise special house cleaning. Most of the time the corpsmen didn't pay any attention to her.

One morning, as she stood just outside my door, she gave them detailed instructions of what to do. She went back to the duty station and went on checking other patients. After a bit, I got up and went to the door and said, in as firm a voice as I could muster, "Didn't you men hear Mrs. Rossacar?"

A couple of them in unison says, "Yessir."

I says, "Go do what she told you on the double," and they scattered to go do it.

Mrs. Rossacar came into my room and says, "Commander, I wish I could do that."

I said, "When they hear you they don't really believe they have to do it. When they heard me, they knew it was their hide if they didn't do it."

As time moved along I got a little better and one day the doctor said I could go down to the first floor to the officer's mess to have lunch. A little rocky and woozy, I got into my uniform and went down to the first floor.

There I was told to step over to the pantry for the ulcer diet. As they handed me out a tray of scrambled eggs and toast, there was a sailor there, real sad lookin'. He says, "Commander, I see you're having scrambled eggs, too." He said he'd had nothing but scrambled eggs for five days.

I really didn't know what I'd had because my mental processes were very sluggish from taking that belladonna. But after lunch I went on back to my room on the 11th floor and looked at a copy of the menu that I was getting, and it showed scrambled eggs for breakfast, but it showed baked fish or turkey or chicken for lunch and dinner. I asked the nurses what I'd been having. They couldn't remember.

I anxiously waited for the evening meal, and so help me, it was scrambled eggs. I was fit to be tied that it wasn't baked fish, according to the menu. But next morning breakfast, of course, was scrambled eggs again. When lunch came and it was scrambled eggs, I hit the ceiling. I told the nurses to call the hospital dietician and tell her I wanted to see her immediately. She told them that she didn't have time to come up and see me and that I had a menu. With this I told the nurse to get my uniform.

She says, "Commander, you're supposed to stay in bed. The doctor gave you permission to get out yesterday as more or less of a test."

I said to her, "I'm going down to the captain's office, and if you don't get me my uniform, I'm going to go in these unhealthy pajamas."

While reluctantly getting the uniform and telling me I shouldn't go, mumbling that she was going to have to tell the doctor, I got dressed and went down to the first floor and into the captain's office.

I told the captain who I was and what had happened. He asked somebody to go get the dietician, and in came a lieutenant commander Wave. The captain told her, "When anybody on the 11th floor calls you, don't you ever again tell them you don't have time to go see them." He says, "Now, go immediately and find out what's happened."

The Wave says, "Well, here's my menu."

The captain says, "Well, Commander Ashe says the menu's not being followed."

I went back to my room and in a couple of hours the Wave came in and says the captain had told her to come up and personally apologize. "And I certainly do apologize, commander. What was happening was that the cooks were taking the chicken, turkey and fish home with them and were serving you scrambled eggs." I told her that I wouldn't have noticed it if it had not been for the sailor.

48

End of Blimp Program

Back at Lakehurst, as time rolled along, in spite of all of my efforts to prevent it, Admiral Perry decided to eliminate airship research and my two research airships. He chose August 31, 1962, as the day when all operations would cease and the airships would be deflated.

I had the two airships each working on a very high priority project, and we continued to work and fly day and night to get as much data as possible, but finally, the night of August 30, Lieutenant Commander Heindrickson made the last all-night flight with the infra-red airship.

Now, I had been told by message and in phone conversation that we were not to have any closing ceremony for phasing out the airships. The commanding officer of the Air Station, Lakehurst, had likewise been informed that no closing ceremony was to be performed. I decided to have the final flight and chose a crew to make it.

One of the last NAN ships in service is shown leaving hangar one at Lakehurst NAS.

I wanted Admiral Rosendahl to be on board, and I chose Captain Kline and the then commanding officer of Lakehurst, Captain Stoltz, to go as passengers. After much deliberation, I chose Commander Bob Shannon, a long-time airship pilot and AT&D operation officer, as pilot. I chose myself as co-pilot. As honorary co-pilots, I chose Max Colley, the current exec of Lakehurst, Gordon Burke, my old fishing buddy, and Henry Alrich, from years before, as my radioman. I chose for crew people there at research that had been with airships for many years, such as Chief Eye for rigger, and Chief Hayes for electrician.

I wrote up a little schedule of flight take-off time and the events. Someone in research took it on themselves to print this schedule and to hand it out to people who came on board at the air station. By word-of-mouth hundreds of long-time airshippers were on the station to witness the last flight. It came to Captain Stolz's attention that this document was being handed out at the main gate and he gave me orders to retrieve all copies and destroy them.

Without further ado, we made about a two-hour flight out over Toms River and Lakewood. We came back to base and Dave Hayes landed us and put the airship into Dock One. A very, very sad day, and the next day even sadder as I witnessed the quiet and stillness of what had been a noisy operation.

I had my orders to the Bureau of Weapons in Washington. I was sorrowful, saddened, but ready to leave.

As word was received and rumors kicked around the station that the airships were about to be phased out of the Navy, I received a message from the Pentagon stating that there would be no more free ballooning. I decided that we would have one last flight in which I would carry the commanding officers of the various activities on the station. And I included one of my officers, Lieutenant Deal, who had never had a free-balloon ride.

On the day designated for this flight, the passengers all gathered out on Mat 1 and got into the balloon basket. I was pilot, Captain Epps was co-pilot, Captain Little, Captain Fortune and Jim Deal were passengers.

As we were about to take off, I looked out across Mat 1 and I saw a figure running that proved to be Dr. Dave Hazen from Princeton. I told Captain Epps, "We've got to take old Dave!" I said, "I'll get out and you be the pilot."

He says, "Oh, no, I'll get out and you be the pilot." I said, "No, RHIP [rank hath its privilege]." I got out of the basket, Dr. Hazen breathlessly got in, Captain Epps gave some last-minute instructions about dropping sand. That is, he told those aboard that when he said put out a little sand, they should take a handful and drop it over the side.

Despite being told that the event should not be publicized, word got out about the last blimp flight, and people who had been involved in the program showed up.

Well, they were ready to go. We turned them loose, they got up into the air a bit and commenced to fall. I heard Captain Epps say, "A little sand out." And Captain Fortune dropped a whole 50 lb. bag. The airship shot up. Mrs. Epps and Evaline had planned to follow the balloon, so I got into the car with them and we proceeded on out the main gate.

Mrs. Epps glanced up and said, "Walt, there's something wrong with that balloon."

I looked, and sure enough, it was falling. As it fell farther and the speed picked up the balloon became a parachute, and it crashed into a farm a few miles from the air station.

Well, as it hit the ground, Captain Fortune tumbled out. The loss of his weight caused the balloon to go back up to about

500 feet, where it began to descend again. This time, it landed in some briars and shrubs and Captain Little tumbled out. It bounced up to about 300 feet and fell again and remained on the ground.

As we came sweeping up the road, we first saw Captain Fortune, as he was crawling out of the bushes. He looked at me and stated he had had both of his balloon rides at the same time—the first and the last.

We proceeded on up, saw Captain Little crawling out of the briars and bushes and noted that he was all right, and then we arrived at the site of the crashed balloon. Captain Epps and the rest of his crew and passengers were shaken up but all right, and the balloon had draped over a farmhouse and knocked down the TV antenna that was on the house.

I was terribly concerned because I had made this flight after being told not to. I told Chief Applegate, who had just arrived in one of the trucks, to go to ship's service and buy a new antenna for that house and install it. I handed him some money and he left. We looked around at the damage to the trees that had been hit and what have you, and I came over to see if an outbuilding that the balloon had draped over was damaged. Lo and behold, that outbuilding was a poultry house. The frightened chickens had piled up on one another and suffocated.

I told the farmer that I'd pay the damage and on carefully reviewing the situation and talking to each member, the only complaint that I got was from Dr. Hazen who stated that they knocked him down in the bottom of that basket, and every time they hit the ground, three or four Navy captains stomped him in the back!

While we were cleaning up the mess Chief Applegate came back with the TV antenna, and he and his men went up on the house and installed it.

He asked the lady of the house for permission to go in and connect it up to her TV. She said, "We hain't got no TV!"

It was with sad feelings that we left Lakehurst. We were sorry that the airship program was canceled. But it was with a feeling of challenge that I headed for Washington for my duties in the Bureau of Weapons. In order for Walt and Susan to enter school on time, we had gone to Washington, purchased a house, bought furniture for it and moved in even though I had a few more weeks before being detached from Lakehurst.

One of the things we discussed at length was whether or not Evaline was going to teach school. After considerable discussion it was decided that she wouldn't teach. It was with considerable surprise that at our very first dinner Susan says, "Daddy, I'm not supposed to tell you, but Momma's teaching school."

Well, I hit the ceiling, but soon calmed down when Evaline told me that she enjoyed teaching school, she was trained to do so, and she wanted to do it. The next day, September 20, 1962, I reported in to BuWeaps.

I thought I'd go by and say hello to my old friend Jean Childes before reporting down to personnel to learn what my new duties would be. Jean Childes greeted me with real and true friendship and told me that she had the new assignment and everything for me there in a folder. She told me that I was going to be the assistant to the guided missile production head, and gave me my parking permit and such other items of interest.

I says, "Jean, I failed a promotion. I was passed over."

She said, "We know it, but the admiral said to assign and treat you just as if you'd been promoted."

Needless to say, I welcomed the much-desired parking permit that only medium-rank captains got and used it for my two years in the Bureau.

I'd always wanted to go to guided missiles production, and here it was! My dream had come true. But I was assigned as assistant to one Captain Mott that really shouldn't have been the division head. His claim to fame was that he became a Flying Tiger back in 1940, went to China, flew P-40's early in the war until the Japs captured him, and he spent the rest of the time as a prisoner of war. Those POWs were badly treated and deserved every consideration for what happened to them, but I wonder at the wisdom of the Navy that made all of them the rank that they would've attained if they had been on active duty.

A few days after arriving in BuWeaps, I was walking down the passageway, looked up and saw Admiral Reich. He says, "Hello, Walt! What're you doing down here?"

I said, "I'm over in Missile Production."

He says, "The hell you say! I want you on my staff."

The next thing I know, I have additional duty on Admiral Reich's staff.

He had orders from the Secretary of the Navy to form a staff whose duties were to quickly determine any problems and solve them for surface-to-air missiles.

I had known Admiral Reich back when we were both commanders in the Bureau of Ordinance. He was one of the sources of information I used to get answers for Captain Robinson and Admiral Schoffel. While I was there at the Bureau he was promoted to captain. During the months that I'd been away, he had gone to sea and been selected as rear admiral.

The admiral had a conference every week attended by all research and production staff, and frequently, users of the missiles. During the week there had been an accumulation of problem areas, and these he addressed by calling on people in the conference. Quite a few of the problems were directly in the missile production area, and I found myself called upon frequently to explain the reasons for the problem and how it was going to be solved.

Time moved along and Captain Mott was retired and Captain Gallagher replaced him. Captain Gallagher was an aeronautical engineer and had been the head of aviation missile production. After approximately a year, Captain Gallagher asked me if I had rather be in the staff position as his assistant or a branch head. I told him branch head, and I quickly became head of the surface-to-air missile production.

One of my duties while assistant division head was to be the Bureau of Weapons representative in charge of some five naval ordinance plants. These included the Naval Ordinance Plant, Forrest Park, Ill., the NOP, York, Pa., the NOP, Louisville, Ky., the NOP, Macon, Ga., as well as the Naval Powder Factory in Maryland.

I occasionally visited each of these plants and became actively involved in the many contracts that these plants had. Included among them was the decision to build a Polaris missile booster plant at the powder factory. A situation developed as I tried to get industrial companies to build the missile booster. I traveled to many companies, including General Dynamics, the Electric Boat division of General Electric, and Thiokol, attempting to get any one of these companies to build the booster.

Although it was illegal to do so, I offered them cost plus fixed-fee profit to produce them. Because of the danger associated with the use of nitroglycerin, they all backed off from producing the booster.

Well, at the time, the Navy was proclaiming across the world that we had submarines loaded with the Polaris missile, ready to make a mess out of Russia. The only problem was that we didn't have the booster to kick the missile out of the sub.

Well, very quietly, secretly, and illegally, I ordered the building of a plant at the Naval Powder Factory. This decision came back to haunt me. One day I learned via a phone call from the administrative officer at the Powder Plant that the inspectors who were looking through the files, trying to find who ordered the building of that illegal plant, were very close to finding out. He said he had periodically moved the files, to keep them from finding what they sought, but he didn't know how long he would be successful.

I told him, "Go hand it to them." He says, "Never would I do that!"

The inspectors got into the act when one of the little igloos blew up.

The laborers in the igloos were instructed that in the event something looked amiss to push a button that turned off everything and to get out of the igloo. It so happened one day that a rather over-weight woman pushed the button and got to the one door of the igloo just as it went off, and she had become a flying projectile.

Some disgruntled Powder Factory person reported to Congress that the building had been constructed illegally, and the congressional inspectors took it from there.

Well, sure enough, shortly the inspectors came to the file that showed that I was the one that directed the construction of the booster plant. They had already canned the commanding officer of the Powder Factory and ordered him out of the Navy. He had, in answers to questions, insisted that he didn't know that he was not supposed to build new construction that wasn't in the budget.

I promptly got orders to appear at Indian Head, Maryland, where I was seated at the wrong end of the green table. The lawyer, incidentally the same lawyer that later grilled Ollie North, looked me in the eye and said he would read me my rights. I said, "No need to. I know 'em." He proceeded to read them anyway.

Then he said, "The way we're going to conduct this investigation is, I will ask you a question and you'll answer yes or no."

I said, "Nooo, we won't." I said, "The way we'll conduct it, is I'll tell the board what happened."

He pulled his hair, jumped up and down, and said I would answer his questions.

I looked then at the congressional board members, related my difficulties trying to get the boosters built by industry and my lack of success. I told how, with the matter so highly classified, I didn't seem to have any alternative to building the booster plant at Indian Head.

I went on, explaining that the many problems that existed boiled down to that we simply couldn't fire the missiles from the submarines. After about an hour, during which time this lawyer kept trying to interrupt me, I told the board members that, yes, I knew that it was illegal, but if any of you had been faced with the same problem, if you had been worth the powder to blow you to hell, would've done the same thing!

A few questions were asked and the lawyer commenced grilling me again. Really, he was trying to find out who in the Bureau ordered me to do it. Well, there hadn't been anybody, but he kept wanting to know if Admiral Stroop had been informed and I assured him that I hadn't informed him, and he marveled that some commander had authority to take such action without the chief of the Bureau knowing it. Then he asked me if had I ever done anything like that before.

"Well," I told him, "Not to this magnitude, but back in '48 I was having difficulty meeting the schedule of producing 3-inch shells and needed two electric furnaces, and I had called up and worked a deal with the chief executive officer of General Electric whereby he would send the foundries to me then and we'd pay for them after we got it put in the budget."

Those two little fluffs of hair that he had on the side of his head were getting mistreated as he pulled them every time he heard something he didn't like. He asked if I had ever done it before that.

I said, "No, but Congress had passed a law back in the fifties and sixties that said that any line item costing more that $25,000 couldn't be purchased unless it had been put in the budget, and that I routinely, at Lakehurst, broke down an item that cost more than $25,000 into two or more parts and paid for them separately."

The whole day was spent at Indian Head. After which time I was excused and went back to Washington. About two weeks later a representative from the congressional board came over to my office, asked me to shut all the doors, and told me that the board had decided that they were going to drop this matter, that it seemed to be to the best interest of the naval service if it were treated as never having existed. He looked at me and grinned and said, "I'm glad we've got the boosters!"

I continued on attending Admiral Reich's conferences, but my chief concern was to get my 73 civilian engineers organized into subsections and promoted to the proper civil service position. I carefully reviewed and, over a few months, wrote the job description and justification that promoted all but two of them. My deputy was a GS-14 and I couldn't justify his promotion to a GS-15. One of my GS-12 engineers was next to useless and I didn't think he deserved to be promoted.

After a bit, Captain Gallagher was transferred and a Captain Now, who had been a branch head in the PWS division, took over as division head. Starting with the very first conference with Admiral Reich, when in the course of any of the meetings there would be a problem, the admiral would say, "What about that, PWS?" And I had become accustomed to answering it or stating that I didn't know the answer. When Captain Now became division head he took the lead when he asked for PWS to give the answer. After a bit, Admiral Reich turned around in this big conference and says, "When I say PWS I mean Walt Ashe and I want everybody else to shut up!"

One day, while on temporary duty as a student at Vandenberg Air Force Base at the Missile, Space, and Astronautics School, the students went down and spent the entire morning observing the firing of one of the first Polaris missiles. This one, unfortunately, veered off toward Australia and had to be destroyed.

The students all came back to the Officer's Mess to have lunch. After lunch I strolled out in front of the Officer's Mess and looked out across the beautiful blue Pacific. As I slowly turned, looking westward over the Vandenberg Base, I suddenly stopped and intently looked at something that I thought was steam at first. Then, it occurred to me that it was fuming nitric acid.

I had a rental car and I quickly got into it and headed for the source of the fumes. I came driving up to the missile compound and there were two Titan missiles, one standing upright, and the other lying on its side, and they were loading a hydrogen bomb on one and the bomb was already on the other. And they in turn, as they got them upright, were pumping in the fuming nitric acid.

In less time than it takes to tell it, two Air Force MPs arrived and came whipping over alongside my car and says, "Sir, you are not permitted in this area."

I said, "I know it, I'm leaving."

I turned and drove out, thinking, "My, my, my, my, my! They're actually loading intercontinental missiles." I hurried to the BOQ, called the Los Angeles airport, found when the next plane was out to Washington, made a reservation, jumped into the car and drove at 100 m.p.h. to Los Angeles. I barely made the plane and flew to Washington.

On arrival home, I found Evaline's mother and father there visiting with her. But I said to her, "What's going on?" She stated, "I don't know!" I said, "Well, come and look."

We lived in an area that was also home to numbers of high defense officials, and it was common in times of crisis for the husbands to stay nights in their offices. When this happened, the wives, being rather concerned, turned on the lights in the house and grounds. Waynewood, our neighborhood, was lit up like a Christmas tree!

I immediately called my office. Mr. Axelson answered and I asked him, "What's going on, Axe?" He says, "I don't know. The admiral called for you. I told him you were in California, and he said to be sure and know the location of all the missiles."

Well, it so happened that the Navy had been the producer of all the air-to-air and air-to-ground missiles for the Navy, Army and Air Force. And it so happened in the organization that my branch had custody of the storage sites of these missiles.

Axe said that they'd been in, going through the Cardex, and checking on the location of the missiles. I told him I'd be in in a few minutes, and he told me, "No reason to. We're about to go home." So I said I'd be in first thing in the morning.

The next day was Saturday. We sat around the office all day and nothing happened, not even any leaking of news. The next day, the same thing.

Monday we came in for a workday and at about 9:30 Assistant Secretary of the Navy Belew came into my office and showed me a message. It read, "This is no drill. Sec. Air Force requests Sec. Navy supply all air missiles south Florida immediately." The Assistant Secretary said to me, "Start movin' 'em out."

I said, "Mr. Secretary, what's going on?" He says, "I don't know."

I got busy on the phones, attempting to locate air wings and squadrons of transport planes to move the missiles. I was successful in getting a Marine air wing at Cherry Point, N.C., to start moving Bull Pup missiles to south Florida. As the day wore on and after many failures to raise anybody that had availability, I finally got Westover Field, Mass., and they told me that an air wing was en route from Germany and they would put my requirements first on the list.

The next morning, Secretary Belew sent a Lieutenant Commander to my office who told me the secretary wanted to see me right away. I went into his office and he showed me another message. It was from Sec. Air Force to Sec. Navy and stated, "This is no drill. Urgent, urgent, urgent. All air missiles south Florida immediately."

The secretary asked me how I was doing and I said, "Not doing too hot." I said, "I don't believe we can get those missiles down there by air. I believe we're going to have to use the rails." He says, "Just get them down there."

I went back to my office and called the president of Florida East Coast Railroads. I told him, "I'm exercising the War Powers Act. I want trains moving non-stop to south Florida."

He says, "I have two lines, one going south and one north; and the passengers that are stuck in Miami will need to be coming back north."

I told him, "Well, they'll have to wait until we get the missiles to south Florida."

Then he said to me, "Commander, what's going on?"

I said, "I truthfully do not know. All I know is that I'm ordered to get the missiles to south Florida."

Normally in Washington when there's some crisis booming the scuttlebutt keeps you informed of what's going on, but here I knew nothing. Just those two messages.

Well, on Wednesday my concern became the same kind of concern that those in the nation that were aware of what was happening were concerned about, and that was a Russian attack by ballistic missiles. Well, I couldn't do much of anything except strengthen the basement of my house in Waynewood. I went to the lumber company and got some two by tens and six by sixes to build a little shelter in the corner of the basement. Wednesday evening I stocked this little shelter with food and liquids—water and soft drinks, and food that wouldn't spoil. I took a shotgun and a box of shells and I took Walter down and told him that if he was lucky enough to make it in the event of an attack to go in there in that basement and to not let anybody in unless they had been decontaminated.

Evaline said, "You can't tell a young boy to shoot people."

I said, "You have to, because if they're contaminated, the ones here will die, too."

I told Walter and Susan and Evaline that, if they had a chance in the event of an attack, to try to make it to that basement.

Each night the radio news came on at 11:30, and I had been waiting to hear any news on the 11:30 broadcast. Just before 11:30 the news came on with an excited announcer, stating, "Mr. and Mrs. America, we're in some sort of a crisis. Commercial airlines, planes, are landing at Boca Chica Air Station, Key West, Florida, one every 30 seconds, loaded with combat Marines." He excitedly said, "The Panama Canal has been closed to all east-bound traffic. Amphibious ships from the Pacific Fleet are coming through the canal loaded with Marines." He went on to discuss other movements that were occurring, including that the 101st Airborne Division equipment was moving by train from Louisville to south Florida.

The next day, Thursday, there was just an absolute dearth of news.

My missiles, by the thousands, were pouring into south Florida. Suddenly, Friday at about noon, President Kennedy declared by radio that Russian missiles were in Cuba and that he had ordered a Navy blockade of Cuba. I didn't think that the Russians would stand still for a naval blockade, and when I learned that our ships were stopping Russian ships and searching them, and, if they had contraband, were sending them back to Russia, I thought, surely, we were in for retaliation.

But they took it. An interesting thing occurred a couple of days later there in Waynewood when several of us were having a few drinks out on the lawn. Some Air Force colonel told me that we're going to have a new Chairman of the Joint Chiefs shortly. I said, "How's that?" He said he had been in the boardroom a couple of hours earlier. Admiral Burke, Chairman of the Joint Chiefs, was in there, and Secretary of Defense MacNamara came in and he was looking at the disposition of the ships, and Secretary MacNamara said to Admiral Burke, "I want this destroyer [marked on the board] to move over and investigate these ships [also marked on the board]."

Admiral Burke said, "Mr. Secretary, I have Admiral Ward down there in command, and if he wants to move that destroyer, he'll move it."

He said to Admiral Burke, "I want that destroyer moved." And Admiral Burke says, "Well all right, move it,'" and walked out.

Well, what was going to happen was the secretary was going to the president and either MacNamara or Burke would have to resign. The next morning it was announced that Admiral Burke had resigned.

Let me say here and now that Burke was one of the finest admirals that I ever knew, and with equal vim and vigor let me say that Sec. MacNamara was the sorriest excuse for a secretary of defense that this nation has ever known. The only thing, apparently, he was any good at was being the head of the World Bank, where his job was to see how much of our money he could give away. He helped Johnson get us defeated in Vietnam. All in all, MacNamara materially contributed to the fiasco we had in southeast Asia.

My little bit, the extent of which was unusual, came about because my branch held the storage of the missiles. President Kennedy was able to solve the problem with the Russians without a nuclear conflagration that would have destroyed the world as we know it.

One thing that was of considerable interest. On Wednesday night, before the news broke, one of my former officers at Key West, Lieutenant Commander Ed Verberg, had retired from the Navy and gone to work for Thompson-Ramo-Woolridge. Ed was in Washington for a minute and he drove by to say hi.

We both were talking about something that was highly classified when he asked me, "How many submarine missiles can you get into the air?"

I put my fingers up and made a circle of zero. He said, "We can't do much better," and stuck three fingers up. The reason for his hurry as he left was that he was urgently, along with his crew, trying to get our silo missiles in readiness to attack.

49

I Leave the Navy

I had done pretty well in my job with missile production, to the extent that a special letter was sent to the next captain's selection board, pointing out that I should be promoted to four stripes. When the selection board names were announced, my boss, Rear Admiral Reich, was one of the board. I immediately had hopes that I might be selected.

Commander Ashe at home in Bristol, Tennessee, in uniform one more time, for a picture.

When the board finished its work and Admiral Reich returned to his office in BuWeaps, he called and asked me to come over and see him. He said, "Well, Walt, what happened in the selection board proceedings is not to be divulged. But I want to tell you that the brown-shoe aviators are not going to let a lighter-than-air pilot take one of the aviation billets." He said, "The board consisted of four line admirals and five aviation admirals and the board's vote on my selection was four for it and five against. Next year the board will consist of five general line and four aviators. You'll make it, then."

I said, "No, admiral, I won't make it because I won't be here. I'm going to retire."

He says, "You can't retire. You are in a special billet and I won't let you retire."

I said, "Admiral, all you want is for me to remain here and run this missile production program for you. I have finished my obligated service and I can retire immediately."

I turned and walked out, made my way back to my office, went in and told my administrative assistant to dash me off a letter requesting immediate retirement. She says, "Commander, I'll do nothing of the sort."

I said, "Yes, you will. I'm going to retire." She says, "Sit on it a few days."

And later, how I wished I had taken her advice.

There were representatives of three companies in my office waiting to see me on various phases of their missile production: General Dynamics of Ponoma, Calif.; Bendix of Misshawauka, Ind.; and Sperry-Rand of Bristol, Tenn. Each of these representatives questioned me regarding what they had overheard as I came into my office and each of them expressed a desire for me to join their respective companies.

The next morning I received a call from the head of the General Dynamics plant, stating that he would have an offer in the mail immediately. I received a phone call from George Stolz of Bendix stating that he had seven plants and I could go to any one that I chose and we would work out what my position would be after I arrived. Sperry's sales manager called me the next morning and said an offer would be in the mail to me that day.

I felt highly elated that they would show the considerable confidence in my ability, but I was still terribly sad that I hadn't been promoted to captain. On receipt I reviewed each of the offers and considered every angle that I could conceive of—potential for promotion, location, salary, tax considerations—

and finally decided to accept the offer from Sperry-Rand as soon as I could arrange my retirement.

I called an acquaintance in the Bureau of Personnel, asking him to expedite my retirement. I took leave and went to Memphis, and en route back to Washington I stopped off at the Sperry Farragut plant in Bristol. I met the top management people, liked what I saw, and returned to Washington.

My assistant welcomed me most enthusiastically on my return and told me that Captain Now had been driving him crazy. When a problem came up, Captain Now would call him in, tell him to get a message prepared to send out with the solution, and have it in his office in two hours.

Just about that time, over the squawk box, Captain Now says, "Jones, get in here!"

I says, "Captain, this is Walt. I'm back." He says, "Get in here!"

He showed me a message and, with a considerable degree of agitation, told me to get him a message and have it on his desk in two hours. I said, "Captain, I've served in this Bureau a number of years. I can be counted on for a rapid solution and rapidly informing the interested parties concerning any problem that comes up." I said, "Don't give me any deadlines."

He said, "I'm sorry, Walt. This job is over my head. I don't know how to handle it."

I said, "Where my branch is concerned, have the action messages routed to me, and I'll have them answered as expeditiously as possible."

Well, in a few days I got my orders saying I would retire on October 31, 1964. They threw a very large party in my honor. Several people on Admiral Reich's staff spoke and quite a number of the civilians in the division spoke. By this time I was having some very pressing second thoughts about leaving the Navy, and surely wished that I hadn't done so.

Walter was about to go to college and he had chosen Cornell. We took him up, went through the trauma of leaving him on the campus, proceeded back to Washington, and moved to Bristol.

I arrived at Bristol and we had numerous opportunities to purchase a home. It was a question of deciding which one we liked the most. Susan enrolled in school and I reported in to Sperry-Farragut.

I was assigned duties as assistant to the chief engineer, a very competent and likable fellow named Ed Wagner. I quickly became competent in the infighting that went on in the preparation of bids for new business. A previous bid to the Bureau to build Shrike missiles resulted in a contract being let to Sperry-Farragut.

The contract called for building 10 missiles, passing tests to qualify production, then producing 40 of the missiles. After a bit, I approached the Vice-President and General Manager, Earl McCormick, with a request that he assign me responsibilities of Shrike Project Officer. With considerable doubt he approved my request, but with misgivings in that he felt that I hadn't been at the plant a sufficient length of time.

Well, away to the races! We built those 10 missiles, shipped them to China Lake, Calif., for tests. Sperry had a policy that all travel would be tourist class. I informed Mr. McCormick that the travels for the Shrike engineers and myself would be first class. Otherwise, we'd stay at home and handle it by phone. He reluctantly agreed to permit this and a number of the engineers and myself kept the road hot between Bristol and China Lake.

We would leave Bristol, fly to Memphis, get on American Airlines from Memphis to Los Angeles, rent cars at Los Angeles to drive up into the desert, and when our business was finished, we would drive back to Los Angeles, get Delta Airlines to Atlanta, and back to Bristol.

In record time the Navy completed preparations for testing our missiles and I followed the movement of the missiles through the Navy test program. I learned the evening before the first test that the Navy had learned the missiles were not set sensitive enough for the guidance system.

I learned that the missiles were actually at the China Lake Air Station, and the first one would be flight tested on the next day. The information that I received on sensitivity I considered very valid and attempted to do something about it.

I went to one of the officers on the air station and told him my problem and that I wanted those missiles back. He reluctantly agreed to let me have them, and on the Q.T. arranged for me to pick them up. In the back of my rental car we took the missiles to a little shop on China Lake, removed the guidance portion of the missile, cut into the rubber seal, and moved the sensitivity up one quarter turn. We put the missiles back together, took them to the back door of testing at the air station, and left them.

By "we" I mean Jon Coppedge from Sperry, Gene Kearns, the government inspector at Sperry, and myself. This was totally illegal and a terrific gamble, but after working on them all night, I called Mr. McCormick back at Bristol, told him what I had done, and he nearly died. He said, "Hold up the test and I'll get engineers on the plane immediately."

I said, "Mr. McCormick, you can't hold up the test. They're already on the test line. Furthermore, one of 'em that they select is going to be flown this morning."

He was quite interested in that Shrike contract, and I think that he considered his chances of qualifying had changed from possible to impossible. In a bit, the airplane with our missile on board came in over the air station and fired at the target. The target was several miles out in the desert and the missile, to be successful, was required to come in and hit within 50 feet of the target.

We drove to the test site and there the missile had hit within 20 feet of the target. As was customary with contractors successfully completing a test, I invited most of the Shrike engineers and other people at Naval Ordinance Test Station

(NOTS) China Lake to come by the motel where we were staying to have a few refreshments and drinks.

Evaline and Ruth Cooper had decided to accompany us to China Lake and they acted as hostesses for the party.

The information that we had been successful spread throughout the China Lake establishment, and two days later they decided to test a second missile. This too was a rip-roaring success, and the resulting party was larger, noisier, and congratulations were more numerous.

Two days later they decided to flight-test two of our missiles. Same routine, the plane came in over the air station, fired at the range. Along with China Lake test personnel, Wally Cooper and myself were at one of the observation test points and the word coming in from the test site stated that we had missed. Well, I thought my tired old eyes were having trouble, because it looked to me that both the missiles hit mighty close to the site.

They made a big to-do and many vehicles approached the test site, and I got out feeling very sad. I went over to look, and there both missiles were about 30 feet from the target. And the China Lake project engineers and test personnel commenced congratulating me and singing that I was a jolly good fellow, and that night we had one heck of a party. Ran out of drinks twice before the people, about 4 o'clock, decided to disband.

Well, China Lake decided that since all four missiles had hit they were going to accept the other six missiles and not test them to destruction. I flew back to Bristol, accepting my accolades of success, and we made preparations to build the 40 new missiles.

Along about this time I learned that it was the Sperry-Farragut policy that expense money—travel, food, and the like—was kept very limited. It had cost quite a few dollars to have these parties there in my motel suite, and I sent in an expense account just like it was.

The treasurer of Sperry-Farragut was a fellow named Patterson, and I watched to see his action as he started to review my expense account. In a little bit, I saw him pick it up and head up to the corner office where the vice-president and general manager was. In a little bit I decided that I'd better go up there myself.

As I entered Mr. McCormick's office, Patterson says, "And you should let this guy know that he can't come in here with any expense accounts like this."

Patterson's back was to me and McCormick looked at me and held up the expense account papers and said, "Walter, what is this all about?'"

I said, "Every time we had a missile hit we had a party. And when two of 'em hit a number of people came to the party. If you think this expense account is large, you wait until we get into the swing of this. I have no intention of presiding over 50 missiles a year. I plan to produce 200 missiles a month."

Mr. McCormick reached over and got his pen and signed the expense account. In about a month, he called me in and told me that he was promoting me from Shrike Project Officer to Shrike Program Manager. I became a red bar manager in the Sperry hierarchy and got about a $3,000 a year pay increase.

At Sperry-Farragut our missile production rapidly increased each month and after about two years we had reached over 200 deliveries each month. There were numerous problems arising daily with Washington. Not the least of which was the annual distribution of production orders to Sperry-Farragut and Texas Instruments.

One day a big conference was called in Washington, and along with John Coppedge I attended the meeting. Quite surprisingly, there was a large room filled with BuWeaps, NOTS China Lake, and Texas Instruments personnel. The meeting started with a statement from Captain Botwell, the BuWeaps program manager, that a determination had to be made regarding the use of polyolefin in the missiles and an allocation of how many missiles would be contracted to Sperry and how many to Texas Instruments.

There were several learned and highly technical dissertations from NOTS engineers, followed by Texas Instruments, regarding the use of polyolefin. They asked what were Sperry's comments? I rose and stated, "Using polyolefin was something like placing a wooly-worm on a bowl of Jello and trying to hold the wooly-worm in place without either squishing him or breaking the surface of the Jello."

It was agreed by all that my colloquial description of the situation was appropriate.

The discussion on allocating numbers of missiles to Sperry and Texas Instruments became quite heated among representatives from NOTS China Lake. The president of Texas Instruments was himself present at the conference, and of course, really couldn't see the need for allocating any number to Sperry.

After a bit, Captain Botwell got up and recessed the meeting and announced that he would like to see Commander Ashe, Mr. Bowbeck and Commander Carter in an adjoining conference room.

Well, of course, the president of Texas Instruments thought that I was going in to get the lion's share of the missiles. What actually occurred was that the Bureau representatives didn't know how to use the Bureau's War Preparation figures.

I quickly showed 'em how to do it, and then they figured out how many missiles would go to Texas Instruments and how many to Sperry. We went back into the conference room. Captain Botwell got up and announced the number of missiles allocated to each of the producers and closed the conference.

It so happened that Sperry's portion of the total production was very close to exceeding our capacity, but contrary to Texas Instruments' representatives' natural feelings on the subject, I really had nothing to do with the allocation.

Texas Instruments' president wrote a letter to the Bureau of Weapons stating that I was illegally using my previous duty in the Bureau of Weapons to negotiate missile production to Sperry. Captain Botwell wrote him back a letter, copy to me, that stated that Commander Ashe has never participated in Shrike contractual matters.

Down at Bristol, I was assigned additional responsibilities and took over as Program Manager for all defense production at Sperry-Farragut.

One of these contracts had to do with the covers on some special atomic weapons. I decided to travel to Fort McAllister, Okla., along with Gene Kearns, the government inspector at Bristol, and resolve the difficulties with the contract.

We drove into McAllister, spent the night, and the next day accompanied the station commanding officer on a tour of that very large base. As we traveled along for miles on end, looking at what seemed to be new construction, Mr. Kearns asked the captain, "What in the world is all that stuff I've been seeing for the last several miles?"

A Christmas card photo at the time showed my transition to civilian life.

The captain said it was determined in Washington that bomb stowage facilities would be constructed at McAllister. All Navy bombs were to be delivered to McAllister and sold on bids to contractors to use the bombs to make fertilizer. Then the Vietnam War came along and used up the bombs and there weren't any to stow, so he had all those facilities empty.

I wasn't saying a word because it so happened that, during my first tour at the Bureau of Ordinance, Secretary McNamara issued a directive that stated we were going into a missile age, there wouldn't be any further use for bombs, and the Navy was to collect the bombs at some location and sell them on high bids to contractors to use in making fertilizer. Admiral Stroop had called a conference, disgustedly read Sec. McNamara's directive to his four planning chiefs and their assistants, and stated, "When the Secretary of Defense issues a directive, the Navy has to comply. And you gentlemen know how to comply."

Captain Robinson and myself went back to our office. He sat down at his desk and stated, "Walt, take care of this. You know how to handle it."

Well, I really didn't. But I decided that I would have to have storage facilities, and that by the time construction of the facilities reached the budget, and the facilities were constructed, more than likely we'd have a new Secretary of Defense, and at any rate, wouldn't need to get rid of all of our bombs. I had chosen McAllister as the storage site and had issued instructions that stated, "When magazines are ready, all bombs will be shipped to McAllister and bids opened for the production of fertilizer."

That had been approximately 12 years previous to my visit, and is about the normal lead time to get anything done in Washington.

A few weeks later, back at Sperry, I was promoted to gold bar manager in charge of all defense production at Sperry-Farragut. For this I got a little bonus and a couple thousand dollars pay increase.

50

Univac

About this time, 1968, Sperry-Univac top management out of St. Paul, Minn., decided that Sperry-Farragut would be transferred to Univac. All defense programs would be transferred to Univac, Salt Lake City, and the Sperry facilities would be converted to the production of computers.

This I did not like, but was asked to transfer to Salt Lake City. After reviewing the situation at Salt Lake, I decided to remain at Bristol. The wheels of Univac at St. Paul decided to put someone in charge of both Bristol and Salt Lake City's production.

The first I heard of this was McCormick one day angrily telling me that if I took that job I wouldn't be permitted to move around in the Bristol plant except to go into my office. I said, "Mr. McCormick, I haven't been offered the job, but I tell you one thing. Should I take such a job, I would go to any and every spot in the Bristol plant and the Salt Lake City plant as often as I saw fit!"

A few days later, I was called from St. Paul and told that I had the job. This was another sizable promotion and I found myself reporting to Mr. Probst, the head of Univac, as did Mr. McCormick. With vim and vigor I tackled the job, shortly to learn that I was to try to transfer the production of Shrike from Bristol to Salt Lake City, maintain minimum prices, and keep up the schedule.

I traveled repeatedly to Salt Lake City, transferred a number of people from Bristol to Salt Lake, and was expecting to transfer some more when I decided that this situation looked untenable. About this time, one of the vice presidents in St. Paul called to tell me, "You and Evaline get that new Lincoln of yours, proceed to Minnesota, and take over as program manager for the Poseidon missile. Don't worry about house, furniture. Sperry will take care of all of it."

For about an hour I was elated at this promotion. And then I began to think of the difficulties of living in Minnesota, and decided that wasn't for me. I called back Verne Lease in Minnesota and told him that I was going to resign. He tried to talk me out of it. He told me he was putting one of his troubleshooters on the plane that night to Bristol, but I had decided that I wanted to be a stockbroker.

One of my Navy friends, Joe Willamette, had gone to work for Merrill-Lynch. On one of his visits in the area, he suggested that I come work for him as a stockbroker. A while later, the offer appealed to me.

I thought there might be some things that one had to do to become a stockbroker, so I called my stockbroker, Bob Hobbs, at Abbott, Procter & Paine, and asked him if there was anything I had to do. He said, "Why do you ask?"

I said, "I'm considering going to Merrill-Lynch in Memphis."

In about 15 minutes Prentiss Hollenbeck, manager of the Abbott, Procter & Paine office in Bristol, gave me a call and asked what I was doing for lunch. I said, "Nothing particular. Why?"

He said, "Meet me at the Country Club."

Since I had nothing better to do, I agreed to join him, and at the ripe old age of 48, I was hired to become a stockbroker.

I agreed to join Abbott, Procter & Paine July 15, 1968. In a few weeks Prentiss told me that they wanted me to come over to Richmond for a 12-weeks study course, preparatory to taking the broker's exam in New York. I hit the ceiling and stated I wasn't going, that I'd been hired on the premise that I could prepare for the exam on my own here in the Bristol office. Later, I did agree to go over to Richmond for a week to acquaint myself with the workings of Abbott, Proctor & Paine.

Three months later I began to clamor to take the exam for stockbroker. I was told that a minimum of six month's training was required before I could take the exam. This didn't set well with me, and I frequently pointed out that I was ready for the exam.

Finally, the day after Thanksgiving, the Abbott, Proctor & Paine New York office informed me to come to New York and prepare to take the exam. I had the feeling that they planned a cram session for me in New York, and I had no intention of going along with it.

Come Sunday after Thanksgiving I flew to New York, and Monday morning, went to the examining center and took the broker's examination. After completing the exam, I went down to Abbott, Proctor & Paine's New York offices. I went in and presented myself to Mr. Proctor's administrative assistant, and from her got a quiz on where in the hell I'd been, that she'd had a training course ready for me.

She took me over to introduce me to Mr. Proctor, and his comment was, "What you do on your off hours is your business, but we expect you to be at the office at 8 o'clock."

Before I could even answer, Mr. Paine came through his office door, and said, "Where's that guy from Bristol?"

Mr. Proctor introduced me to Mr. Paine, and Mr. Paine lit in on me, asking me where had I been? Finally I got in a word edgeways and told them that I had taken the brokerage exam that morning. Such surprise, consternation, and disbelief I saw written across their faces.

Mr. Paine said that they had a training course set up for me to prepare me for the exam, that I wouldn't come to Richmond for the training course, but that I damn well would now. He said he would give me one more chance to pass that exam, and this time I would be prepared for it.

I said, "Mr. Paine, I passed the exam. But if I didn't, I wouldn't take it the second time."

He lit into a dissertation, the gist of which was that 30 percent of their brokers failed the first time and some 15 percent failed the second time, and this was even after the 12-week training course was used in trying to prepare the embryo broker. He said, "When do you get your grades?"

I told him that the examining center said I'd get them in approximately two weeks. "Well," he says, "I'll get 'em quicker than that!" And he went walking out, all 300 pounds of him.

Mr. Proctor told me that his administrative assistant ran the program and for me to report over to her. This I did, and you know, that tall, thought-she-was-sexy Puerto Rican sent me up to their trading center where I commenced buying and selling stock on eight telephones that were there in the office because the guy that did it had called in sick. What a strange and unusual situation.

But, as best I could, I handled it for that afternoon. The next morning when I reported in she told me to go back and do the same job for the day.

I told her, "Oh, no, no, hold it!" I said, "I did that yesterday. I'm going over to watch commodity trading."

She stomped her foot and said, "You'll go where I send you!"

I said, "Stick around, sister, and see!"

What an eye-opener commodity trading was! In the silver pits with brokers screaming at the top of their lungs, buying and selling contracts of silver. I came back to the office after lunch just in time to see ol' Hugh Paine comin' down the hall, wavin' a piece of paper, looking like he was the father of a new baby. And, practically breathless, stuck that paper out to Ron Proctor and said, "Lookee here, he made an 'A' on that exam!"

He congratulated me, and said that they had never had anybody from Abbott, Proctor & Paine make an 'A.' He told Ron Proctor to change the course for the brokers there in training and have me tell them the questions and the answers that I could remember from the exam.

Ron Proctor told me to have the brokers there under training to meet me there in the large conference room and to do the best I could at recalling the questions and being sure that the students had the answers. I went across the hall and into the office of "Stompin' Matilda." She greeted me explosively, telling me to get up to the trading desk. As calmly as I could, I told her that I wanted the student brokers to meet me in the conference room, and to repeat this the rest of the week.

She went flying over to Ron Proctor's office, came out completely subdued, and went about getting the student brokers into the conference room. Once there I learned that about a dozen students were being subjected to that week's cram session in preparation for the exam the following Monday.

I returned to Bristol on Saturday and commenced making ready to commence operating as a registered broker. I immediately began trading commodities as well as stocks, but doing it in Hallenbeck's name. On the arrival of my registration I told Hallenbeck that I wanted to come off salary and go on commission immediately. He cautioned me to wait six months, but, as I told him, I wasn't interested. If I couldn't beat my salary in commissions then I had no business being there.

The next thing I know, a New York exchange full service brokerage firm bought Abbott, Proctor & Paine.

There were many highlights, errors and pitfalls that I made during my 31 years as a Paine-Webber stockbroker. I made all the errors common for a broker. I put down 1,000 shares when I meant 100. I put down buy when I meant sell. But over the years I saw some of my customers' accounts change from a few thousand dollars to several million. I had clients who bought $10,000 worth of mutual funds, 25 years later cash in at $400,000.

I established the reputation of being a serious, completely honest stockbroker. I only wish that, during those years, I had practiced on my own account what I preached to my clients. For me, I played long shots and seemed to have the ability to pick a stock that was about to go broke. Certainly in my commodity playing, I was a steady and stupid loser. I enjoyed my long tour with Paine-Webber, and only can say that I regret that I can't do it again.

51

Church

Shortly after arriving in Bristol, Evaline, Susan and myself joined the First Baptist Church. We seemed to be happy in this church. Evaline taught Sunday school in the primary department, and I taught the senior boys' class.

In the young people's department the girl's class was taught by the wife of the president of Virginia Intermont College.

I noticed that each time the occasion arose where the Sunday school subject matter had to do with temperance, which, as we all know in the Baptist Church, is total abstinence from several things, that each time such a temperance class was scheduled in the Sunday school quarterly, Mrs. Turner would suggest to me that I teach the combined boys and girls classes.

These two classes were very active, with high percentage attendance, and consisted of a total of about 50 boys and girls. One time after a few years, when I was teaching the combined classes, the kids came in armed with many of the questions that troubled Baptist young people.

The first question came from one of the girls. "Commander Ashe, is it a sin to dance?" I said, "Well it's certainly a sin to dance like I do! But biblically there's no reference that associates dancing with wrong-doing in the Bible. In fact, there are a few references like where David danced in the street nude. Well, there might be some objection to the men dancing in the nude, but even that, scripturally, is not associated with wrong-doing."

And so it went. A boy asked, "Is it wrong to drink beer?"

I said, "Drinking beer can be wrong if it's taken to excess, to the point where it makes one drunk." I said, "Bible Proverbs repeatedly points out that a drunkard is wrong. It even mentions that people who get up in the morning and commence to drink are wrong. But," I said, "aside from the social and economic problems that can be generated by drinking excessive alcohol, drinking beer is not wrong, and the scriptures clearly state that Jesus' first miracle was making wine, and that Jesus attended a party with his mother, a wedding party, that lasted about two weeks, at the end of which time the crowd had consumed all of the wine. And when Mary told them to check with Jesus for more wine, the Bible further states the wine that He made was even better than the wine that the host had provided in the first place."

I said, "Now here you will get from many people that the Bible was referring to grape juice. The Bible was not referring to grape juice. It was calling wine, wine. As a matter of fact, they had no way of keeping grape juice. As you know, grape juice exposed to the air will shortly become wine, and if the exposure continues, it will become vinegar. Man had not discovered ways and means of keeping the grape juice free from the air. And in fact, they made a champagne by taking the grape juice and putting it in oxen intestine where the intestine will expand as the wine becomes champagne and it mentions that you can't reuse these wineskins."

Many of the other questions that confront Baptist young people were kicked around and discussed before we finally went overtime and had to dismiss the class. The very next Sunday, as I came walking by the pastor's study heading for my class, the assistant pastor was there waiting for me and said the pastor wanted to see me.

The two of them in the pastor's study with the door closed began to tell me what I must do. The pastor said, "You will get those classes together and disavow the things you told them last Sunday."

I said, "I'll do nothing of the sort. I told them exactly what the scriptures say in answer to their questions."

He said, "This question of dancing and drinking is disallowed in the Baptist church." He says, "The membership of the First Baptist Church won't stand for it."

I said, "I told them exactly what the scriptures say."

He said, "You know that and I know it, but the membership of the church doesn't know it."

I said, "It's your job to teach them! To teach them what the Bible says!"

He says, "I want you to retract what you said."

I said, "I won't do it!" I said, "Under the circumstances I'll tell you I won't take a class again next year, but I won't resign from teaching the class that I have until the term's over." And I said, "If you and/or the deacons push for my resignation, I'll appear before the whole church." And, I says, "And let me tell you something, preacher, your attitude and position reminds me of a used car salesman. In fact, I suspect it would be better if you went into another line of business!"

It suffices to say that three months later he resigned as pastor, went out to the Ford car dealership, and became an automobile salesman.

It was about this time that Susan and Evaline became interested in, and later joined the Worldwide Church of God. They accepted Herbert W. Armstrong's teachings and interpretations of the Bible. One of these teachings and beliefs was that it was wrong for people to go to doctors—surgeons as well as medical—for treatment. For this reason it literally broke Evaline's heart for her number one son to become a doctor.

During the course of an annual physical exam, our doctor found that Evaline was losing calcium, potassium, magnesium, and other minerals from her bones. He finally decided that Evaline had difficulties with one or more of her parathyroids. I found that there were three hospitals in the nation that did this rare parathyroid surgery—Houston General, Mayo Clinic, and Duke.

Life became miserable for poor Evaline as she was subjected to the continuous badgering by Walter and myself to go to Duke for surgery. The members of her church were highly supportive of her as she stood by her decision not to have surgery.

After about a year or so, Evaline decided to have her pastor over to have dinner with us. The prime objective was for him to convince me that her position on surgery was correct. By the time we had drinks before dinner, then dinner, and a couple of bottles of wine after dinner, I had convinced him that she should have the surgery, and he told her, "Mrs. Ashe, as the church teaches, it's a matter of individual preference, but I believe, if I were you, I would have the surgery."

Evaline seemed to be relaxed and in concurrence as we arranged to go to Duke for parathyroid surgery. Aside from my chewing out one of the ward doctors for gouging around on her arm while trying to obtain blood samples, all went well at Duke and she was scheduled to go into surgery at 7:00 in the morning.

They had told me that the surgery would probably take 30 minutes to an hour. In some instances it would go over that if they had difficulties in locating all the parathyroids. While Evaline was in surgery I went in to her room and stretched out on her bed while waiting for the time to pass. Some smart-aleck nurse came in and told me to get up out of her bed and stay out of it.

I said, "Now listen, sister, let me tell you something. I'm paying for this room as well as this bed and as long as she's not back from surgery, I'll stay in it as long as I damn well please!"

She says, "I'm reporting you to the head nurse."

In a few minutes, the head nurse came in and told me, "Mr. Ashe, you're right, it's your bed and you can use it as you please. Of course, we expect you to vacate it when Mrs. Ashe gets out of surgery."

I asked her to find out what's going on in surgery. I said, "It's been over two hours."

She says, "Well, I can't very well go into surgery."

"Well," I says, "you can. And if you don't, I will!"

She came back to say that the doctor said that he had had difficulty locating the last parathyroid, but that she would soon be coming out of surgery into the recovery room.

In a bit, he came in to tell me that she had six parathyroids, five good ones, and one bad one, which was about as big as half of a chicken egg.

They put Evaline on several different minerals and they were able to stop her bone deterioration, but could never replace the bone that she had lost.

Commander and Mrs. Ashe in front of their Bristol, Tennessee, home.

Of course, I'm no doctor, but that matters not. I am convinced that her delay in the parathyroid surgery was a large contributing factor to her later coming down with Alzheimer's.

Susan went to Tennessee High where she excelled scholastically. In fact, was the school class valedictorian. Poor girl was deprived of many of the thrills and spills of high school weekends in that her Friday nights and Saturdays were tied up with the keeping of the Sabbath. She, early in the 12th grade, commenced to explain that she wanted to go to college at Ambassador College in Pasadena, the Worldwide Church of God's pastor-training school.

I was bitterly opposed to her going to Ambassador College, but her heart was so set on it that she declared that if she didn't go to Ambassador College she wouldn't go anywhere. *{Transcriptionist's comment: I don 't remember saying that—but I was determined to go.}*

In due time she was registered at Ambassador College and prepared to leave Bristol to go to school. While at the airport waiting for her plane, I told her to listen to some advice that I would give her. I said, "You were deprived of many of the social activities in high school. You should plan to make up for that while at college." I said, "You can study a little bit and make straight A's, or you can study none at all, listen in class, and make B's. May I suggest to you that if time comes along and you have a test the next day and a party that night that you just go ahead to the party and make B's instead of A's.

I thought Evaline would pass out. But under the circumstances I thought it was good advice.

She went on to Pasadena and very soon met her future husband who had been ear-marked to be in charge of a dig that was to be conducted in Jerusalem, associated with the Hebrew University. She very soon began to pressure me to go to Israel for the summer in order to participate in that archeological dig.

My fear and concern of a new Arab attack on Israel caused me to flat-out put my foot down and say no to Israel. During that summer and fall and the next winter, she continued to pressure me to go to Israel for the next summer's dig. I was still concerned about what I believed to be an imminent attack by the Arabs on Israel. But I weakened to the extent that I called Admiral Siberlich, one of my former junior officers, who was then in command of the Sixth Fleet aircraft carriers. I discussed with him that Susan was planning to go to Jerusalem for the summer, but that I wanted to know that in the event of an Arab attack could he get her out of Jerusalem?

He shared my concern for an Arab war, but told me he would get her out if he had to use helicopters guarded by Sixth Fleet carrier planes. So it was all set. Susan prepared to go to Jerusalem. I was still a bit concerned and decided that

Evaline and myself would go to Israel and, at least for a few days during the summer, keep our eye on any hostile Arab developments.

We took off from Bristol to New York, where we were earmarked for a tour with British Airways (BOAC) and listed as a Jew. Kosher food, the works. We flew to London where we were required to have all of our baggage re-inspected before going on to Israel. On arrival at Israel we were held at the intersection of the runways while the Israelis came on board, came down the line in the airplane, searching for terrorists that might be on the plane.

Susan and Brent met Evaline and me at the airport and took us to the hotel to begin our tour of Israel. It isn't necessary to list the many things we saw and did, except to point out, in all my world travels, the trip to Israel was the most impressive.

During the course of the tour, we met Susan and Brent in Jerusalem.

One thing particularly caught my attention. While outside the students' hotel, Evaline and I, along with Brent, were waiting for Susan to come up from the dig. The students were singing hymns. The music and the singing were absolutely beautiful. After a little bit they stopped singing. And about this time Susan came up and sat down to join us under the giant grape arbor.

I told Brent to go ask the students to start singing again. He says, "They won't do it. Susan has come up, and none of them will play the piano if Susan can hear 'em."

A lot of highlights and points of interest were on the tour, but one particular afternoon after touring the Golan Heights, as our tour bus was about to leave, I called for everybody's attention and pointed out that where we sat, Israel, Syria, and Jordan come together. "See those mountains to the east, and the valley between them?" I said, "One of the days shortly after we get back home we're going to see TV of a morning and we're going to see the Israeli army trying to attack the Syrian troops up that crooked road from the Jordan Valley to the Golan Heights." I said, "The Israeli Air Force will be using napalm and the Israeli Army will be trying to get up the Golan Heights with their tanks."

Our guide says to the people, "Don't pay any attention to Commander Ashe of the U.S. Army. We have this pass heavily defended and we'll stop anything the Syrians have."

I said to him, "I see your defenses. I see the 155 mm cannon. I see the 75 mm's along that ridge over here. And I saw your tanks as we came down the highway to Kinestra. But they will choose a time and a place and surprise you." I said, "Your reaction time is swift, but it isn't sufficient to prevent the Syrian army from reaching the Jordan Valley before you can stop them."

We went on back to Jerusalem, saw Susan and Brent again, and, by that time, Susan planned a tour of Europe with several of the students. And she really couldn't understand why Evaline and myself didn't go with them.

Susan, with the students, took off for Greece a little before we did, but on arrival in Athens we contacted her, had dinner, and joined the students the next day on a trip from Athens to Corinth. A couple of days later we took off for New York. Susan, with the students, proceeded to tour Europe.

We arrived back in Bristol, glad to be home, and doubted very seriously I'd ever make an extended tour again.

One interesting feature of touring Israel was correcting the tour guide as he answered questions regarding what crops were growing alongside the road. He didn't know agricultural crops at all. I corrected him a few times, pointing out that we were seeing cotton, or tobacco, or whatever the case might be. He got on the loud speaker and said he'd like to announce that Commander Ashe from the U.S. Army was the tour agricultural guide.

As we traveled along the Golan Heights area I commenced to notice that around each of the oases I'd see tanks three-quarter buried, with the only thing sticking out being their guns. Most of the men on the tour were rabbis and much of the time the rabbi from Atlanta sat in front of me, and I would hit him on the shoulder and say, "See those tanks dug in?" And he'd look and couldn't see them. And Egal, the guide, would say, "How do you see those tanks? I know that they're there, but I can't see them."

But one day, as we were traveling from the kibbutz in the Jordan Valley, rockets out of Lebanon the night before had hit Tiberias near our kibbutz. The guide got alongside the bus and told us that in recent weeks we had had several incidents where hand grenades were thrown into tour buses, and other instances where Israelis as well as tourists were killed, and that we were going to go on across to Kinestra, but if anyone didn't want to go, they would come back by with the bus that evening and pick them up and proceed on with the tour. I'm pleased to relive my fond memory that Evaline and myself, along with the other 39 members of our tour, filed on the bus and made the trip.

Egal told us that the defenses along the highway were such that the window shades were supposed to be down and no pictures were allowed. Despite that, he said, "It's so hot that I will leave the shades up, but certainly no pictures."

As we plodded along, I kept jumping up, hitting the rabbi in front of me, calling his attention to buried tank positions. It wasn't long before Egal went forward and got the loud speaker and said, "If Commander Ashe of the U.S. Army doesn't stop pointing out our defense positions, I'm going to have to lower the shades!"

He came back alongside of me and says, "How can you see those? I know they're in here and I can't see 'em."

And I said, "Egal, for some reason, camouflage doesn't bother me very much."

For several months after we arrived back in Bristol nothing significant happened in Israel, and then, sure enough, one morning I came down for breakfast, turned on the TV and there were the cameras on that crooked road coming up from the Jordan Valley to the Golan Heights, jam-packed with Israeli

Army, airplanes flying at tree-top levels, dropping napalm, as they tried to stop the Syrian Army's attack that had surged across the Golan Heights.

Of course, this Holy War, as it was called, was a combined attack by Egypt, Syria, Jordan, and Lebanon. And before it was over, the Iraqis came across Syria with their tanks.

52

Farming

Shortly after arriving at Bristol to work for Sperry, I began to look into tobacco farming in the area. I looked at various ads in the newspaper and one day saw an ad for 100+ acres of land with a house and a barn for $2,500. I went out to look at this farm and found the house to be in pretty good shape, the barn was passable for hanging tobacco, and though the farm was mostly high, timbered hills, it had a plot of land for growing half an acre of tobacco.

I bought it!

Two or three days later, a fellow out in the area came by the house and told me that he would like to sell me his farm. I drove out, looked it over, and bought his farm, including the barn, but without the house, for $4,000.

Now these amounts were very small, but they represented a half-acre tobacco allotment, a place to grow it and additional land.

Now the second farm I bought had 140 acres and included a cemetery.

The church members were terribly disturbed when they learned that Mr. Charlie Barker, the farm owner, had sold the cemetery. A committee of three men called on me at my office, wanting to arrange to purchase the cemetery land.

I told them I'd gladly sell them the cemetery plot for $1, and I'd furnish the dollar.

I needed someone to work on these farms. After I bought the first farm I hired a fellow named Necessary. As Evaline says, he was totally "un." On the second farm I inquired among the neighbors regarding Charlie Barker's work habits. I learned that he was a good worker as long as you could keep him from going fishing.

I later learned that that was nearly impossible.

There were several plots of good farmland on the Barker farm. I had him plant, in addition to the half-acre of tobacco, corn, potatoes and strawberries. I soon over-taxed him, but learned that he wouldn't allow either his wife or two daughters to work outside the house.

Rather funny, Malc and Mr. Corbett came to visit us and I went out to the farm to get some new potatoes and roasting ear corn. We visited up and down the creek. Mr. Corbett asked Charlie Barker if there were any fish in that creek, a tributary of the Holston River.

Charlie exclaimed, "Oh, my Lord, yes!" He says, "See right over there at the bend in that creek? I caught a four-pound fish." He looked up at me and he says, "But mind you, it was at night!"

I soon had Charlie fencing that farm while having "un" Necessary put a pond on his farm. Well, about a year passed and another Barker about a quarter-mile down the road had a rather nice house and an excellent barn. And he sold me his farm for $5,000.

Well, here I had three half-acre plots of tobacco, strawberries, corn and potatoes, and I put cattle on the Charlie Barker farm. At this time, through an ad in the paper, I purchased another farm nearer to Bristol, with the basic requirement of a half-acre of tobacco, but this one had pasture land and I put a pond on it.

Well in short order I'd gone rather heavily into the farming business, and by the time I got this farm fenced I also had a couple of productive cattle farms.

I inventoried the farms and the cattle, and found that I had a total of $18,000 invested in all my land and cattle.

Then, lo and behold, I learn that I'm about to be transferred to Salt Lake City. So, in one day, I sold all four farms for $50,000. As previously mentioned, after a few shakes, rattles, and rolls, it was determined that I wasn't going to Salt Lake City, so I invested my funds in the stock market.

A few days later, a couple of men appeared. One had a farm for sale and the other was going to finance it. So after looking over a farm out north of Abingdon, Va., I purchased about 120 acres with a house and two barns and a half-acre tobacco allotment for $6,000.

Time passed along. I built another barn and fenced the farm for cattle and purchased, at two different times, another 269 acres.

As I started collecting cattle, I had several unusual incidents occur.

One day, I heard some trail bikes coming across the farm. I got on my tractor, went out to intercept the cyclists. They stopped and I told them to turn around, go back off of that farm, and never return. They didn't make any movement to leave, so I told them that if they weren't out in one minute, I'd take my tractor and run over their motorcycles.

This started a grand exodus and I never saw them again.

One day at the beginning of the deer season, I arrived on the farm, looked across the hill, and there were two men following a dog, and the dog was not far behind a deer.

I took my rifle, took careful aim, and hit close enough to the dog that he turned and headed back toward the men. The men came across the valley up to where I was standing, and one said, "You shoot my dog and you'll have me to shoot!"

I said, "That can be handled. And if you don't get you and that dog off this farm, that's what'll happen"

The two men each had rifles, but I had carefully handled my shotgun into position. They looked at the shotgun and decided to turn and leave.

Well, by this time I had 399 acres of land that surrounded a farm that belonged to an estate. It consisted of 18 acres, had a half-acre allotment and a barn to stow the tobacco.

The estate put the farm up for sale with Judge Hutton of Abingdon as the auctioneer. About 50 people arrived one morning and we began bidding on the farm. Each time I made a bid, someone in that crowd would raise my bid price by $50. This continued until the price had reached $4,000.

I asked the judge for his mike, and I told those people, "I understand what you're doing. I don't really want this farm. I just don't want it inside my farms. I'm going to make one more bid, and then leave. Whoever bids after I do will buy the farm."

I left, and about an hour later the judge came by my house over on the other side of the farm and says, "You bought the farm. Nobody else bid."

I started a program to reduce the population of the groundhogs. At the same time, I planted a garden with corn, squash, cantaloupe, tomatoes and what have you. Evaline objected strenuously to my shooting the groundhogs. But one day the corn and cantaloupe were ready to be picked.

I took Evaline out to get enough for us to fill our deep freeze. What a shock on arrival! The groundhogs had picked the night before to commence their own harvest of the garden.

Needless to say, Evaline offered no more objections to my eliminating the groundhogs.

I leased a farm nearby to grow cattle and tobacco. After a bit, I was approached and offered the sale of the farm for $18,000. I went with the owner, carefully looking at the farm. As he went across it, pointing out the fine pasture land, I was in the edge of the trees, counting the number of poplar trees ready to be sawed.

After a bit, I bought the farm. A next-door neighbor, an old man Grubb, in a couple of days asked me, "How much did you pay for that farm?"

I told him I paid $18,000. He says, "Brother, you got taken. I've lived here all of my life. That farm doesn't even have any timber on it."

I said, "Yeah, I guess I did, Mr. Grubb."

The next day, I approached a logger that cut and delivered lumber on halves. In a few short weeks, he sold $41,000 worth of timber off my little plot of land.

It was on this farm that I decided to determine by actual experience the cost of growing half an acre of tobacco. Only by then, the quota system had changed from acreage to poundage. I carefully calculated the hours and cost of producing the tobacco and found that for each hour and dollar I spent in the tobacco, I got a sale of $10 an hour for the time I spent.

It was during the gathering of these figures that it looked like the remnants of a hurricane was going to hit the Mountain Empire of east Tennessee and southwest Virginia, and I was hurriedly trying to harvest my tobacco. I hired two men to help me and I inquired from them, did they know anyone else that I could hire?

One boy said I "might could" hire his sister and boyfriend. I said, "Where are they?" He said, "At home." I said, "Get in the truck with me and show me where they are and I'll go see them."

They said yes, they could help, and they'd be over to the farm in a few minutes. Shortly after my arriving at the farm, they drove up. The girl, rather attractive incidentally, and about 20 years old, came out to that tobacco field wearing a white brassiere and a pair of white panties. That's all—no shoes, no nothin'.

Well, they worked in the tobacco that afternoon. When nightfall came I paid them all and they promised to meet me there the next morning at 7:00.

I went home and Evaline prepared sandwiches and we got cold drinks together. The next morning they arrived at about 9:00. She was still wearing the same brassiere and panties.

There were two boys with her, and they couldn't stay away from the cold drinks. I asked her, "Why in the world are those fellows so thirsty?"

She paused, and I says, "What did y'all do after you left here last night?"

She said, "We went to the river and took a bath. And the boys went and bought some whiskey."

I said, "Didn't you have anything to eat?"

She says, "No sir." She says, "We went over to the car. I got into the back seat. One of the boys slept in the front seat. The other one was in the back seat with me."

She says, "About every hour or two they would change positions." I said, "Then you haven't had any dinner or breakfast, either."

She says, "No sir."

I said, "Well, get over here and we'll get something to eat." She says no, she would wait till 12:00.

Later, on that same farm, I rented it to a share-cropper and I went out to see how things were coming at tobacco harvesting time. I found eight or 10 men helping the share-cropper.

Upon a closer look, his wife's granddaughter was helping with the harvesting, wearing only a brassiere and a pair of panties.

I left, came back a week later. I asked where were all of his hands?

He said, "They didn't show up."

In a little bit his wife says, "Mr. Ashe, my granddaughter gave all those men the clap and they're gettin' shots."

Well, well, well.

Well, back on one of the other farms, this unsavory character named Necessary was giving me a bit of trouble. One of the neighbors stopped me one day and warned me to be careful with that fella, that he had a reputation of cuttin' people with that knife that he carried along on his hip.

A few days later, on a Saturday, I was out inspecting the farms and I noted that his tobacco had neither been hoed nor plowed. I told him, "Next week, take care of that."

The following Saturday, I appeared at the farm, and it still hadn't been hoed nor plowed, and he was sittin' up on the front porch of his house, rocking back and forth. I went up to the house, and while standing near the porch, I says, "Howard, I told you to plow and hoe that tobacco. Now you get out there and do it, and if you don't, I'll hire it done and take it out of your part."

He stood up, put his hand on that knife, and says, "Nobody talks to me like that. I'll cut your guts out!"

I said, "Howard, you pull that knife, I'll shoot you through the head three times before you hit the floor. Now, right now, get out there and hitch up that mule."

And I followed him, watched him, and waited while he started to plow that tobacco. Then I turned to go back to the car and somehow reached back to touch my pistol, and my pistol wasn't in my pocket.

Needless to say, I almost had a laundry problem, but I never set foot on that farm again without that gun being in my right hip pocket.

Many instances, some pleasant, some dangerous. My farm operations were beginning to be more than a hobby. One day I went out to the big farm to gather some roasting ears and put in the deep freeze. I came up and looked out across the corn field, and it was picked clean. The gate from the pasture was open, and beside the gate was my bush hog, all busted up.

Just at this instant, a realtor with a client come driving up, and asked me, "Mr. Ashe, do you know of any farms for sale?"

I said, "Yes, this one!"

After about two hours I sold the farm, cattle and equipment for $100,000.

As the fall wore on and the winter arrived, one cold day I was at the other farm, and a man came up and asked me the same question—did I know of a farm for sale?

I told him I'd sell him mine. A little bit later I had sold him my farm for $50,000, and the cattle on it for $10,000 more.

It was with glee that I figured that I had less than $50,000 invested in the big farm, and $20,000 in the little farm, and that I had received over $20,000 for my lumber, plus $160,000 for my cattle and equipment.

I was out of the farming business, footloose and fancy-free. Suddenly, I didn't have anything to do with my time except be a stockbroker.

In early spring, I noted an ad for a farm to be sold at auction. I went out, looked it over, and bought that farm at auction for $153,000. I got some good bulls, some excellent cows, and started improving the pastures.

By the end of ten years, that farm was a beautiful, productive cattle farm. I had built a lake around the springs on the farm and had a pump that was delivering water to various troughs across the farm, with thermostatically controlled heaters to keep the water from freezing in the barn as the cattle continuously ate hay inside the barn.

In 1998 I had a stroke. I had difficulty getting around on level land.

My farming days were over, and I sold the farm at auction, followed by auctioning my equipment and my cattle. Again, I made a substantial percentage profit on the sale of the farm and the cattle.

The only thing that I wish is that I could do it all over again.

The End

Cast of Characters

Walter Dee Ashe, Jr.—our hero, W.D., "Dub," the boy commander.

Evaline Paseur Ashe—my wife.

Walter Dee Ashe—my father, who died young, when I was almost seven.

Audelle Keathley Ashe Bryant—my mother, who raised four boys.

John Ashe—my grandfather. Sawmill operator, sharecropper, small farmer, sometime bootlegger.

A.J. Ashe—my brother, third son, who became a B.F. Goodrich Co. vice president; M.S., Ph.D., Cornell University.

Malcolm Ashe—My brother Malc, second brother, operations manager, Keathley Pie Co., Memphis.

Farris Ashe—my youngest brother, earned M.S, U. of Tennessee, an executive with Frito-Lay.

Uncle Maurice Keathley—a mentor to all the Ashe boys.

Vice Admiral Charles E. Rosendahl—in charge of the lighter-than-air fleet from WWI until retirement. A great mentor and friend.

Vice Admiral John Perry—deputy chief of Naval Operations, Air. Didn't like airships, or me.

Vice Admiral Paul D. Stroop—head of the Navy's Bureau of Weapons, who assigned our group all sorts of interesting challenges, usually involving other than airships.

Professor David Hazen—head of the Forrestal Lab at Princeton University, worked with us to develop a more useful and accurate wind tunnel inside and behind a flying airship, a modified NAN ship. A good friend to me and to airships.

Glossary

Macedonia—a rural community 126 miles northeast of Memphis where Dub and his brothers were raised, surrounded by many Ashes and Keathleys.

Ensign—the lowest commissioned naval officer rank, one gold bar on collar or one stripe on epaulet or coat sleeve.

Lieutenant (junior grade) or Lt. (j.g.)—the second lowest Navy officer rank, one silver bar on collar and/or one regular and one narrow gold stripe on epaulet or sleeve.

Lieutenant—two silver bars and/or two gold stripes, equivalent to an Army or Marine captain.

Lieutenant Commander—one gold oak leaf cluster on collar and/or two and a half gold stripes, equivalent to major.

Commander—silver oak leaf cluster on collar and/or three gold stripes on epaulet or sleeve.

Captain—one silver eagle on collar and/or four gold stripes, equivalent to colonel.

Rear Admiral, lower half—one star on collar and/or gold epaulet, wide gold sleeve band.

Rear Admiral, upper half—two stars on gold epaulet and/or one gold stripe above wide band.

Vice Admiral—three stars on wide gold epaulet, and/or two gold stripes above wide band.

Admiral—four stars on wide gold epaulet and/or three narrow gold stripes above wide band.

Fleet Admiral—five stars over wide gold epaulet (wartime only).

K-ship—The K-class non-rigid airship was a class of blimps built by the Goodyear Aircraft Co. of Akron, Ohio. These airships were powered by two Pratt & Whitney Wasp nine-cylinder air-cooled engines, each mounted on twin-strut outriggers on either side of the control car that hung under the rubber envelope. Before and during World War II, 134 K-ships were built and configured for patrol and anti-submarine warfare. They were used extensively in the Navy's anti-submarine operations in the Atlantic and Pacific Ocean areas.

Smaller than the Nan-ship, K-ships had a much more colorful and longer history. K-ships made 55,900 operational flights, a total of over 550,000 hours during WWII, escorting surface ships 89,000 times.

NAN ship—A line of large, non-rigid airships built by the Goodyear Aircraft Co. for the U.S. Navy, with the first delivery in 1952. This line was developed through many versions designed for anti-submarine warfare and airborne early warning missions. In 1957 this airship departed Naval Air Station South Weymouth, Mass., on March 4, reached Casablanca, Morocco, the morning of March 8, and without landing or refueling re-crossed the Atlantic, landing at Key West NAS the evening of 15 March. It covered 9,448 miles in 262 hours, breaking the Graf Zeppelin's 1929 lighter-than-air distance record (6,980 miles), and the endurance record without refueling for all aircraft.

www.ingramcontent.com/pod-product-compliance
Lightning Source LLC
Chambersburg PA
CBHW070117100426
42744CB00010B/1849